**Volume 1
Chapters 1-16**

Working Papers Plus

for use with
Accounting
Warren, Reeve, Fess 19e
Chapters 1-16

Graphical Integration
of
Learning Objectives,
Exercises,
Selected Problems,
and
Working Papers

Prepared by John Wanlass – Interactive Learning

Accounting Team Director: Richard Lindgren
Senior Acquisitions Editor: David L. Shaut
Senior Marketing Manager: Sharon Oblinger
Senior Developmental Editor: Ken Martin
Production Editor: Mark Sears

Copyright © 1999
by South-Western College Publishing
Cincinnati, Ohio

International Thomson Publishing
South-Western is an ITP Company. The ITP trademark is used under license.

Portions of the material in all chapters copyrighted by John W. Wanlass, 1998.

Portions of clip art used in this manual are from CorelDraw! and 3G Graphics.

ISBN: 0-538-87417-1

   3 4 5 6 7 PN 4 3 2 1 0 9

Printed in the United States of America

Working Papers Plus

For the Student – Questions and Answers

Question .... What is <u>Working Papers Plus</u> and what does it include?

Answer .... <u>Working Papers Plus</u> is designed to be used with your textbook, **Accounting**, 19e, by Carl S. Warren, James M. Reeve, and Philip E. Fess. It includes the following:

1. Chapter learning objectives.
2. Textbook exercises with appropriate forms.
3. Selected textbook problems with appropriate forms.
4. Blank forms for other textbook problems.

These components are integrated into a graphical format with appropriate pictures and business dialogue. The forms have been designed to fade into the background as you write on them.

Question .... If <u>Working Papers Plus</u> includes only selected textbook problems, how can I work other problems that are not included?

Answer .... **Working Papers Plus** includes blank forms which can be used to work any textbook problem. The table of contents lists the problems, showing the textbook page and suggested blank forms.

Question .... What are the advantages of using working papers that restate the problem together with appropriate forms on the same page?

Answer .... There are two major advantages. First, you will not have to flip your textbook pages between the textbook problem and the textbook topic discussion. Second, and more importantly, because the problem statement is integrated with your solution, your work is quick and easy to review — a real plus when preparing for an exam.

For the Instructor – Questions and Answers

Question .... **How is <u>Working Papers Plus</u> different from traditional working papers?**

Answer .... Traditional working papers contain blank forms for use in solving textbook problems and do not include forms for textbook exercises. <u>Working Papers Plus</u> is a graphical integration of learning objectives, all exercises, selected problems, and blank forms for other problems. <u>Working Papers Plus</u> restates the textbook exercises and problems together with the appropriate forms, providing an ease-of-use not found in the traditional papers.

Question .... **How can I effectively use Working Papers Plus in the classroom?**

Answer .... Here are a few ideas we have found to be effective.

1. Make transparencies of selected exercises. Develop a solution together with the class as they use the working papers.

2. Give a student an overhead marker and a transparency of a selected exercise. Have the student write their solution on the transparency and then present it to the class. This works well for exercises that have been assigned as homework.

3. Organize in-class teams of three or four members and have them remove the appropriate pages. Because the <u>Working Papers Plus</u> contains both the problem and related forms, textbooks and other materials can be removed from the desk, leaving an uncluttered work area.

Acknowledgments

<u>Working Papers Plus</u> is the result of many years of development and experimentation in the classroom. The contributions of accounting faculty and students have greatly influenced this project. I am indebted to the South-Western accounting team for the opportunity to develop materials that enhance accounting education. It is my hope that by using these working papers you will enjoy your accounting studies and be better prepared to face the challenges of the business world.

John Wanlass

Interactive Learning

Working Papers Plus

ACCOUNTING
Warren, Reeve, Fess, 19e

Brief Contents – Volume 1

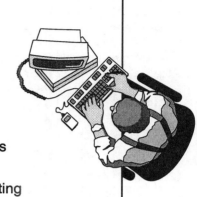

Working Papers Plus – Contents

Blank Forms

How to Use Your Working Papers

" I'm Amy McKeague. I would like to explain how Working Papers Plus can be used effectively in your first accounting course. The basic design centers around the concept that behind each textbook exercise and problem there are real people in real business settings, requiring your ability to analyze and develop reasonable solutions. Many of the problems introduce you to individuals within the business organization. In the pages that follow, I've asked Donna Ulmer, our learning specialist, to share some suggestions on how to study accounting. I've also asked Robert Lynch, our enthusiastic accounting instructor, to share his thoughts on the first accounting course. I have outlined the steps below that will help you gain the intended benefits of the working papers. We hope you enjoy your studies. "

Amy McKeague
Planning Director

Step 1 .... **Understand Your Assignment.** Make sure that you know which exercise or problem you are expected to complete. Are you expected to have the work completed before coming to class or will the work be completed during the class period? Your instructor may work some exercises together with you in class.

Step 2 .... **Organize your study materials.** Remove the appropriate working papers and place them in front of you. Integrated into each of the exercises and problems you will find the problem statement and related forms. You will see the accounting topic, learning objective, and text page where the objective is discussed. Open your textbook to the appropriate page and you are ready to work.

Step 3 .... **Prepare your solution.** Because your working papers contain both the problem and forms, you will need to refer to your textbook only to get some help with the specific topic. Try to formulate what you think would be a reasonable solution and then compare your work with the textbook presentation.

Note: Not all of your textbook problems are included. We have added blank forms at the back of the working papers for those problems that are not included. The table of contents lists forms for each problem.

How to Study Accounting — Some Suggestions

" I'm learning specialist Donna Ulmer. When I first attended college my motivation and study habits were terrible. Someone suggested that maybe I wasn't just lazy but that I lacked the necessary study skills to be successful. Acting on that suggestion I enrolled in a study skills class—one of the best decisions I've ever made. From that class I discovered that I had never received the proper training and had no idea how to organize my time and study efforts. After applying some simple concepts, I began to not only enjoy my studies but I also decided to specialize in the field of 'learning technology' so that I could help others develop their own learning skills. Although the study of accounting can be technical, there are some basic study skills that you will find helpful. I have outlined several in the section below. Good luck! "

Donna Ulmer
Learning Specialist

Getting Organized

Get the Appropriate Study Materials .... This may sound obvious but it is often overlooked. Buy the required materials and review all other recommended or suggested materials.

Organize Your Papers in a 3-Ring Binder .... A 3-ring binder is an excellent way to organize your class notes, working papers, quizzes, and exams. We have designed the working papers to be easily reviewed in preparation for quizzes and exams. Having these organized in your binder will be very helpful.

Ask About Other Resources .... Your textbook is supported by a wide range of learning aids such as videotapes, practice cases, and study guides. Your school may provide a tutorial service or other resources that may facilitate your studies. Ask about these resources and ask students that have successfully completed the class for their advice.

Using Your Class Time Effectively

Be Prepared for Class .... The most obvious way to benefit from your classroom experience is to be well prepared. When you are behind in your work you won't be ready to learn new material and you will seem to always be in a 'catch-up' mode. Working ahead of what is expected pays great dividends for some students. Try it!

Take Notes .... Listening and observing are very important. Unfortunately, we quickly forget what we hear—writing it down is a must. However, many of us cannot listen and write at the same time without missing important information. If your instructor allows you to tape record the class session, you would be free to concentrate on the lecture, and later, write it down while listening to the tape. This technique really helped me—it's worth a try.

Tackling Your Homework Assignments

Accounting is a Cumulative Study .... Each new topic relies heavily on what you have learned before. Your textbook is organized to introduce basic concepts first and then build on these concepts. The first five chapters dealing with the accounting cycle are cumulative. Understanding this will provide motivation to keep up with your work.

Form a Study Group .... If you do all of your studying by yourself, you may be making a big mistake. An important educational goal is to prepare yourself for employment in the so-called real world. The ability to work in a team setting is crucial. As part of a team, you need to learn to actively listen and communicate your ideas to others. This is one of the most important skills you can acquire. A word of caution— do not do all of your studying in a group setting. A balance between individual study and group study is important.

Taking Quizzes and Examinations

An Effective Review is the Key .... Preparing for and taking exams can be a very personal situation— we all have different styles. Some people seem to naturally have an aptitude for taking exams. In this short review of study skills we don't have time for a complete discussion on this important topic. If this seems to be a problem for you, please consider taking a study skills class—it could make a big difference.

The First Accounting Course — What To Expect

"I m accounting instructor Robert Lynch. I remember my first accounting class as if it happened yesterday. I was planning to major in business administration and just wanted to get accounting 'out-of-the-way,' so to speak, so I could take some interesting classes. Some of my friends were convinced that accounting was only for those who didn't like working with people—and I wasn't one of those; I love working with people. Anyway, I had a great accounting teacher who brought accounting to life and helped me realize that successful accountants not only have good technical skills but also are able to work with and communicate effectively with others. After working in the accounting profession for a few years, I decided that my real interest in life was sharing my accounting knowledge and experience with others. Your first accounting class can be as rewarding as mine—it's really up to you. "

Robert Lynch
Accounting Instructor

Working Papers Plus and Your Textbook

Working Papers Plus Volume 1 — Textbook Chapters 1 to 16

Working Papers Plus Volume 2 — Textbook Chapters 17 to 24

Get a Good Start and Stay Ahead of the Game

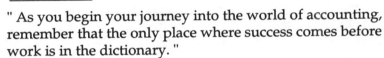

" Starting with Chapter 1 on the following page,
plan to spend the extra time to get a good start.
Here are some suggestions:

1. Make sure that you understand what is required of you.
2. Understand your homework assignments. How are they to be prepared? When are they due?
3. Schedule more time than you think will be necessary.
4. Make one or two friends. Exchange phone numbers and call for help if you don't understand an assignment.
5. And most importantly, relax and plan to enjoy your first accounting course. "

" As you begin your journey into the world of accounting, remember that the only place where success comes before work is in the dictionary. "

Robert Lynch
Accounting Instructor

Chapter 1

Introduction to Accounting and Business

Accounting provides and interprets economic data for economic units within society. These economic units include profit enterprises and non-profit entities, such as churches, government agencies, and charities. In addition, accounting provides information for individual persons and family units. Regardless of the type of economic unit, accounting must provide economic data that are reliable and accurate.

Learning objectives are listed for the exercises and problems that follow. Use the information to the right to determine the nature of the objective and the page number to refer to your textbook for a discussion of the topic.

Objective 1 — Nature of a Business 2
Describe the nature of a business.

Objective 2 — The Role of Accounting in Business 5
Describe the role of accounting in business.

Objective 3 — Business Ethics 6
Describe the importance of business ethics and the basic principles of proper ethical conduct.

Objective 4 — Profession of Accounting 7
Describe the profession of accounting.

Objective 5 — Generally Accepted Accounting Principles 9
Summarize the development of accounting principles and relate them to practice.

Objective 6 — Assets, Liabilities, and Owner's Equity 11
State the accounting equation and define each element of the equation.

Objective 7 — Business Transactions and the Accounting Equation 11
Explain how business transactions can be stated in terms of the resulting changes in the three basic elements of the accounting equation.

Objective 8 — Financial Statements 16
Describe the financial statements of a proprietorship and explain how they interrelate.

Objective 9 — Financial Analysis and Interpretation 19
Use the ratio of liabilities to owner's equity to analyze the ability of a business to withstand poor business conditions.

Completing Homework Assignments — Some Tips

" I remember doing my first accounting assignments. I would spend too much time just getting ready to do the work and then once I began, it seemed that a lot of time was wasted. I would read over the homework problem, then take five minutes flipping pages in the textbook trying to find where the topic was presented. Moving between the working papers, the problem in the textbook, and the reference material where the topic was presented created some frustration for me. After a while I got use to it, but it never seemed very efficient—too much moving back and forth. We have designed the <u>Working Papers Plus</u> to eliminate much of this wasted effort. Here's how to use the working papers.

1. Remove the appropriate pages and place them in front of you. The learning objective number and related textbook page are printed at the top of each exercise and problem.

2. Open your textbook to the appropriate page number.

That's it. Within seconds you are ready to work. While preparing your solution, refer to your textbook to get some help with the specific topic *only* if you really need to. "

Important suggestion: " Try to prepare what you think would be a reasonable solution and then compare your work with the textbook presentation. Enjoy yourself. "

Robert Lynch
Accounting Instructor

Professional ethics
Objective 3 - Text page 6

A fertilizer manufacturing company wants to relocate to Collier County. A 13-year-old report from a fired researcher at the company says the company's product is releasing toxic by-products. The company has suppressed that report. A second report commissioned by the company shows there is no problem with the fertilizer.

Should the company's chief executive officer reveal the context of the unfavorable report in discussions with Collier County representatives? Discuss.

Working
Papers
Plus

Chapter 1

Exercise 1–2

Accounting equation
Objective 6 - Text page 11   ✔ a. $62,000

Determine the missing amount for each of the following:

	Assets	=	Liabilities	+	Owner's Equity
a.	_____	=	$20,500	+	$41,500
b.	$32,750	=	_____	+	10,000
c.	57,000	=	18,000	+	_____

Exercise 1–3

Accounting equation
Objectives 6, 8 - Text pages 11 and 16   ✔ b. $303,000

David Plymouth is the owner and operator of Dyn-A-Go, a motivational consulting business. At the end of its accounting period, December 31, 1999, Dyn-A-Go has assets of $325,000 and liabilities of $85,000. Using the accounting equation and considering each case independently, determine the following amounts:

a. David Plymouth, capital, as of December 31, 1999.

b. David Plymouth, capital, as of December 31, 2000, assuming that during 2000, assets increased by $84,000 and liabilities increased by $21,000.

c. David Plymouth, capital, as of December 31, 2000, assuming that during 2000, assets decreased by $5,000 and liabilities increased by $17,000.

d. David Plymouth, capital, as of December 31, 2000, assuming that during 2000, assets increased by $75,000 and liabilities decreased by $35,000.

e. Net income (or net loss) during 2000, assuming that as of December 31, 2000, assets were $425,000, liabilities were $105,000, and there were no additional investments or withdrawals.

Exercise 1–4

Asset, liability, owner's equity items
Objective 7 - Text page 11

Indicate whether each of the following is identified with (1) an asset, (2) a liability, or (3) owner's equity:

_____ a. fees earned   _____ d. land

_____ b. supplies   _____ e. accounts payable

_____ c. wages expense   _____ f. cash

Exercise 1–5

Effect of transactions on accounting equation
Objective 7 - Text page 11

Describe how the following business transactions
affect the three elements of the accounting equation.

a. Invested cash in business.

b. Received cash for services performed.

c. Purchased supplies for cash.

d. Paid for utilities used in the business.

e. Purchased supplies on account.

Exercise 1–6

Effect of transactions on accounting equation
Objective 7 - Text page 11   ✔ a. (1) increase $70,000

a. A vacant lot acquired for $90,000, on which there is a balance owed of
$30,000, is sold for $160,000 in cash. What is the effect of the sale on the
total amount of the seller's:

(1) assets? ....

(2) liabilities? ....

(3) owner's equity? .....

b. After receiving the $160,000 cash in (a), the seller pays the $30,000 owed.
What is the effect of the payment on the total amount of the seller's:

(1) assets? ....

(2) liabilities? ....

(3) owner's equity? .....

Exercise 1–7

Effect of transactions on owner's equity
Objective 7 - Text page 11

Indicate whether each of the following types of transactions
will (a) increase owner's equity or (b) decrease owner's equity:

____1. owner's investments
____2. revenues
____3. expenses
____4. owner's withdrawals

Exercise 1–8

Transactions
Objective 7 - Text page 11

The following selected transactions were completed by On Time Delivery Service during May:

_____ 1. Received cash from cash customers, $6,250.
_____ 2. Paid creditors on account, $250.
_____ 3. Received cash from owner as additional investment, $25,000.
_____ 4. Paid advertising expense, $625.
_____ 5. Billed customers for delivery services on account, $2,900.
_____ 6. Purchased supplies for cash, $750.
_____ 7. Paid rent for July, $2,500.
_____ 8. Received cash from customers on account, $900.
_____ 9. Determined that the cost of supplies on hand was $180; therefore, $570 of supplies had been used during the month.
_____ 10. Paid cash to owner for personal use, $1,000.

Indicate the effect of each transaction on the accounting equation by inserting at the left of each number the appropriate letter from the following list:

  a. Increase in an asset, decrease in another asset.
  b. Increase in an asset, increase in a liability.
  c. Increase in an asset, increase in owner's equity.
  d. Decrease in an asset, decrease in a liability.
  e. Decrease in an asset, decrease in owner's equity.

Exercise 1–9

Nature of transactions
Objective 7 - Text page 11   ✔ d. $3,950

Joe Norwood operates his own catering service. Summary financial data for August are presented in equation form as follows. Each line designated by a number indicates the effect of a transaction on the equation. Each increase and decrease in owner's equity, except transaction (5), affects net income.

	Cash	Supplies	Land	Liabilities	Owner's Equity	Description
Bal.	5,500	750	29,000	3,750	31,500	
1.	+16,000				+16,000	1._____
2.	-2,000		+2,000			2._____
3.	-11,250				-11,250	3._____
4.		+600		+ 600		4._____
5.	-1,950				-1,950	5._____
6.	-2,300			-2,300		6._____
7.		-800			- 800	7._____
Bal.	4,000	550	31,000	2,050	33,500	

a. Describe each transaction.
b. What is the amount of net decrease in cash during the month? $_____
c. What is the amount of net increase in owner's equity during the month? $_____
d. What is the amount of the net income for the month? $_____
e. How much of the net income for the month was retained in the business? $_____

Net income and owner's withdrawals
Objective 8 - Text page 16

The income statement of a proprietorship for the month of February indicates a net income of $28,000. During the same period, the owner withdrew $35,000 in cash from the business for personal use.

Would it be correct
to say that the
business incurred a
net loss of $7,000
during the month?
Discuss.

Exercise 1–11 _____

Net income and owner's equity for four businesses
Objective 8 - Text page 16   ✔ Company G: Net loss, $60,000

Four different proprietorships, E, F, G, and H, show the same balance sheet data at the beginning and end of a year. These data, exclusive of the amount of owner's equity, are summarized as follows:

	Total Assets	Total Liabilities
Beginning of the year	$325,000	$120,000
End of the year	570,000	325,000

On the basis of the above data and the following additional information for the year, determine the net income (or loss) of each company for the year. (Suggestion: First determine the amount of increase or decrease in owner's equity during the year.) Enter the appropriate answer to the left of each company.

$_____ Company E: The owner had made no additional investments in the business and had made no withdrawals from the business.

$_____ Company F: The owner had made no additional investments in the business but had withdrawn $25,000.

$_____ Company G: The owner had made an additional investment of $100,000 but had made no withdrawals.

$_____ Company H: The owner had made an additional investment of $100,000 and had withdrawn $25,000.

Exercise 1–12 and 13

Balance sheet items and Income statement items
Objective 8 - Text page 16

From the following list of selected items taken from the records of Reliable Appliance Service as of a specific date, indicate to the left of the item if it would appear on the balance sheet (BS) or on the income statement (IS).

_____ 1. Utilities Expense   _____ 6. Cash

_____ 2. Fees Earned   _____ 7. Supplies Expense

_____ 3. Supplies   _____ 8. Land

_____ 4. Wages Expense   _____ 9. Julie McCarthy, Capital

_____ 5. Accounts Payable   _____ 10. Wages Payable

Exercise 1–14

Statement of owner's equity
Objective 8 - Text page 16   ✔ Meg Tewksbury, capital September 30, 2000: $350,250

Financial information related to Eldora Company, a proprietorship, for the month ended September 30, 2000, is as follows:

Net income for September ....$ 91,250
Meg Tewksbury's withdrawals during September 12,000
Meg Tewksbury, capital, September 1, 2000 271,000

Prepare a statement of owner's equity for the month ended September 30, 2000. Include the appropriate heading.

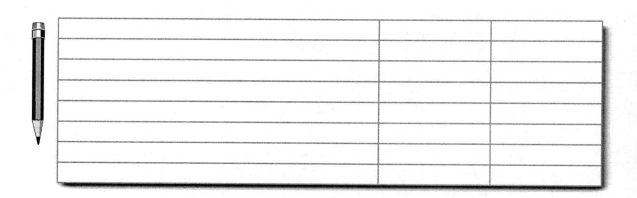

Exercise 1–15 Name: _____

Income statement
Objective 8 - Text page 16   ✔ Net income: $19,700

Temporary Help Services was organized on November 1. A summary of the revenue and expense transactions for November are as follows:

Prepare an income statement for the month ended November 30. Include the appropriate heading.	Fees earned $75,400
	Wages expense 37,700
	Miscellaneous expense 2,250
	Rent expense 12,500
	Supplies expense 3,250

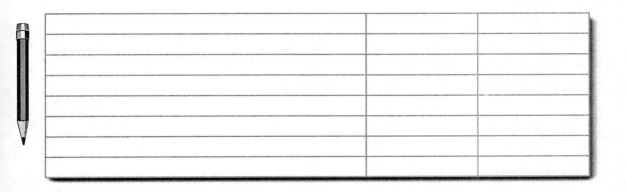

Exercise 1–16

Missing amounts from balance sheet and income statement data
Objective 8 - Text page 16   ✔ (a) $211,000, (d) $335,000

One item is omitted in each of the following summaries of balance sheet and income statement data for four different proprietorships, I, II, III, and IV.

	I	II	III	IV
Beginning of the year:				
Assets	$500,000	$ 95,000	$90,000	**(d)**_____
Liabilities	360,000	45,000	76,000	$150,000
End of the year:				
Assets	855,000	125,000	94,000	310,000
Liabilities	465,000	35,000	87,000	170,000
During the year:				
Additional investment	**(a)**_____	22,000	5,000	50,000
Withdrawals	46,750	8,000	**(c)**_____	75,000
Revenue	197,750	**(b)**_____	88,100	140,000
Expenses	112,000	52,000	89,600	160,000

Determine the amounts of the missing items, labeled (a) through (d). (Suggestion: First determine the amount of increase or decrease in owner's equity during the year.)

Balance sheets, net income
Objective 8 - Text page 16 ✔ b. $10,170

Financial information related to the proprietorship of Lynch Interiors for May and June of the current year is as follows:

	May 31, 20__	June 30, 20__
Accounts payable	$ 5,720	$ 6,900
Accounts receivable	9,300	10,400
Kate Lynch, capital	_____	_____
Cash	15,000	25,500
Supplies	1,000	750

Kate Lynch, Owner

a. Prepare balance sheets for Lynch Interiors as of May 31 and as of June 30 of the current year. Ms. Lynch is anxiously awaiting your calculation of her capital balance. Use a separate column for each month.

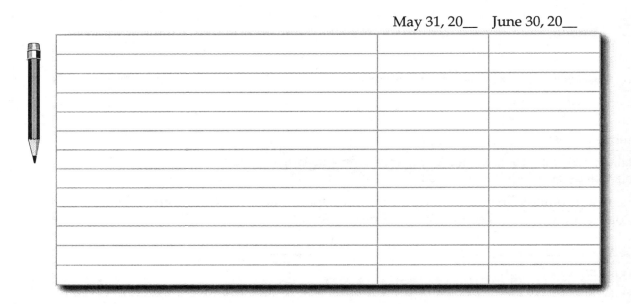

	May 31, 20__	June 30, 20__

$_____ b. Determine the amount of net income for June, assuming that the owner made no additional investments or withdrawals during the month.

$_____ c. Determine the amount of net income for June, assuming that the owner made no additional investments but withdrew $5,000 during the month.

Financial statements
Objective 8 - Text page 16

Each of the following items is shown in the financial statements of
Exxon Corporation. Identify the financial statement—balance sheet (BS)
or income statement (IS)—in which each item would appear.

____ a. Operating expenses   ____ i. Cash equivalents

____ b. Crude oil inventory   ____ j. Long-term debt

____ c. Income taxes payable   ____ k. Selling expenses

____ d. Sales   ____ l. Notes receivable

____ e. Investments   ____ m. Equipment

____ f. Marketable securities   ____ n. Accounts payable

____ g. Exploration expenses   ____ o. Prepaid taxes

____ h. Notes and loans payable

Exercise 1–19

Statement of cash flows
Objective 8 - Text page 16

Indicate whether each of the following activities would be reported on the
statement of cash flows as (a) an operating activity, (b) an investing activity,
or (c) a financing activity:

____ 1. Cash received as owner's investment

____ 2. Cash paid for land

____ 3. Cash received from fees earned

____ 4. Cash paid for expenses

Exercise 1–20

Financial statements

Objective 8 - Text page 16   ✔ Correct Amount of Total Assets is $13,875

Vineyard Realty, organized July 1, 2000, is owned and operated by Barbara Straud. How many errors can you find in the following financial statements for Vineyard Realty, prepared after its second month of operations?

Vineyard Realty
Income Statement
August 31, 2000

Sales commissions		$26,100.00
Operating expenses:		
Office salaries expense	$18,150.00	
Rent expense	2,800.00	
Automobile expense	1,750.00	
Miscellaneous expense	550.00	
Supplies expense	225.00	
Total operating expenses		23,475.00
Net income		$12,625.00

Barbara Straud
Statement of Owner's Equity
August 31, 1999

Barbara Straud, capital, August 1, 2000	$ 8,450.00
Less withdrawals during August	1,000.00
	$ 7,450.00
Additional investment during August	2,500.00
	$ 9,950.00
Net income for the month	12,625.00
Barbara Straud, capital, August 31, 2000	$22,575.00

Balance Sheet
For the Month Ended August 31, 2000

Assets		Liabilities	
Cash	$ 3,350.00	Accounts receivable	$ 9,200.00
Accounts payable	1,300.00	Supplies	1,325.00
		Owner's Equity	
		Barbara Straud, capital	22,575.00
Total assets	$ 4,650.00	Total liabilities and owner's equity	$33,100.00

Financial Analysis and Interpretation

Ratio of Liabilities to Owner's Equity

Objective: Use the ratio of liabilities to owner's equity to analyze the ability of a business to withstand poor business conditions.

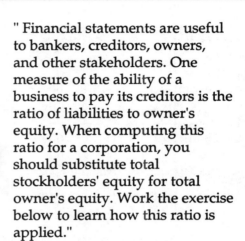

Formula

$$\text{Ratio of liabilities to owner's equity} = \frac{\text{Total liabilities}}{\text{Total owner's equity}}$$

Example

Computer King $\dfrac{\$400}{\$16,050} = .025$ or 2.5%

" Financial statements are useful to bankers, creditors, owners, and other stakeholders. One measure of the ability of a business to pay its creditors is the ratio of liabilities to owner's equity. When computing this ratio for a corporation, you should substitute total stockholders' equity for total owner's equity. Work the exercise below to learn how this ratio is applied."

Ken Harper
Financial Analyst

Exercise 1–21

Ratio of liabilities to stockholders' equity
Objective 9 - Text page 19

The financial statements for **Hershey Foods Corporation** are presented in Appendix G at the end of the text.

a. Determine the ratio of liabilities to stockholders' equity for **Hershey Foods Corporation** at the end of 1996 and 1995.

b. What conclusions regarding the margin of protection to the creditors can you draw from your analysis?

By satisfying certain specific requirements, accountants may become certified as public accountants (CPAs), management accountants (CMAs), or internal auditors (CIAs). Find the certification requirements for *one* of these accounting groups by accessing the appropriate Internet site listed below.

www.ais-cpa.com

This site lists the address and/or Internet link for each state's board of accountancy. Find your state's requirements.

www.rutgers.edu/Accounting/raw/ima/icma.htm

This site lists the requirements for becoming a CMA.

www.rutgers.edu/Accounting/raw/iia

This site lists the requirements for becoming a CIA.

Transactions

Objective 7 - Text page 11   ✔ Cash Bal. at End of July: $23,895

Chris Oxnard established an insurance agency on July 1 of the current year and completed the following transactions during July:

a. Opened a business bank account with a deposit of $25,000.

b. Purchased supplies on account, $850.

c. Paid creditors on account, $625.

d. Received cash from fees earned, $4,250.

e. Paid rent on office and equipment for the month, $1,000.

f. Paid automobile expenses for month, $780, and miscellaneous expenses, $250.

g. Paid office salaries, $1,200.

h. Determined that the cost of supplies on hand was $275; therefore, the cost of supplies used was $575.

i. Billed insurance companies for sales commissions earned, $3,350.

j. Withdrew cash for personal use, $1,500.

Chris Oxnard, Owner

| | Assets | | | | Liabilities and Owner's Equity | | |
	Cash	+ Accounts Receivable	+ Supplies	=	Accounts Payable	+ Chris Oxnard, Capital	Nature of Equity Change
a.							
b.							
Bal.							
c.							
Bal.							
d.							
Bal.							
e.							
Bal.							
f.							
Bal.							
g.							
Bal.							
h.							
Bal.							
i.							
Bal.							
j.							
Bal.							

Instructions

1. Using the table above, indicate the effect of each transaction and the balances after each transaction. Indicate the nature of each increase and decrease in owner's equity by an appropriate notation in the equity change column.

Continued

" I'm glad to have my first month behind me. Your analysis of my transactions is interesting. Most of your work is easy to follow, but would you briefly explain why my investment and revenues increased my owner's equity, while withdrawals and expenses decreased my owner's equity. "

Chris Oxnard, Owner

Memo To: Chris Oxnard

Problem 1–2A Las Posas Travel Service   Name:

Financial statements
Objective 8 - Text page 16   ✔ Net income: $26,300

Shown on the right are the amounts of the assets and liabilities of Las Posas Travel Service at June 30, 2000, the end of the current year, and its revenue and expenses for the year ended on that date. The capital of Gabriela Sanchez, owner, was $18,000 at July 1, 1999, the beginning of the current year, and the owner withdrew $15,000 during the current year.

Accounts payable ..... $	6,100
Cash	33,725
Fees earned	108,775
Misc. expense	1,825
Rent expense	18,900
Supplies	1,675
Supplies expense	3,550
Taxes expense	2,800
Utilities expense	10,500
Wages expense	44,900

Instructions

Include the appropriate headings.

1. Prepare an income statement for the current year ended June 30, 2000.

2. Prepare a statement of owner's equity for the current year ended June 30, 2000.

3. Prepare a balance sheet as of June 30, 2000.

Blank Page

Problem 1–4A Rabbit Realty

Name: _____

Transactions; financial statements

Objectives 7, 8 - Text pages 11 and 16   ✔ Net income: $5,775

On May 1 of the current year, Tom O'Hare established Rabbit Realty. O'Hare completed the following transactions during the month of May:

Tom O'Hare, Realtor

a. Opened a business bank account with a deposit of $7,000.
b. Paid rent on office and equipment for the month, $4,600.
c. Paid automobile expenses (including rental charge) for month, $900, and miscellaneous expenses, $550.
d. Purchased supplies (pens, file folders, and copy paper) on account, $1,325.
e. Earned sales commissions, receiving cash, $16,500.
f. Paid creditor on account, $800.
g. Paid office salaries, $3,950.
h. Withdrew cash for personal use, $2,000.
i. Determined that the cost of supplies on hand was $600; therefore, the cost of supplies used was $725.

	Assets			Liabilities and Owner's Equity		
Item	+ Cash	+ Supplies	=	Accounts Payable	Tom O'Hare, + Capital	Nature of Equity Change

Instructions

1. Using the table above, indicate the effect of each transaction and the balances after each transaction. Indicate the nature of each increase and decrease in owner's equity by an appropriate notation in the equity change column.

Continued

Continued

2. Prepare an income statement for May, a statement of owner's equity for May, and a balance sheet as of May 31.

Transactions

Objective 7 - Text page 11   ✔ Cash Bal. at End of Feb. $27,670

On February 1 of the current year, Diane Winn established a business to manage rental property. She completed the following transactions during February:

a. Opened a business bank account with a deposit of $30,000.
b. Purchased supplies (pens, file folders, and copy paper) on account, $1,250.
c. Received cash from fees earned, $5,500.
d. Paid rent on office and equipment for the month, $3,000.
e. Paid creditors on account, $575.
f. Billed customers for fees earned, $3,250.
g. Paid automobile expenses (including rental charges) for month, $980, and miscellaneous expenses, $775.
h. Paid office salaries, $1,500.
i. Determined that the cost of supplies on hand was $315; therefore, the cost of supplies used was $935.
j. Withdrew cash for personal use, $1,000.

Diane Winn, Owner

	Assets				Liabilities and Owner's Equity		
	Cash +	Accounts Receivable +	Supplies	=	Accounts Payable +	Diane Winn, Capital	Nature of Equity Change
a.							
b.							
Bal.							
c.							
Bal.							
d.							
Bal.							
e.							
Bal.							
f.							
Bal.							
g.							
Bal.							
h.							
Bal.							
i.							
Bal.							
j.							
Bal.							

Instructions

1. Using the table above, indicate the effect of each transaction and the balances after each transaction. Indicate the nature of each increase and decrease in owner's equity by an appropriate notation in the equity change column.

Continued

" Thanks for completing my transactions for the month of June. Because I'm new to the business world, I'm not sure that I understand all of your calculations. I would appreciate it if you would briefly explain why my investment and revenues increased my owner's equity, while withdrawals and expenses decreased my owner's equity. "

Diane Winn, Owner

Memo To: Diane Winn

Financial statements
Objective 8 - Text page 16   ✔ Net income: $46,655

Shown on the right are the amounts of the assets and liabilities of Seven Seas Travel Agency at December 31, 2000, the end of the current year, and its revenue and expenses for the year ended on that date. The capital of Trent Baker, owner, was $24,500 on January 1, 2000, the beginning of the current year. During the current year, Trent withdrew $30,000.

Accounts payable............$ 3,200
Cash 42,490
Fees earned 127,530
Miscellaneous expense..........1,750
Rent expense........................27,000
Supplies 1,865
Supplies expense....................2,125
Utilities expense 4,500
Wages expense 45,500

Instructions
Include the appropriate headings.

1. Prepare an income statement for the current year ended December 31, 2000.

2. Prepare a statement of owner's equity for the current year ended December 31, 2000.

3. Prepare a balance sheet as of December 31, 2000.

Blank Page

Transactions; financial statements
Objectives 7, 8 - Text pages 11 and 16   ✔ Net income: $9,250

On September 1 of the current year, Corean Pace established Rapid
Realty. Pace completed the following transactions during the month of
September:

a. Opened a business bank account with a deposit of $8,500.
b. Purchased supplies (pens, file folders, and fax paper, etc.)
   on account, $1,250.
c. Paid creditor on account, $750.
d. Earned sales commissions, receiving cash, $18,200.
e. Paid rent on office and equipment for the month, $2,000.
f. Withdrew cash for personal use, $3,000.
g. Paid automobile expenses (including rental charge) for
   month, $1,900, and miscellaneous expenses, $350.
h. Paid office salaries, $4,150.
i. Determined that the cost of supplies on hand was $700;
   therefore, the cost of supplies used was $550.

Corean Pace, Realtor

		Assets			Liabilities and Owner's Equity		
Item	+ Cash	+ Supplies	=	Accounts Payable	+	Corean Pace, Capital	Nature of Equity Change

Instructions

1. Using the table above, indicate the effect of each transaction and the balances
   after each transaction. Indicate the nature of each increase and decrease in
   owner's equity by an appropriate notation in the equity change column.

Continued

2. Prepare an income statement for September, a statement of owner's equity for September, and a balance sheet as of September 30. Include appropriate report headings and draw a line showing the connection between each report.

Chapter 2

Analyzing Transactions

Basic concepts, principles, and methods of recording transactions were presented in Chapter 1. The preparation of financial statements summarizing the effects of transactions on an enterprise was also illustrated.

This chapter describes additional concepts, principles, forms, and methods used to initially record transactions. The chapter also discusses how errors may occur and how they are detected by the accounting process. Finally, methods of correcting errors are presented.

Learning objectives are listed for the exercises and problems that follow. Use the information to the right to determine the nature of the objective and the page number to refer to your textbook for a discussion of the topic.

A Handy Visual Aid

" When I started my first accounting class, I found it difficult to remember how debits and credits related to the five financial statement categories. Let me describe a visual aid that you will always have with you—your left hand. In the first diagram below, you will see that the thumb of your left hand represents total assets (that is, all of the resources available to the business enterprise). Your four fingers represent the ownership equities in the total assets.

In the second diagram below, you will see that debits (assets and expenses) are represented toward the left side by your thumb and little finger. Credits are represented by the three fingers to the right: the index, middle, and ring fingers.

As described below, your left hand represents all of the important parts of the financial accounting model. I hope this visual aid will help you remember some important relationships. "

Robert Lynch
Accounting Instructor

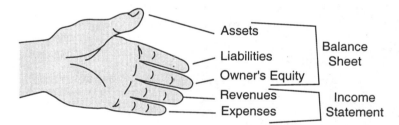

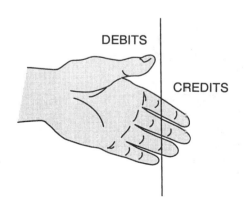

DEBITS

CREDITS

Your left hand represents:

1. A trial balance and a general ledger showing the major account categories listed in the proper order: assets, liabilities, owner's equity, revenues, and expenses.

2. The balance sheet and income statement.

3. Accounts with normal debit and credit balances. Debits (assets and expenses) are to the left, and credits (liabilities, owner's equity, and revenues) are to the right.

When you look at the revenue and expense fingers, the tip of the ring finger represents the amount of net income—the excess of revenues over expenses. There are many other ways to group the fingers to show relationships; try to find some yourself.

Understanding Double-Entry Accounting

" My name is Luca Pacioli. Some say that I'm the father of the balance sheet and that I invented what is known as the double-entry system of accounting. This system of accounting was strongly influenced by the financial needs of the Venetian merchants and was developed while I taught mathematics in various universities in Italy. In 1494 a friend of mine, Leonardo da Vinci, and I collaborated on a mathematics book in which I described the nature of the double-entry system. Leonardo drew the illustrations and I wrote the text. "

" Like most valuable and lasting ideas, **double-entry accounting** is based on a simple concept. When completing a business transaction, each party to the transaction will **receive** something and will also **give** something in return. For both parties, the value of what is received must equal the value of what is given. When this happens both parties to the transaction are satisfied. "

" The device we use to measure what is received and given is called a scale or a balance and is shown below. Your modern-day T account is a representation of this device. Like your T account, the scale has two sides. Using the right hand, a seller places commodities on the right side of the scale. Standing on the other side of the scale, a potential buyer (or trader) places commodities or monetary value, also using the right hand. Both parties have given their respective offerings on the right side of the scale using the right hand. When the value is balanced and acceptable to both parties, each party then accepts or receives the commodities or monetary value using the left hand. The **right hand** is used to **give**—the **credit** side of the transaction. The **left hand** is used to **receive**—the **debit** side of the transaction. This concept is explained further on the following page. "

Luca Pacioli
Father of the
Balance Sheet

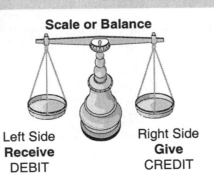

Scale or Balance

Left Side
Receive
DEBIT

Right Side
Give
CREDIT

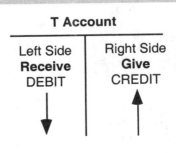

T Account

Left Side **Receive** DEBIT	Right Side **Give** CREDIT

" When learning to use the double-entry accounting system, you will always record **debits** on the **left-hand** side and **credits** on the **right-hand** side of a ledger account. Debits are often abbreviated as Dr. and credits as Cr. These terms are derived from the Latin *debere* and *credere*. Some followers of the double-entry system will tell you that there is no particular reason for this left and right placement. This is not the case; the justification for **left-hand receiving** and **right-hand giving** has existed throughout history and is extremely important. "

The Left Hand Receives (Debits)

" The left hand has always been considered evil or unsanitary. In Latin, left is spelled 'sinister.' Never give or offer anything with the left hand; this would be the ultimate insult, and you may find yourself in a grave situation. The left hand is only used for receiving and represents the debit side of the transaction. "

The Right Hand Gives (Credits)

" The right hand has always been used for giving or offering of everything from commodities for sale to food for a hungry stranger. The right hand is raised to indicate giving support, and a right-hand handshake implies that both parties give their word on a business deal. Table etiquette requires that you give (offer) food with your right hand and receive (accept) it with your left hand. There are many other examples; perhaps you can think of a few yourself. "

Rules for Recording Double-Entry Transactions

" What is received is recorded on the left (debit) side of the appropriate ledger account, and what is given is recorded on the right (credit) side of the ledger account. Because we read from left to right, in the journal we record the debits first and then the credits. If you understand, in simple terms, what is received and given, you are on your way to using the double-entry system of accounting. Carefully study the examples that follow. Best wishes. "

Luca Pacioli
Inventor of
Double-Entry
Accounting

Computer King — Service Company Transactions

" On November 1, 1999, I started a sole proprietorship called Computer King. I plan to use my knowledge of microcomputers and offer computer consulting services for a fee. The following transactions describe the November activity in terms of double-entry accounting. As you study these transactions, you will see how the amounts received (debits) always equals the amounts given (credits). "

Pat King, Owner

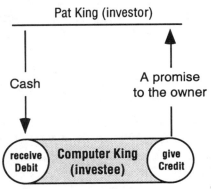

Transaction A. King's first transaction is to deposit $15,000 in a bank account in the name of Computer King. Notice that Computer King is a separate entity. Pat King, as an individual, is investing cash into Computer King.

Account	Debit	Credit
Cash	15,000	
Pat King, Capital		15,000

✓ **Note:** In exchange for receiving an investment of cash, the company gives a promise to the owner. This promise consists of an obligation to manage and periodically report the status of the investment.

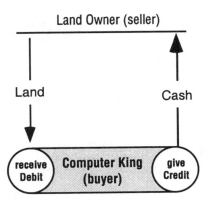

Transaction B. Computer King's next transaction is to purchase land for $10,000 cash. The land is located near a shopping mall that contains three microcomputer stores. Computer King's current plans are to rent equipment and office space near the shopping mall for several months. If the business is a success, a building will be built on the land.

Account	Debit	Credit
Land	10,000	
Cash		10,000

✓ **Note:** When one asset (cash) is exchanged for another (land), total assets do not change.

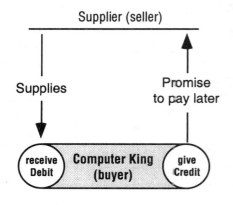

Supplier (seller)

Supplies

Promise
to pay later

receive
Debit — Computer King
(buyer) — give
Credit

Transaction C. Computer King purchased supplies for $1,350 from a supplier, agreeing to pay in the near future. This type of transaction is called a purchase on account. There are only two ways to pay for what is purchased: (1) pay now—credit Cash, or (2) promise to pay later—credit a payable.

Account	Debit	Credit
Supplies 1,350		
Accounts Payable..1,350		

✓ **Note:** Payables represent promises given to pay cash later. The company states that it is able to pay.

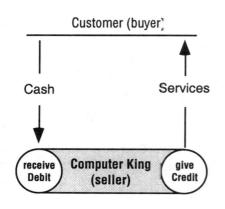

Customer (buyer)

Cash

Services

receive
Debit — Computer King
(seller) — give
Credit

Transaction D. During its first month of operations, Computer King earned fees of $7,500, receiving the amount in cash. When selling goods or services, there are two ways to receive payment: (1) receive cash now—debit Cash, or (2) receive a promise to collect cash later—debit a receivable.

Account	Debit	Credit
Cash 7,500		
Fees Earned 7,500		

✓ **Note:** Fees earned are revenues. Revenues represent goods or services given in a selling transaction.

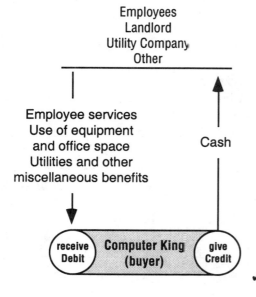

Employees
Landlord
Utility Company
Other

Employee services
Use of equipment
and office space
Utilities and other
miscellaneous benefits

Cash

receive
Debit — Computer King
(buyer) — give
Credit

Transaction E. The expenses paid during the month were as follows: wages, $2,125; rent, $800; utilities, $450; miscellaneous, $275. Miscellaneous expenses include small amounts paid for postage due, coffee, and newspaper and magazine purchases.

Account	Debit	Credit
Wages Expense 2,125		
Rent Expense 800		
Utilities Expense 450		
Miscellaneous Expense........................ 275		
Cash 3,650		

✓ **Note:** Expenses represent services, goods, and benefits received in a buying transaction.

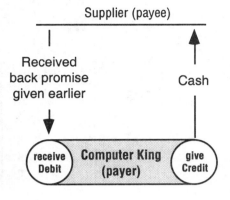

Supplier (payee)

Received back promise given earlier ← | Cash ↑

receive **Debit** | **Computer King (payer)** | give **Credit**

Transaction F. During the month, $950 is paid to creditors on account. In the prior Transaction C, a promise was given to pay later. Now that a portion of that obligation is paid, Computer King receives a reduction of that obligation by receiving back part of the promise given earlier.

Account	Debit	Credit
Accounts Payable................................950		
Cash 950		

✓ **Note:** When payment is made on account, the company receives a reduction in their obligation in exchange for cash given.

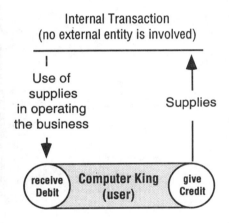

Internal Transaction (no external entity is involved)

Use of supplies in operating the business ← | Supplies ↑

receive **Debit** | **Computer King (user)** | give **Credit**

Transaction G. At the end of the month, it is determined that the cost of the supplies on hand is $550. The remainder of the supplies ($1,350-$550) were used in the operations of the business. This is an internal transaction; no outside entity is involved. A portion of the supplies has been used up in operating the company.

Account	Debit	Credit
Supplies Expense................................. 800		
Supplies..800		

✓ **Note:** Supplies are an asset which represent future benefits to the company. As supplies are used, the company gives up the supplies and receives the benefit of using the supplies. Expenses represent services or benefits received by the company.

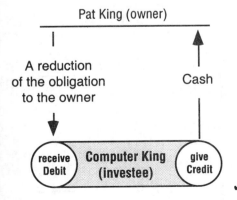

Pat King (owner)

A reduction of the obligation to the owner ← | Cash ↑

receive **Debit** | **Computer King (investee)** | give **Credit**

Transaction H. At the end of the month, Pat King withdraws $2,000 in cash from the business for personal use. This is the exact opposite of the investment in the business by the owner.

Account	Debit	Credit
Pat King, Drawing............................ 2,000		
Cash 2,000		

✓ **Note:** The owner's drawing account is not an expense of the company.

General Journal

All transactions for Computer King for the first month of operations are shown to the right. This general journal is a listing of resources and obligations received and given in chronological order.

General Ledger

The transactions have been classified by account in the general ledger accounts below. In a manual accounting system the classification process is called posting. Using a computer system, this is accomplished by sorting or indexing.

General Journal

		Received Column	Gave Column
Account		**Debit**	**Credit**
a. Cash		15,000	
Pat King, Capital			15,000
b. Land		10,000	
Cash			10,000
c. Supplies		1,350	
Accounts Payable			1,350
d. Cash		7,500	
Fees Earned			7,500
e. Wages Expense		2,125	
Rent Expense		800	
Utilities Expense		450	
Miscellaneous Expense		275	
Cash			3,650
f. Accounts Payable		950	
Cash			950
g. Supplies Expense		800	
Supplies			800
h. Pat King, Drawing		2,000	
Cash			2,000

ASSETS

Cash

a. 15,000	b. 10,000
d. 7,500	e. 3,650
	f. 950
	h. 2,000
5,900	

Supplies

c. 1,350	g. 800
550	

Land

b. 10,000	

LIABILITIES

Accounts Payable

f. 950	c. 1,350
	400

OWNER'S EQUITY

Pat King, Capital

	a. 15,000

Pat King, Drawing

h. 2,000	

REVENUES

Fees Earned

	d. 7,500

EXPENSES

Wages Expense

e. 2,125	

Rent Expense

e. 800	

Supplies Expense

g. 800	

Utilities Expense

e. 450	

Misc. Expense

e. 275	

Summary of Transactions by Accounts and Categories

Computer King Trial Balance November 30, 1999	Received Column — Debit	Gave Column — Credit	Description
Accounts	**Debit**	**Credit**	**Description**
Cash	5,900		net amount of cash **received**
Supplies	550		**received** supplies with future benefits
Land	10,000		**received** land for future use
Accounts Payable		400	**gave** promise to suppliers
Pat King, Capital		15,000	**gave** promise to owner
Pat King, Drawing	2,000		**received** reduction in obligation
Fees Earned		7,500	**gave** services to customers
Wages Expense	2,125		**received** services from employees
Rent Expense	800		**received** use of equipment and space
Supplies Expense	800		**received** benefit of supplies used
Utilities Expense	450		**received** benefit of utilities
Miscellaneous Expense	275		**received** other services or benefits
Totals	**22,900**	**22,900**	

Categories	**Debit**	**Credit**	**Description**
ASSETS	16,450		total resources **received**
LIABILITIES		400	total promises **given** to creditors
OWNER'S EQUITY		13,000	obligation **given** to owner
REVENUES		7,500	total services **given** to customers
EXPENSES	4,450		total services and benefits **received**

✓ **Note:** The total dollar amounts **received** (debits) must equal the amounts **given** (credits). This basic equality is fundamental to the double-entry system of accounting and is evident in all of the accounting records.

Basic Financial Statements

Income Statement

Revenues represent the value of services given to customers in selling transactions.

Expenses represent the value of services and benefits received in buying transactions.

Net income is the result of giving more value than the value received.

Statement of Owner's Equity

Three types of transactions affect the owner's equity:
(1) owner investments
(2) net income
(3) owner withdrawals

Balance Sheet

Assets are economic resources received and owned by the business which are expected to benefit future operations.

Liabilities are debts owed to creditors evidenced by promises given by the business.

Owner's Equity is the excess of total assets over total liabilities and represents obligations given to the owner for resources invested by the owner.

Computer King
Income Statement
For Month Ended November 30, 1999

Fees earned		$ 7,500
Operating expenses:		
Wages expense	$ 2,125	
Rent expense	800	
Supplies expense	800	
Utilities expense	450	
Miscellaneous expense	275	
Total expenses		4,450
Net income		$ 3,050

Computer King
Statement of Owner's Equity
For Month Ended November 30, 1999

Pat King, capital, November 1, 1999		$ 0
Investment on November 1, 1999	$15,000	
Net income for November	3,050	
Less withdrawals	2,000	
Increase in owner's equity		16,050
Pat King, capital, November 30, 1999		$16,050

Computer King
Balance Sheet
November 30, 1999

Assets:		
Cash		$ 5,900
Supplies		550
Land		10,000
Total assets		$16,450
Liabilities:		
Accounts payable		$ 400
Owner's Equity:		
Pat King, capital		16,050
Total liabilities and owner's equity		$16,450

" The double-entry system of accounting involves a series of processing steps. Source documents are analyzed and recorded in a journal and then classified by account in the general ledger. Ledger accounts are summarized in a trial balance and then categorized in the financial statements. "

Procedures	Accounting Records
Analyze Transactions	Source Documents
Record Transactions	General Journal
Classify Accounts	General Ledger
Summarize Accounts	Trial Balance
Categorize Accounts	Financial Statements

" These processing steps are not the most important aspect of the double-entry system. It is much more important to understand and be able to structure and negotiate basic business transactions as a buyer or seller, or as a lender or borrower. All personal or business relationships involve at least four parts as shown below. Although you will account for only two of the four parts (one set of books), understanding and satisfying all four parts is necessary for a healthy relationship. Understanding the two parts that you do not record is very important. For example, a successful entrepreneur knows the needs of others must be satisfied in order to complete any transaction. When you satisfy the needs of others, you build strong and trusting relationships which will lead to many satisfying and profitable business transactions. "

Luca Pacioli
Inventor of
Double-Entry
Accounting

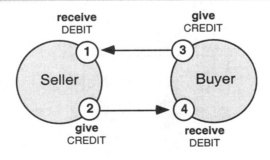

Model of a Successful Enterprise

" The successful company or individual is always looking for ways to serve others by providing for their needs. **Revenues** are a measure of our services or goods given in a selling transaction. **Expenses** are not considered a negative factor—expenses are necessary services or benefits received which allow us to better serve others. When the value of services and goods **given** (revenues) is greater than the value of services and benefits **received** (expenses), you are profitable. Study the model below and you will see how the pieces fit together. "

" As you begin your study of the double-entry system, analyze each transaction carefully. If the transaction is an external one involving another entity, determine whom you are dealing with and take a moment to reflect on how the transaction affects them. Only in looking beyond your own situation will you find satisfaction in business. When both entities are satisfied with transactions, true value will be added at each step of the transformation process from producer to the ultimate consumer. Best wishes for your business success and accurate accounting! "

Luca Pacioli
Father of the
Balance Sheet

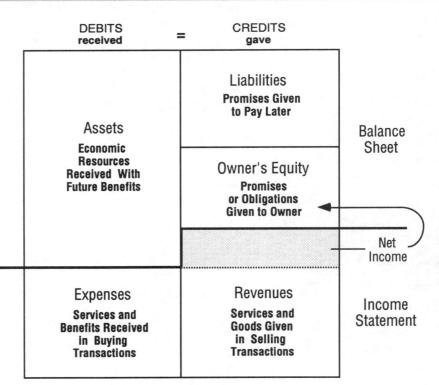

Exercise 2–1

Chart of accounts
Objective 1 - Text page 44

Adcock Interiors is owned and operated by Harold Adcock, an interior decorator. In the ledger of Adcock Interiors, the first digit of the account number indicates its major account classification (1-assets, 2-liabilities, 3-owner's equity, 4-revenues, 5-expenses). The second digit of the account number indicates the specific account within each of the preceding major account classifications.

Working Papers Plus

Chapter 2

Match each account number with its most likely account in the list below.

Account Numbers: 11, 12, 13, 21, 31, 32, 41, 51, 52, 53

Accounts:

____	Accounts Payable	____	Harold Adcock, Drawing
____	Accounts Receivable	____	Land
____	Cash	____	Miscellaneous Expense
____	Fees Earned	____	Supplies Expense
____	Harold Adcock, Capital	____	Wages Expense

Exercise 2–2

Chart of accounts
Objective 1 - Text page 44

The Charm School is a newly organized business that teaches young people how to behave in a socially acceptable way. The list of accounts to be opened in the general ledger is as follows:

Accounts Payable	Heather Mock, Capital	Supplies
Accounts Receivable	Heather Mock, Drawing	Supplies Expense
Cash	Miscellaneous Expense	Unearned Rent
Equipment	Prepaid Insurance	Wages Expense
Fees Earned	Rent Expense	

List the accounts in the order in which they should appear in the ledger of The Charm School and assign account numbers. Each account number is to have two digits: the first digit is to indicate the major classification (1 for assets, etc.), and the second digit is to identify the specific account within each major classification (11 for Cash, etc.).

Balance Sheet Accounts   Income Statement Accounts

#	NAME

#	NAME

Exercise 2–3

Identifying transactions
Objectives 2, 3 - Text pages 46 and 47

Sunrise Co. is a travel agency. The nine transactions recorded by Sunrise during June, its first month of operations, are indicated in the following T accounts:

Cash				Equipment		Cheng Sun, Drawing	
(1) 50,000	(2)	2,500		(3) 30,500		(8) 2,500	
(7) 9,500	(3)	10,000					
	(4)	6,050					
	(6)	6,000					
	(8)	2,500					

Accounts Receivable			Accounts Payable			Service Revenue	
(5) 12,500	(7) 9,500		(6) 6,000	(3) 20,000			(5) 12,500

Supplies			Cheng Sun, Capital		Operating Expenses	
(2) 2,500	(9) 1,450			(1) 50,000	(4) 6,050	
					(9) 1,450	

Indicate for each debit and each credit: (a) whether an asset, liability, owner's equity, drawing, revenue, or expense account was affected and (b) whether the account was increased (+) or decreased (-). Present your answers in the following form [transaction (1) is given as an example]:

	Account Debited		Account Credited	
Transaction	Type	Effect	Type	Effect
(1)...........	asset	+	owner's equity	+
(2)...........				
(3)...........				
(4)...........				
(5)...........				
(6)...........				
(7)...........				
(8)...........				
(9)...........				

Exercise 2–4

Journal entries
Objectives 3, 4 - Text pages 47 and 51

Based upon the T accounts in Exercise 2-3, prepare the nine journal entries from which the postings were made. Journal entry explanations may be omitted.

NO.	DESCRIPTION	DEBIT	CREDIT

Continued

Continued

Based upon the T accounts in Exercise 2-3, prepare the nine journal entries from which the postings were made. Journal entry explanations may be omitted.

NO.	DESCRIPTION	DEBIT	CREDIT

Exercise 2–5

Trial balance
Objective 5 - Text page 64
✔ Total Debit Column:
$76,500

Based upon the data presented in Exercise 2-3, prepare a trial balance, listing the accounts in their proper order.

Sunrise Co.
Trial Balance
June 30, 20__

ACCOUNT NAME	DEBIT	CREDIT

Exercise 2–6

Normal entries for accounts
Objective 3 - Text page 47

During the month, Dexter Labs Co. has a substantial number of transactions affecting each of the following accounts. State for each account whether it is likely to have (a) debit entries only, (b) credit entries only, or (c) both debit and credit entries.

____ 1. Accounts Payable   ____ 5. Justin Sykes, Drawing

____ 2. Accounts Receivable   ____ 6. Miscellaneous Expense

____ 3. Cash   ____ 7. Supplies Expense

____ 4. Fees Earned

Exercise 2–7

Normal balances of accounts
Objective 3 - Text page 47

Identify each of the following accounts of Elrod Services Co. as an asset, liability, owner's equity, revenue, or expense, and state in each case whether the normal balance is a debit or a credit.

	Type	Balance
a. Accounts Payable	_____	_____
b. Accounts Receivable	_____	_____
c. Cash	_____	_____
d. Chester Elrod, Capital	_____	_____
e. Chester Elrod, Drawing	_____	_____
f. Equipment	_____	_____
g. Fees Earned	_____	_____
h. Rent Expense	_____	_____
i. Salary Expense	_____	_____
j. Supplies	_____	_____

Exercise 2–8

Rules of debit and credit
Objective 3 - Text page 47

The following table summarizes the rules of debit and credit. For each of the items (a) through (l), indicate whether the proper answer is a debit or a credit.

	Increase	Decrease	Normal Balance
Balance sheet accounts:			
Asset	(a)_____	Credit	Debit
Liability	(b)_____	(c)_____	(d)_____
Owner's Equity:			
Capital	(e)_____	(f)_____	Credit
Drawing	(g)_____	(h)_____	Debit
Income statement accounts:			
Revenue	Credit	(i)_____	(j)_____
Expense	(k)_____	Credit	(l)_____

Capital account balance

Objective 2 - Text page 46   ✔ Negative $7,000

As of January 1, Wanda Deaton, Capital had a credit balance of $8,000. During the year, withdrawals totaled $10,000 and the business incurred a net loss of $5,000.

a. Calculate the balance of Wanda Deaton, Capital as of the end of the year.

b. Assuming that there have been no recording errors, will the balance sheet prepared at December 31 balance? Explain.

Exercise 2–10

Cash account balance

Objective 2 - Text page 46   ✔ b. $100,000

During the month, a business received $712,800 in cash and paid out $630,000 in cash.

a. Does the data indicate that the business earned $82,800 during the month? Explain.

b. If the balance of the cash account was $17,200 at the beginning of the month, what was the cash balance at the end of the month?

Exercise 2–11

Account balances

Objective 2 - Text page 46   ✔ c. $13,800

a. On April 1, the cash account balance was $11,250. During April, cash receipts totaled $31,800 and the April 30 balance was $12,500. Determine the cash payments made during April.

b. On June 1, the accounts receivable account balance was $23,900. During June, $21,000 was collected from customers on account. If the June 30 balance was $27,500, determine the fees billed to customers on account during June.

c. During August, $40,500 was paid to creditors on account and purchases on account were $77,700. If the August 31 balance of Accounts Payable was $51,000, determine the account balance on August 1.

Exercise 2–12

Transactions
Objectives 3, 4 - Text pages 47 and 51

The Wildlife Co. has the following accounts in its ledger: Cash; Accounts Receivable; Supplies; Office Equipment; Accounts Payable; Erin Fox, Capital; Erin Fox, Drawing; Fees Earned; Rent Expense; Advertising Expense; Utilities Expense; Miscellaneous Expense.

Journalize the following selected transactions in the two-column journal below. Journal entry explanations may be omitted.

July Transactions

1. Paid rent for the month, $3,000.

2. Paid advertising expense, $500.

4. Paid cash for supplies, $770.

6. Purchased office equipment on account, $8,500.

8. Received cash from customers on account, $3,600.

12. Paid creditor on account, $2,150.

20. Withdrew cash for personal use, $1,500.

25. Paid cash for repairs to office equipment, $120.

30. Paid telephone bill for the month, $195.

31. Fees earned and billed to customers for the month, $11,150.

31. Paid electricity bill for the month, $430.

DATE	DESCRIPTION	DEBIT	CREDIT

Journalizing and posting
Objectives 3, 4 - Text pages 47 and 51

On April 8, 2000, Parshall Co. purchased $2,720 of supplies on account. In Parshall Co.'s chart of accounts, the supplies account is No. 15 and the accounts payable account is No. 21.

a. Journalize the April 8, 2000 transaction on page 12 of Parshall Co.'s
   two-column journal. Include an explanation of the entry.

GENERAL JOURNAL　　　　　　　　　Page

Date	Description	Post. Ref.	Debit	Credit

b. Prepare a four-column account for Supplies. Enter a debit balance of $1,200
   as of April 1, 2000. Place a check mark (✓) in the posting reference column.

ACCOUNT　　　　　　　　　　　　　　　　　　　　NO.

Date	Description	Post. Ref.	Debit	Credit	Balance Debit	Balance Credit

c. Prepare a four-column account for Accounts Payable. Enter a credit balance of
   $11,734 as of April 1, 2000. Place a check mark (✓) in the posting reference column.

ACCOUNT　　　　　　　　　　　　　　　　　　　　NO.

Date	Description	Post. Ref.	Debit	Credit	Balance Debit	Balance Credit

d. Post the April 8, 2000 transaction to the accounts.

Exercise 2–14

Transactions and T accounts
Objectives 2, 3, 4 - Text pages 46, 47, and 51

The following selected transactions were completed during February of the current year:

1. Billed customers for fees earned, $5,210.
2. Purchased supplies on account, $520.
3. Received cash from customers on account, $3,200.
4. Paid creditors on account, $400.

a. Journalize the foregoing transactions in a two-column journal, using the appropriate number to identify the transactions. Journal entry explanations may be omitted.

DATE	DESCRIPTION	DEBIT	CREDIT

b. Post the entries prepared in (a) to the following T accounts: Cash, Supplies, Accounts Receivable, Accounts Payable, Fees Earned. To the left of each amount posted in the accounts, place the appropriate number to identify the transactions.

Cash

Accounts Payable

Supplies

Fees Earned

Accounts Receivable

Trial balance

Objective 5 - Text page 64   ✔ Total Debit Column: $485,000

Dillon Garcia
Consultant

" The accounts in the ledger of my company as of August 31 of the current year are listed in alphabetical order below. All accounts have normal balances. The balance of the cash account has been intentionally omitted, as I have temporarily misplaced the cash records. Please prepare a trial balance, listing the accounts in their proper order and inserting the missing figure for cash. "

Accounts Payable $18,710	Notes Payable .... $ 35,000
Accounts Receivable 20,500	Prepaid Insurance 3,150
Cash ....?	Rent Expense 58,000
Dillon Garcia, Capital 110,290	Supplies 4,100
Dillon Garcia, Drawing ... 20,000	Supplies Expense 5,900
Fees Earned 315,000	Unearned Rent 6,000
Insurance Expense 5,000	Utilities Expense 41,500
Land 125,000	Wages Expense 175,000
Miscellaneous Expense 9,900	

Asbury Park Co.
Trial Balance
August 31, 20__

ACCOUNT NAME	DEBIT	CREDIT

Exercise 2–16

Effect of errors on trial balance
Objective 5 - Text page 64

Indicate which of the following errors, each considered individually, would cause the trial balance totals to be unequal:

a. Payment of a cash withdrawal of $2,000 was journalized and posted as a debit of $200 to Salary Expense and a credit of $200 to Cash.

b. A payment of $5,000 for equipment purchased was posted as a debit of $5,000 to Equipment and a credit of $50,000 to Cash.

c. A fee of $3,100 earned and due from a client was not debited to Accounts Receivable cr credited to a revenue account, because the cash had not been received.

d. A receipt of $500 from an account receivable was journalized and posted as a debit of $500 to Cash and a credit of $500 to Fees Earned.

e. A payment of $850 to a creditor was posted as a debit of $850 to Accounts Payable and a debit of $850 to Cash.

Errors in trial balance
Objective 5 - Text page 64　　✔ Total of Credit Column: $143,280

The following preliminary trial balance of The Montana Co.,
a sports ticket agency, does not balance:

The Montana Co.
Trial Balance
December 31, 20____　　　　　　　　Corrected Trial Balance

ACCOUNT NAME	DEBIT	CREDIT	DEBIT	CREDIT
Cash	83,000			
Accounts Receivable	23,600			
Prepaid Insurance		3,300		
Equipment	4,500			
Accounts Payable		9,450		
Unearned Rent		1,480		
Ted Turner, Capital	68,550			
Ted Turner, Drawing	10,000			
Service Revenue		64,940		
Wages Expense		33,400		
Advertising Expense	5,200			
Miscellaneous Expense		1,380		
	194,850	113,950		

When the ledger and other records are reviewed, you discover the following:

(1) The debits and credits in the cash account total $83,000 and $65,300, respectively.
(2) A billing of $3,700 to a customer on account was not posted to the accounts
    receivable account.
(3) A payment of $1,500 made to a creditor on account was not posted to the
    accounts payable account.
(4) The balance of the unearned rent account is $1,840.
(5) The correct balance of the equipment account is $45,000.
(6) Each account has a normal balance.

Prepare a corrected trial balance using the columns provided.

Exercise 2–18

Effect of errors on trial balance
Objective 5 - Text page 64

The following errors occurred in posting from a two-column journal:

1. A credit of $500 to Accounts Payable was posted as a debit.
2. An entry debiting Accounts Receivable and crediting Fees Earned for $4,500 was not posted.
3. A credit of $250 to Cash was posted as $520.
4. A debit of $750 to Cash was posted to Wages Expense.
5. A debit of $1,200 to Supplies was posted twice.
6. A debit of $1,575 to Wages Expense was posted as $1,755.
7. A credit of $1,830 to Accounts Receivable was not posted.

Considering each case individually (i.e., assuming that no other errors had occurred), indicate:

(a) by "yes" or "no" whether the trial balance would be out of balance;
(b) if answer to (a) is "yes,' the amount by which the trial balance totals would differ;
(c) whether the debit or credit column of the trial balance would have the larger total.

Answers should be presented in the following form [error (1) is given as an example]:

	(a)	(b)	(c)
Error ....Out of Balance		Difference	Larger Total
(1)	yes	$ 1,000	debit
(2)			
(3)			
(4)			
(5)			
(6)			
(7)			

Exercise 2–19

Errors in trial balance
Objective 5 - Text page 64 ✔ Total of Credit Column: $105,100

How many errors can you find in the following trial balance?
All accounts have normal balances.

The Peasley Co.
Trial Balance
For the Month Ending March 31, 20__

Cash	3,010	
Accounts Receivable.............	16,400	
Prepaid Insurance		2,400
Equipment	41,200	
Accounts Payable............._......	1,850	
Salaries Payable.................._...		750
Nikki Swoopes, Capital		34,600
Nikki Swoopes, Drawing ...		5,000
Service Revenue ...._...		67,900
Salary Expense		28,400
Advertising Expense	7,200	
Miscellaneous Expense	1,490	
	139,050	139,050

Exercise 2–20

Name:

Entries to correct errors
Objective 6 - Text page 65

Errors in journalizing and posting transactions are described as follows:

a. A withdrawal of $15,000 by T. Woods, owner of the business, was
    recorded as a debit to Salary Expense and a credit to Cash.

b. Rent of $1,800 paid for the current month was recorded as a debit to
    Accounts Payable and a credit to Cash.

Journalize the entries to correct the errors. Omit explanations.

DATE	DESCRIPTION	DEBIT	CREDIT

Exercise 2–21

Entries to correct errors
Objective 6 - Text page 65

Errors in journalizing and posting transactions are described as follows:

a. A $1,050 purchase of supplies on account was recorded as a debit to
    Cash and a credit to Accounts Payable.
b. Cash of $1,350 received on account was recorded as a debit to
    Accounts Payable and a credit to Cash.

Journalize the entries to correct the errors. Omit explanations.

DATE	DESCRIPTION	DEBIT	CREDIT

Financial Analysis and Interpretation

Objective: Use horizontal analysis to compare financial statements from different periods.

Comparative Balance Sheet
December 31, 2000 and 1999

Assets	2000	1999	Increase (Decrease) Amount	Percent
Current assets	$ 550,000	$ 533,000	$ 17,000	3.2%
Long-term investments				
Fixed assets (net)				
Intangible assets				

Horizontal Analysis:

$$\frac{\text{Current year (2000)} \quad \$550,000}{\text{Base year (1999)} \quad \$533,000} = 103.2\%$$

$$\frac{\text{Increase amount} \quad \$17,000}{\text{Base year (1999)} \quad \$533,000} = 3.2\%$$

Two ways to express the relationship:

The 2000 current assets are 103.2% of the 1999 current assets.

Current assets increased by 3.2% during 2000.

Comparative Income Statement
December 31, 2000 and 1999

	2000	1999	Increase (Decrease) Amount	Percent
Sales	$1,530,500	$1,234,000	$296,500	24.0%
Sales returns	32,500	34,000	(1,500)	(4.4%)
Net sales	$1,498,000	$1,200,000	$298,000	24.8%
Cost of goods sold				
Gross profit				

Horizontal Analysis:

$$\frac{\text{Current year (2000)} \quad \$1,498,000}{\text{Base year (1999)} \quad \$1,200,000} = 124.8\%$$

$$\frac{\text{Increase amount} \quad \$298,000}{\text{Base year (1999)} \quad \$1,200,000} = 24.8\%$$

Exercise 2–22

Horizontal analysis of income statement
Objective 7 - Text page 67

The financial statements for **Hershey Foods Corporation** are presented in Appendix G at the end of the text.

a. For Hershey Foods Corporation, comparing 1996 with 1995, determine the amount of change and the percent of change for:

1. net sales (revenues) and

2. selling, marketing, and administrative expenses.

b. What conclusions can you draw from your analysis of the net sales and the selling, marketing, and administrative expenses?

The increasing complexity of the current business and regulatory environment has created an increased demand for accountants who can analyze business transactions and interpret their effects on the financial statements. In addition, a basic ability to analyze the effects of transactions is necessary to be successful in all fields of business as well as in other disciplines, such as law. To better understand the importance of accounting in today's environment, search the Internet or your local newspaper for job opportunities. One possible Internet site is **www.jobweb.com**. Then do *one* of the following:

1. Print a listing of at least two ads for accounting jobs. Alternatively, bring to class at least two newspaper ads for accounting jobs.

2. Print a listing of at least two ads for nonaccounting jobs for which some knowledge of accounting is preferred or necessary. Alternatively, bring to class at least two newspaper ads for such jobs.

Career Directions on the Web

Do you ever wonder if you are really headed in the right profession for your personality, interest, and skill sets? "To thine own self, be true," noted Socrates. Yet for many of us it's difficult to determine what we are interested in and what we have the skills for. Try the following web sites to learn more about career possibilities and your personality.

A great site to explore:
   www.aboutwork.com

A good site to match your personality to career options:
   www.aboutwork.com/resourcecenter

Based on your research, list a few career possibilities that may match your interests and skills.

Blank Page

Problem 2–1A Robin Reich, Architect   Name:

Entries into T accounts and trial balance
Objectives 2, 3, 4, 5 ✔ 3. Total of Debit Column: $50,100

Robin Reich, an architect, opened an office on April 1 of the current year. During the
month, he completed the following transactions connected with his professional practice:

Robin Reich
Architect

a. Transferred cash from a personal bank account to an account to be used for the business, $30,000.
b. Purchased used automobile for $18,300, paying $6,000 cash and giving a non-interest-bearing note for the remainder.
c. Paid April rent for office and workroom, $2,200.
d. Paid cash for supplies, $300.
e. Purchased office and drafting room equipment on account, $4,200.
f. Paid cash for insurance policies on automobile and equipment, $810.
g. Received cash from a client for plans delivered, $2,725.
h. Paid cash to creditors on account, $2,100.
i. Paid cash for miscellaneous expenses, $120.
j. Received invoice for blueprint service, due in following month, $275.
k. Recorded fee earned on plans delivered, payment to be received in May, $3,500.
l. Paid salary of assistant, $1,500.
m. Paid cash for miscellaneous expenses, $60.
n. Paid installment due on note payable, $800.
o. Paid gas, oil, and repairs on automobile for April, $170.

Instructions

1. Record the foregoing transactions directly in the following T accounts, without journalizing. To the left of each amount entered in the accounts, place the appropriate letter to identify the transaction.

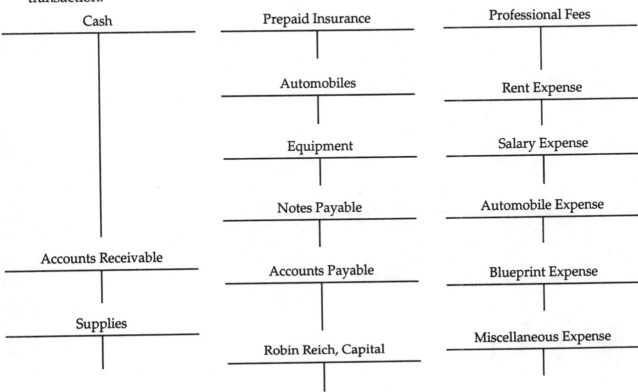

2. Determine the balances of the T accounts having two or more debits or credits.

Continued

3. Using the form below, prepare a trial balance for Robin Reich,
   Architect, as of April 30 of the current year. (Flipping this page back
   and forth a few times will test your concentration.)

Robin Reich, Architect
Trial Balance
April 30, 20__

ACCOUNT NAME	DEBIT	CREDIT

" Is this really as easy as it looks? Maybe
next month I'll record my transactions and
prepare a trial balance. Of course I'll have
you check my work and prepare my
financial statements. "

Robin Reich
Architect

Journal entries and trial balance
Objectives 2, 3, 4, 5 ✔ a. $32,600 b. $12,700

On October 1 of the current year, Clay Bryant established Northside Realty, which completed the following transactions during the month:

a. Clay Bryant transferred cash from his personal bank account to an account to be used for the business, $25,000.
b. Purchased supplies on account, $2,900.
c. Earned sales commissions, receiving cash, $32,600.
d. Paid rent on office and equipment for the month, $4,500.
e. Paid creditor on account, $1,000.
f. Withdrew cash for personal use, $2,000.
g. Paid automobile expenses (including rental charge) for month, $1,900, and miscellaneous expenses, $1,050.
h. Paid office salaries, $4,000.
i. Determined that the cost of supplies used was $1,250.

Clay Bryant, Owner
Northside Realty

Instructions

1. Using a blank **Form GJ**, journalize entries for transactions (a) through (i), using the following account titles: Cash; Supplies; Accounts Payable; Clay Bryant, Capital; Clay Bryant, Drawing; Sales Commissions; Rent Expense; Office Salaries Expense; Automobile Expense; Supplies Expense; Miscellaneous Expense. Journal entry explanations may be omitted.

2. T accounts have been prepared on the back of this page. Post your journal entries to these accounts, placing the appropriate letter to the left of each amount to identify the transactions. Determine the account balances, after all posting is complete, for all accounts having two or more debits or credits. A memorandum balance should also be inserted in accounts having both debits and credits, in the manner illustrated in the chapter. For accounts with entries on one side only, there is no need to insert a memorandum balance in the item column. For accounts containing only a single debit and a single credit, the memorandum balance should be inserted in the appropriate item column.

3. Using the form provided on the back of this page, prepare a trial balance as of October 31, 20___.

4. Determine the following:

   a. Amount of total revenue recorded in the ledger. $_____

   b. Amount of total expenses recorded in the ledger. $_____

   c. Amount of net income for October. $_____

Continued

Post your journal entries to these accounts. See instruction 2
on the front of this page for additional information.

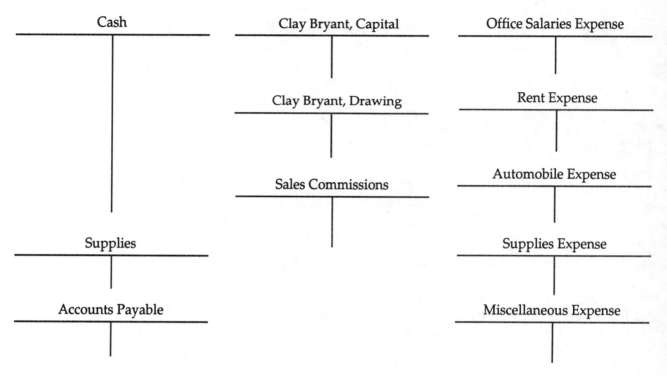

Using the form provided below, prepare a trial balance as of October 31, 20___.

ACCOUNT NAME	DEBIT	CREDIT

Journal entries and trial balance
Objectives 2, 3, 4, 5
✔ 3. Total of Credit Column: $36,425

Name: _____

Note: The working papers that follow this problem may be used with either Problem 2-3A or 2-3B.

On July 10 of the current year, Jong Woo established an interior decorating business, Asian Designs. During the remainder of the month, Jong Woo completed the following transactions related to the business:

Jong Woo
Interior Designer

July 10. Jong transferred cash from a personal bank account to an account to be used for the business, $20,000.

10. Paid rent for period of July 10 to end of month, $1,500.

11. Purchased a truck for $15,000, paying $5,000 cash and giving a note payable for the remainder.

12. Purchased equipment on account, $2,500.

14. Purchased supplies for cash, $1,050.

14. Paid premiums on property and casualty insurance, $750.

15. Received cash for job completed, $3,100.

21. Paid creditor for equipment purchased on July 12, $2,500.

24. Recorded jobs completed on account and sent invoices to customers, $3,100.

26. Received an invoice for truck expenses, to be paid in August, $225.

27. Paid utilities expense, $1,205.

27. Paid miscellaneous expenses, $173.

28. Received cash from customers on account, $1,420.

31. Paid wages of employees, $2,100.

31. Withdrew cash for personal use, $1,500.

Instructions

1. Journalize each transaction in a two-column journal, referring to the following chart of accounts in selecting the accounts to be debited and credited. (Do not insert the account numbers in the journal at this time.) Journal entry explanations may be omitted.

11 Cash	31 Jong Woo, Capital
12 Accounts Receivable	32 Jong Woo, Drawing
13 Supplies	41 Fees Earned
14 Prepaid Insurance	51 Wages Expense
16 Equipment	53 Rent Expense
18 Truck	54 Utilities Expense
21 Notes Payable	55 Truck Expense
22 Accounts Payable	59 Miscellaneous Expense

2. Post the journal to a ledger of four-column accounts, inserting appropriate posting references as each item is posted. Extend the balances to the appropriate balance columns after each transaction is posted.

3. Prepare a trial balance for Asian Designs as of July 31.

Blank Page

GENERAL JOURNAL

Page ____

Date	Description	Post. Ref.	Debit	Credit

Problem 2-3___

1. Journalize transactions.

GENERAL JOURNAL

Page

Date	Description	Post. Ref.	Debit	Credit

Problem 2-3___

Name:

2. Post journal to general ledger.

GENERAL LEDGER

ACCOUNT Cash   NO. 11

Date	Description	Post. Ref.	Debit	Credit	Balance Debit	Balance Credit

ACCOUNT Accounts Receivable   NO. 12

Date	Description	Post. Ref.	Debit	Credit	Balance Debit	Balance Credit

ACCOUNT Supplies   NO. 13

Date	Description	Post. Ref.	Debit	Credit	Balance Debit	Balance Credit

2. Post journal to general ledger.

ACCOUNT Prepaid Insurance   NO. 14

Date	Description	Post. Ref.	Debit	Credit	Balance Debit	Balance Credit

ACCOUNT Equipment   NO. 16

Date	Description	Post. Ref.	Debit	Credit	Balance Debit	Balance Credit

ACCOUNT Truck   NO. 18

Date	Description	Post. Ref.	Debit	Credit	Balance Debit	Balance Credit

ACCOUNT Notes Payable   NO. 21

Date	Description	Post. Ref.	Debit	Credit	Balance Debit	Balance Credit

ACCOUNT Accounts Payable   NO. 22

Date	Description	Post. Ref.	Debit	Credit	Balance Debit	Balance Credit

2. Post journal to general ledger.

ACCOUNT   , Capital   NO. 31

Date		Description	Post. Ref.	Debit	Credit	Balance	
						Debit	Credit

ACCOUNT   , Drawing   NO. 32

Date		Description	Post. Ref.	Debit	Credit	Balance	
						Debit	Credit

ACCOUNT Fees Earned   NO. 41

Date		Description	Post. Ref.	Debit	Credit	Balance	
						Debit	Credit

2. Post journal to general ledger.

ACCOUNT Wages Expense   NO. 51

Date		Description	Post. Ref.	Debit	Credit	Balance	
						Debit	Credit

ACCOUNT Rent Expense   NO. 53

Date		Description	Post. Ref.	Debit	Credit	Balance	
						Debit	Credit

ACCOUNT Utilities Expense   NO. 54

Date		Description	Post. Ref.	Debit	Credit	Balance	
						Debit	Credit

ACCOUNT Truck Expense   NO. 55

Date		Description	Post. Ref.	Debit	Credit	Balance	
						Debit	Credit

ACCOUNT Miscellaneous Expense   NO. 59

Date		Description	Post. Ref.	Debit	Credit	Balance	
						Debit	Credit

3. Prepare a trial balance.

No.	Account	Debit	Credit

Asian Designs
Total Credits $36,425
_____
Modern Designs
Total Credits $46,040

Blank Page

Corrected trial balance

Objectives 5, 6　✔ 1. Total of Debit Column: $103,090

K. C. prepared the trial balance shown to the right as of December 31 of the current year:

K. C.
Part-time Bookkeeper

Newman Photography
Trial Balance
December 31, 20___　　　Corrected Trial Balance

ACCOUNT NAME	DEBIT	CREDIT	DEBIT	CREDIT
Cash	4,025			
Accounts Receivable	9,350			
Supplies	1,277			
Prepaid Insurance	330			
Equipment	12,500			
Notes Payable		12,500		
Accounts Payable		3,025		
Jake Newman, Capital		13,240		
Jake Newman, Drawing	6,000			
Fees Earned		80,750		
Wages Expense	48,150			
Rent Expense	750			
Advertising Expense	5,250			
Gas, Electricity Expense	3,150			
	90,782	109,515		

The debit and credit totals are not equal as a result of the following errors:

a. The balance of cash was overstated by $1,500.

b. A cash receipt of $1,200 was posted as a credit to Cash of $2,100.

c. A debit of $750 to Accounts Receivable was not posted.

d. A return of $252 of defective supplies was erroneously posted as a $225 credit to Supplies.

e. An insurance policy acquired at a cost of $310 was posted as a credit to Prepaid Insurance.

f. The balance of Notes Payable was overstated by $5,000.

g. A credit of $75 in Accounts Payable was overlooked when the balance of the account was determined.

h. A debit of $1,500 for a withdrawal by the owner was posted as a credit to Jake Newman, Capital.

i. The balance of $7,500 in Rent Expense was entered as $750 in the trial balance.

j. Miscellaneous Expense, with a balance of $915, was omitted from the trial balance. (Add this account to the bottom of the trial balance.)

Instructions

1. Prepare a corrected trial balance as of December 31 of the current year.

Continued

" You make this look real easy. Thanks for your help. I do have a question for you—does the fact that our trial balance now balances mean that there are no errors in the accounts? By the way, your suggestion that I should consider majoring in sports medicine is a good one; I've always been interested in that. I'm already signed up for the fall term. Thanks. "

K. C.
Part-time Bookkeeper

Memo
To: K. C.
Re: Trial Balance Errors

Entries into T accounts and trial balance
Objectives 2, 3, 4, 5 ✔ 3. Total of Debit Column: $39,410

Veronica Mays, an architect, opened an office on January 1 of the current year. During the month, she completed the following transactions connected with her professional practice:

Veronica Mays
Architect

a. Transferred cash from a personal bank account to an account to be used for the business, $20,000.
b. Paid January rent for office and workroom, $2,500.
c. Purchased used automobile for $11,500, paying $2,500 cash and giving a non-interest-bearing note for the remainder.
d. Purchased office and drafting room equipment on account, $6,200.
e. Paid cash for supplies, $900.
f. Paid cash for insurance policies, $1,050.
g. Received cash from client for plans delivered, $3,100.
h. Paid cash for miscellaneous expenses, $75.
i. Paid cash to creditors on account, $2,950.
j. Paid installment due on note payable, $400.
k. Received invoice for blueprint service, due in February, $310.
l. Recorded fee earned on plans delivered, payment to be received in February, $4,150.
m. Paid salary of assistant, $1,150.
n. Paid gas, oil, and repairs on automobile for January, $175.

Instructions

1. Record the foregoing transactions directly in the following T accounts, without journalizing. To the left of the amount entered in the accounts, place the appropriate letter to identify the transaction.

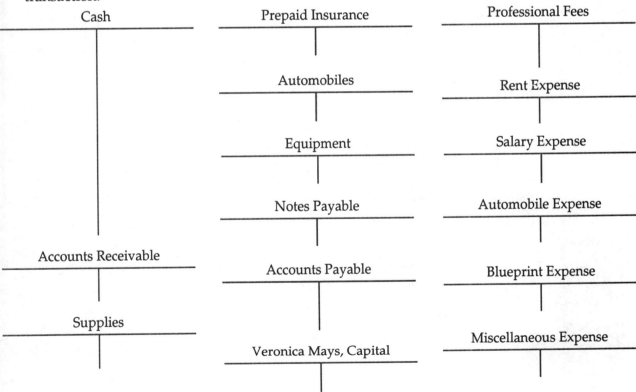

2. Determine the balances of the T accounts having two or more debits or credits.

Continued

3. Using the form below, prepare a trial balance for Veronica Mays, Architect, as of January 31 of the current year. (Flipping this page back and forth a few times will test your concentration.)

Veronica Mays, Architect
Trial Balance
January 31, 20__

ACCOUNT NAME	DEBIT	CREDIT

" I really appreciate you volunteering your time to help with the books. I'm very excited about being my own boss in my own company. Have you ever considered working for yourself? Hopefully, my business will take off and I can pay you a monthly fee for doing my accounting. "

Veronica Mays
Architect

Journal entries and trial balance
Objectives 2, 3, 4, 5 ✔ a. $20,750 b. $11,200

On July 1 of the current year, Lamar Todd established Sky Realty, which
completed the following transactions during the month:

a. Lamar Todd transferred cash from a personal bank account
   to an account to be used for the business, $15,000.
b. Paid rent on office and equipment for the month, $2,500.
c. Purchased supplies on account, $1,500.
d. Paid creditor on account, $900.
e. Earned sales commissions, receiving cash, $20,750.
f. Paid automobile expenses (including rental charge) for
   month, $2,400, and miscellaneous expenses, $1,250.
g. Paid office salaries, $4,000.
h. Determined that the cost of supplies used was $1,050.

Lamar Todd - Realtor   i. Withdrew cash for personal use, $1,500.

Instructions

1. Using a blank **Form GJ**, journalize entries for transactions (a) through (i), using the
   following account titles: Cash; Supplies; Accounts Payable; Lamar Todd, Capital;
   Lamar Todd, Drawing; Sales Commissions; Office Salaries Expense; Rent Expense;
   Automobile Expense; Supplies Expense; Miscellaneous Expense. Explanations may
   be omitted.

2. T accounts have been prepared on the back of this page. Post your journal entries to
   these accounts, placing the appropriate letter to the left of each amount to identify
   the transactions. Determine the account balances, after all posting is complete, for all
   accounts having two or more debits or credits. A memorandum balance should also
   be inserted in accounts having both debits and credits, in the manner illustrated in
   the chapter. For accounts with entries on one side only, there is no need to insert a
   memorandum balance in the item column. For accounts containing only a single
   debit and a single credit, the memorandum balance should be inserted in the
   appropriate item column.

3. Using the form provided on the back of this page, prepare a trial balance as of
   July 31, 20___.

4. Determine the following:

   a. Amount of total revenue recorded in the ledger. $_____

   b. Amount of total expenses recorded in the ledger. $_____

   c. Amount of net income for July. $_____

Continued

Post your journal entries to these accounts. See instruction 2
on the front of this page for additional information.

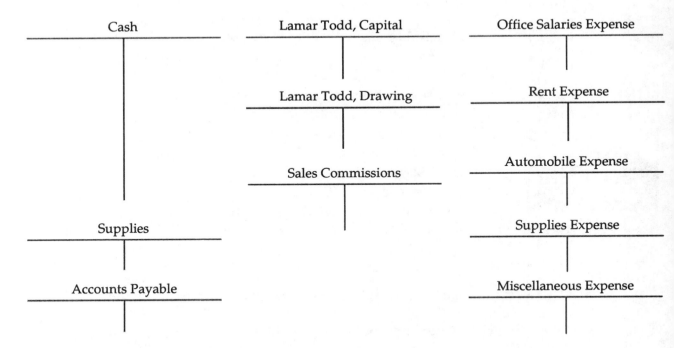

Cash	Lamar Todd, Capital	Office Salaries Expense

| | Lamar Todd, Drawing | Rent Expense |

| | Sales Commissions | Automobile Expense |

| Supplies | | Supplies Expense |

| Accounts Payable | | Miscellaneous Expense |

Using the form provided below, prepare a trial balance as of July 31, 20__.

ACCOUNT NAME	DEBIT	CREDIT

Journal entries and trial balance
Objectives 2, 3, 4, 5

✔ 3. Total of Credit Column: $46,040

Note: The working papers that follow Problem 2-3A may be used with either Problem 2-3A or 2-3B.

On June 5 of the current year, Dave Chapman established an interior decorating business, Modern Designs. During the remainder of the month, Dave completed the following transactions related to the business:

Dave Chapman
Decorator

June   5. Dave transferred cash from a personal bank account to an account to be used for the business, $25,000.
     5. Paid rent for period of June 5 to end of month, $1,700.
     7. Purchased office equipment on account, $10,500.
     8. Purchased a used truck for $18,000, paying $10,000 cash and giving a note payable for the remainder.
    10. Purchased supplies for cash, $1,315.
    12. Received cash for job completed, $3,300.
    20. Paid premiums on property and casualty insurance, $800.
    22. Recorded jobs completed on account and sent invoices to customers, $1,950.
    24. Received an invoice for truck expenses, to be paid in July, $290.
    29. Paid utilities expense, $490.
    29. Paid miscellaneous expenses, $195.
    30. Received cash from customers on account, $1,200.
    30. Paid wages of employees, $1,900.
    30. Paid creditor a portion of the amount owed for equipment purchased on June 7, $3,000
    30. Withdrew cash for personal use, $2,500.

Instructions

1. Journalize each transaction in a two-column journal, referring to the following chart of accounts in selecting the accounts to be debited and credited. (Do not insert the account numbers in the journal at this time.) Explanations may be omitted.

11 Cash	31 Dave Chapman, Capital
12 Accounts Receivable	32 Dave Chapman, Drawing
13 Supplies	41 Fees Earned
14 Prepaid Insurance	51 Wages Expense
16 Equipment	53 Rent Expense
18 Truck	54 Utilities Expense
21 Notes Payable	55 Truck Expense
22 Accounts Payable	59 Miscellaneous Expense

2. Post the journal to a ledger of four-column accounts, inserting appropriate posting references as each item is posted. Extend the balances to the appropriate balance columns after each transaction is posted.

3. Prepare a trial balance for Modern Designs as of June 30.

Blank Page

Corrected trial balance

Objectives 5, 6   ✔ 1. Total of Debit Column: $78,190

Becky Newton prepared the trial balance shown to the right as of March 31 of the current year:

Doolittle Carpet
Trial Balance
March 31, 20___

Corrected Trial Balance

ACCOUNT NAME	DEBIT	CREDIT	DEBIT	CREDIT
Cash	2,070			
Accounts Receivable	6,150			
Supplies	1,010			
Prepaid Insurance	250			
Equipment	15,500			
Notes Payable		15,000		
Accounts Payable		4,810		
Ellisa Doolittle, Capital		16,300		
Ellisa Doolittle, Drawing	6,000			
Fees Earned		49,980		
Wages Expense	28,500			
Rent Expense	6,400			
Advertising Expense	320			
Miscellaneous Expense	945			
	67,145	86,090		

Becky Newton
Novice Bookkeeper

The debit and credit totals are not equal as a result of the following errors:

a. The balance of cash was understated by $750.

b. A cash receipt of $2,100 was posted as a debit to Cash of $1,200.

c. A debit of $2,000 for a withdrawal by the owner was posted as a credit to Ellisa Doolittle, Capital.

d. The balance of $3,200 in Advertising Expense was entered as $320 in the trial balance.

e. A debit of $975 to Accounts Receivable was not posted.

f. A return of $125 of defective supplies was erroneously posted as a $215 credit to Supplies.

g. The balance of Notes Payable was overstated by $5,000.

h. An insurance policy acquired at a cost of $150 was posted as a credit to Prepaid Insurance.

i. Gas, Electricity, and Water Expense, with a balance of $3,150, was omitted from the trial balance. (Add this account to the bottom of the trial balance.)

j. A debit of $900 in Accounts Payable was overlooked when determining the balance of the account.

Instructions

1. Prepare a corrected trial balance as of March 31 of the current year.

Continued

" Thanks for your help in cleaning up my trial balance. I do have a question for you—does the fact that our trial balance is balanced mean that there are no errors in the accounts? By the way, your suggestion that I should enroll in an accounting class at Midtown Community College is a good one. I'm already signed up for the fall term. Thanks. "

Becky
Novice Bookkeeper

Memo
To: Becky
Re: Trial Balance Errors

Chapter 3

The Matching Concept and the Adjusting Process

Transactions are recorded as they occur, as illustrated in Chapter 2. At the end of an accounting period, the ledger accounts must be analyzed and, if necessary, updated to ensure that revenues and expenses are properly matched. This matching concept ensures that the income statement fairly presents the results of operations for a period and the balance sheet fairly presents the financial condition at the end of the period.

This chapter describes the matching concept and how accounts are updated at the end of the accounting period. Accounts that normally require updating are described, and the journal entries necessary to update the accounts are illustrated. The chapter concludes with a discussion of the use of the work sheet in the adjustment process.

Learning objectives are listed for the exercises and problems that follow. Use the information to the right to determine the nature of the objective and the page number to refer to your textbook for a discussion of the topic.

Objective 1 — **The Matching Concept 98**
Explain how the matching concept relates to the accrual basis of accounting.

Objective 2 — **Nature of the Adjusting Process 99**
Explain why adjustments are necessary and list the characteristics of adjusting entries.

Objective 3 — **Recording Adjusting Entries 101**
Journalize entries for accounts requiring adjustment.

Objective 4 — **Summary of Adjustment Process 108**
Summarize the adjustment process and prepare an adjusted trial balance.

Objective 5 — **Financial Analysis and Interpretation 112**
Use vertical analysis to compare financial statement items with each other and with industry averages.

Blank Page

The Matching Process and Adjusting Entries

" Your study of the matching process and your ability to analyze and record adjusting entries will determine, to a large extent, your success in the financial accounting course. The accrual basis of accounting requires that the expenses incurred are properly matched and deducted from the revenues that they helped to generate, resulting in a net income or loss for the period. Adjusting entries are necessary to bring the accounts up to date at the end of the period. By their nature, all adjusting entries affect at least one income statement account and one balance sheet account. Accordingly, an adjusting entry will always involve a **revenue** or an **expense** account and an **asset** or a **liability** account. Adjustments focus on two possibilities — (1) transactions that have already been recorded, sometimes called **deferrals**, and (2) transactions that have not yet been recorded but should be, called **accruals**. Your careful study of these adjustments will play an important role in your study of accounting. "

Robert Lynch
Accounting Instructor

Luca Pacioli's Accounting Model

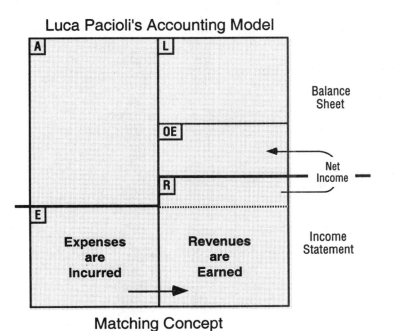

Matching Concept

Deferred Expenses (Prepaid Expenses) — Basic Concepts

Deferred expenses are assets that are expected to become expenses over time or through the normal operations of the enterprise. Supplies and prepaid insurance are examples of deferred expenses. The supplies become an expense as they are used, and the prepaid insurance becomes an expense as time passes and the insurance expires. There are two ways to record what is received in the initial purchase — (1) as an asset, or (2) as an expense. In theory, it makes sense to record the initial purchase as an asset because at the time of the purchase the item has not yet been used or consumed. In practice, however, the purchase is often initially expensed. Either way, an adjustment will update the books to reflect the actual situation at the end of an accounting period.

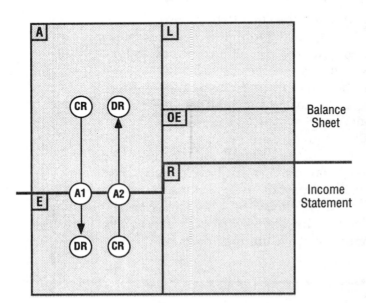

Adjustment A1. The original purchase was recorded as an asset. This adjustment reduces assets and increases expenses, resulting in a reduction in net income.

If this adjustment is **not** recorded, what effect would this have on the financial statements?

Adjustment A2. The original purchase was recorded as an expense. This adjustment reduces expenses and increases assets, resulting in an increase in net income.

If this adjustment is **not** recorded, what effect would this have on the financial statements?

Example P1: Purchase Recorded as an Asset

Assume that on December 1 your company purchased insurance for 24 months at a cost of $2,400 with a debit to **Prepaid Insurance** and a credit to Cash. Using the T accounts below, record the December 31 adjustment.

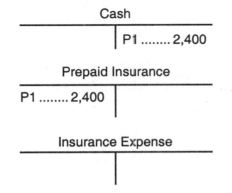

Example P2: Purchase Recorded as an Expense

Assume that on December 1 your company purchased insurance for 24 months at a cost of $2,400 with a debit to **Insurance Expense** and a credit to Cash. Using the T accounts below, record the December 31 adjustment.

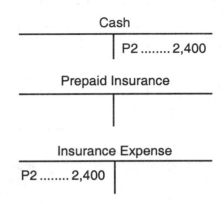

Note: In the two examples above, the adjusted balances should be the same, regardless of how the initial cash was recorded.

Deferred Revenues (Unearned Revenue) — Basic Concepts

Deferred revenues are liabilities that are expected to become revenues over time or through the normal operations of the enterprise. Examples of deferred revenues include fees received by a college at the beginning of a term and magazine subscriptions received in advance by a publisher. There are two ways to record the initial cash collected — (1) as a liability (unearned revenue), or (2) as a revenue. In theory, it makes sense to record the initial sale as a liability because at the time of the sale the item has not yet been earned. In practice, however, the sale is often initially recorded as revenue. Either way, an adjustment will update the books to reflect the actual situation at the end of an accounting period.

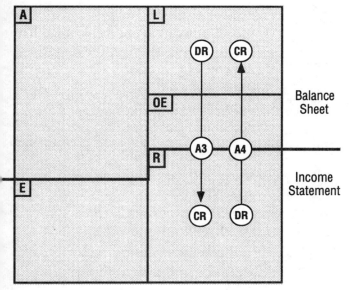

Adjustment A3. The original entry was recorded as a liability (unearned revenue). This adjustment reduces liabilities and increases revenues, resulting in an increase in net income.

If this adjustment is **not** recorded, what effect would this have on the financial statements?

Adjustment A4. The original entry was recorded as a revenue. This adjustment reduces revenues and increases liabilities, resulting in a decrease in net income.

If this adjustment is **not** recorded, what effect would this have on the financial statements?

Example S1: Sale Recorded as a Liability
Assume that on December 1 your company received cash of $360 for rent for three months and credited **Unearned Rent**. Using the T accounts below, record the December 31 adjustment.

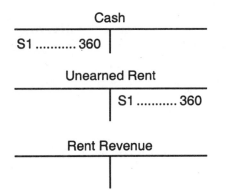

Example S2: Sale Recorded as a Revenue
Assume that on December 1 your company received cash of $360 for rent for three months and credited **Rent Revenue**. Using the T accounts below, record the December 31 adjustment.

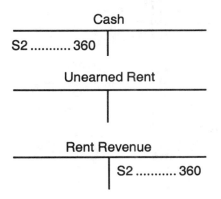

Note: In the two examples above, the adjusted balances should be the same, regardless of how the initial cash was recorded.

Accrued Expenses (Accrued Liabilities) — Basic Concepts

Accrued expenses represent expenses that have been incurred but not yet paid and not yet recorded. As you will remember, expenses should be recorded when they have been incurred, which simply means the services or benefits have been received. In the example below, notice that a debit to an expense account must be offset by a credit to a payable account.

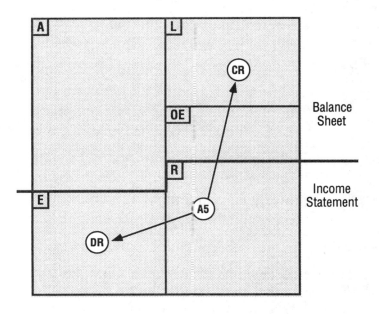

Adjustment A5. This adjustment records expenses that have been incurred but not yet recorded. As a result, this adjustment increases liabilities and increases expenses, resulting in a decrease in net income.

If this adjustment is **not** recorded, what effect would this have on the financial statements?

Balance Sheet
    Assets ....
    Liabilities ....
    Owner's Equity ...

Income Statement
    Revenues ....
    Expense ....
    Net Income ....

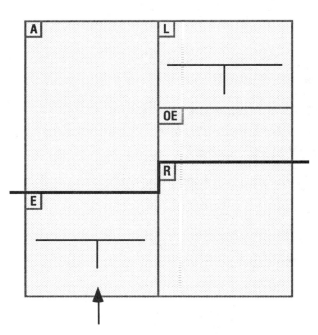

The expense has been incurred.
(Employee services have been received.)

Example
1. Assume that the weekly payroll is $5,000, payable for a five-day work week ending on Friday. December 31 falls on a Tuesday. Using the T accounts shown to the left, label the accounts and record the year-end adjustment.

2. Assume that an expense for advertising services of $3,500 has been incurred but not yet recorded. How would this adjustment be recorded?

The Selling Side of Business

Accrued Revenues (Accrued Assets) — Basic Concepts

Accrued revenues represent revenues that have been earned but not yet received and not yet recorded. As you will remember, revenues should be recorded when they have been earned, which simply means the services or goods have been given. In the example below, notice that a credit to revenues must be offset by a debit to a receivable account.

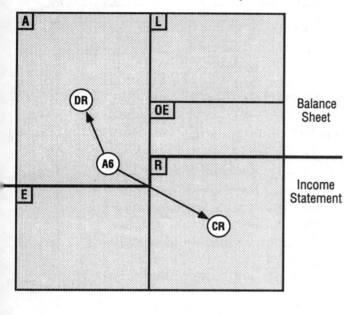

Balance Sheet

Income Statement

Adjustment A6. This adjustment records revenues that have been earned but not yet recorded. As a result, this adjustment increases assets and increases revenues, resulting in an increase in net income.

If this adjustment is **not** recorded, what effect would this have on the financial statements?

Balance Sheet
    Assets ....
    Liabilities ....
    Owner's Equity ...

Income Statement
    Revenues ....
    Expense ....
    Net Income ....

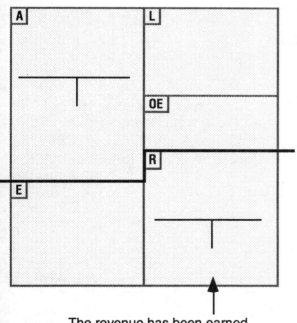

The revenue has been earned.
(The use of funds has been given to borrower.)

Example
1. Assume that we hold a note receivable of $10,000 with interest of 9% per year. At the end of the accounting period we have earned interest of $300. Using the T accounts shown to the left, label the accounts and record the year-end adjustment.

2. Assume that service fees of $2,250 have been earned but not yet recorded. How would this adjustment be recorded?

A Summary of the Adjusting Entries

" At first the adjusting process may be hard to understand. Like most challenging topics, you must first work a few exercises and problems before you begin to put all the pieces together. In my case, it took quite a bit of work before I could analyze and record certain adjustments. Plan to spend extra time studying the adjusting process—it will pay off many times as you continue your accounting studies. "

" There are many ways to view the adjusting process. Below I have organized the six adjustments into two broad groups—adjustments relating to the **buying side** of the business which involve **expenses**, and adjustments relating to the **selling side** of the business which involve **revenues**. In each of these two groups there are **deferrals** and **accruals**. As you study each adjustment, try to determine the effects of the adjustment on the major components of the financial statements, usually starting with net income and then moving to the balance sheet effects. For example, can you determine which adjustments decrease net income and which adjustments increase net income? "

Robert Lynch
Accounting Instructor

Adjustments Relating to the Buying Side of the Business	Adjustments Relating to the Selling Side of the Business

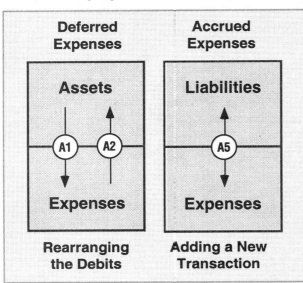

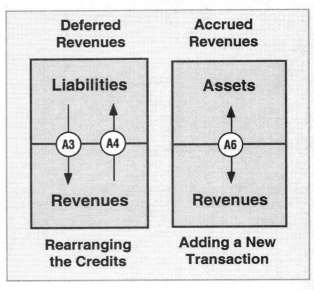

Classify accruals and deferrals
Objectives 2, 3 - Text pages 99 and 101

Classify the following items as (a) deferred expense (prepaid expense), (b) deferred revenue (unearned revenue), (c) accrued expense (accrued liability), or (d) accrued revenue (accrued asset).

Working
Papers
Plus

Chapter 3

_____1. Supplies on hand.

_____2. Fees received but not yet earned.

_____3. Utilities owed but not yet paid.

_____4. A two-year premium paid on a fire insurance policy.

_____5. Fees earned but not yet received.

_____6. Taxes owed but payable in the following period.

_____7. Salary owed but not yet paid.

_____8. Subscriptions received in advance by a magazine.

Exercise 3–2

Classify adjusting entries
Objectives 2, 3 -Text pages 99 and 101

The following accounts were taken from the unadjusted trial balance of O'Dell Co., a congressional lobbying firm. Indicate whether or not each account would normally require an adjusting entry. If the account normally requires an adjusting entry, use the following notation to indicate the type of adjustment:

AE -- Accrued Expense
AR -- Accrued Revenue
DE -- Deferred Expense
DR -- Deferred Revenue

To illustrate, the answers for the first two accounts are shown below:

Account	Answer
George Lee, Drawing	Does not normally require adjustment.
Accounts Receivable	Normally requires adjustment (AR).
Accumulated Depreciation	
Cash	
Interest Payable	
Interest Receivable	
Land	
Office Equipment	
Prepaid Insurance	
Supplies Expense	
Unearned Fees	
Wages Expense	

Exercise 3–3

Adjusting entry for supplies
Objective 3 - Text page 102 ✔ Amount of entry: $1,445

The balance in the supplies account, before adjustment at the end of the year, is $1,820. Journalize the adjusting entry required if the amount of supplies on hand at the end of the year is $375.

Date	Description	Debit	Credit

Exercise 3–4

Determine supplies purchased
Objective 3 - Text page 102 ✔ $1,300

The supplies and supplies expense accounts at December 31, after adjusting entries have been posted at the end of the first year of operations, are shown in the following T accounts:

Supplies		Supplies Expense	
Bal. 280		Bal. 1,020	

Determine the amount of supplies purchased during the year. $_____

Exercise 3–5

Effect of omitting adjusting entry
Objective 3 - Text page 102

At December 31, the end of the first month of operations, the usual adjusting entry transferring supplies used to an expense account is omitted. Which items will be incorrectly stated, because of the error, on:

(a) the income
    statement for
    December;

(b) the balance sheet
    as of December 31?

Also indicate
whether the items
in error will be
overstated or
understated.

Exercise 3-6

Name:

Adjusting entries for prepaid insurance
Objective 3 - Text page 102   ✔ Amount of entry: $1,140

The balance in the prepaid insurance account, before adjustment at the end of the year, is $3,780. Journalize the adjusting entry required under each of the following *alternatives* for determining the amount of the adjustment:
(a) the amount of insurance expired during the year is $1,140;
(b) the amount of unexpired insurance applicable to future periods is $2,640.

Date	Description	Debit	Credit

Exercise 3-7

Adjusting entries for prepaid insurance
Objective 3 - Text page 102   ✔ a. Amount of entry: $1,400

The prepaid insurance account had a balance of $2,400 at the beginning of the year. The account was debited for $1,800 for premiums on policies purchased during the year. Journalize the adjusting entry required at the end of the year for each of the following situations:
(a) the amount of unexpired insurance applicable to future periods is $2,800;
(b) the amount of insurance expired during the year is $1,650.

Date	Description	Debit	Credit

Exercise 3–8

Adjusting entries for unearned fees
Objective 3 - Text page 103   ✔ Amount of entry: $5,500

The balance in the unearned fees account, before adjustment at the end of the year, is $7,000. Journalize the adjusting entry required if the amount of unearned fees at the end of the year is $1,500.

Date	Description	Debit	Credit

Exercise 3–9

Effect of omitting adjusting entry
Objective 3 - Text page 102

At the end of January, the first month of the year, the usual adjusting entry transferring rent earned to a revenue account from the unearned rent account was omitted. Indicate which items will be incorrectly stated, because of the error, on:

(a) the income
   statement for
   January;

(b) the balance sheet
   as of January 31.

Also indicate whether the items in error will be overstated or understated.

Exercise 3–10

Adjusting entries for accrued salaries
Objective 3 - Text page 104   ✔ a. $4,200

River Realty Co. pays weekly salaries of $10,500 on Friday for a five-day week ending on that day. Journalize the necessary adjusting entry at the end of the accounting period, assuming that the period ends (a) on Tuesday, (b) on Wednesday.

Date	Description	Debit	Credit

Determine wages paid
Objective 3 - Text page 104   ✔ $52,520

The wages payable and wages expense accounts at December 31,
after adjusting entries have been posted at the end of the first
year of operations, are shown in the following T accounts:

Wages Payable		Wages Expense	
	Bal. 1,010	Bal. 53,530	

Determine the amount of wages paid during the year. $_____

Exercise 3–12

Effect of omitting adjusting entry
Objective 3 - Text page 104

Accrued salaries of $2,500 owed to employees for December 30 and 31 are
not considered in preparing the financial statements for the year ended
December 31. Indicate which items will be erroneously stated, because of
the error, on:

(a) the income
     statement for
     the year;

(b) the balance
     sheet as of
     December 31.

Also indicate whether
the items in error will
be overstated or
understated.

Exercise 3–13

Effect of omitting adjusting entry
Objective 3 - Text page 104

Assume that the error in Exercise 3-12 was not corrected and that the $2,500 of accrued salaries was included in the first salary payment in January. Indicate which items will be erroneously stated, because of failure to correct the initial error, on:

(a) the income
    statement for the
    month of January;

(b) the balance sheet
    as of January 31.

Also indicate whether
the items in error will
be overstated or
understated.

Exercise 3–14

Adjusting entries for prepaid and accrued taxes
Objective 3 - Text page 102 ✔ b. $8,572

Edwards Financial Planning Co. was organized on April 1 of the current year. On April 2, Edwards prepaid $1,296 to the city for taxes (license fees) for the *next* 12 months and debited the prepaid taxes account. Edwards is also required to pay in January an annual tax (on property) for the *previous* calendar year. The estimated amount of the property tax for the current year (April 1 to December 31) is $7,600.

(a) Journalize the two adjusting entries required to bring the accounts affected by the two taxes up to date as of December 31, the end of the current year.

Date	Description	Debit	Credit

(b) What is the amount
    of tax expense for
    the current year?

Exercise 3–15   Name: _____

Effects of errors on financial statements
Objective 3 - Text page 101   ✔ a. $534,000,000

The balance sheet for **The Quaker Oats Company** as of December 31, 1996, includes the following accrued expenses as liabilities:

Accrued payroll, benefits, bonus	$111,300,000
Accrued advertising and merchandising	130,200,000
Other accrued liabilities	292,500,000

The net income for The Quaker Oats Company for the year ended December 31, 1996, was $247,900,000.

(a) If the accruals had not been recorded at December 31, 1996, by how much would net income have been misstated for the fiscal year ended December 31, 1996?

(b) What is the percentage of the misstatement in (a) to the reported net income of $247,900,000?

Exercise 3–16

Effects of errors on financial statements
Objective 3 - Text page 101   ✔ 1. Revenue understated, $6,800

The accountant for Baskin Medical Co., a medical services consulting firm, mistakenly omitted adjusting entries for (a) unearned revenue ($6,800) and (b) accrued wages ($1,050). Indicate the effect of each error, considered individually, on the income statement for the current year ended December 31. Also indicate the effect of each error on the December 31 balance sheet. Insert a zero if the error does not affect the item.

	Error (a)		Error (b)	
	Over-stated	Under-stated	Over-stated	Under-stated
1. Revenue for the year would be	$_____	$_____	$_____	$_____
2. Expenses for the year would be	$_____	$_____	$_____	$_____
3. Net income for the year would be	$_____	$_____	$_____	$_____
4. Assets at December 31 would be	$_____	$_____	$_____	$_____
5. Liabilities at December 31 would be	$_____	$_____	$_____	$_____
6. Owner's equity at December 31 would be	$_____	$_____	$_____	$_____

Exercise 3–17

Effects of errors on financial statements
Objective 3 - Text page 101   ✔ $121,050

If the net income for the current year had been $115,300 in Exercise 3-16, what would be the correct net income if the proper adjusting entries had been made?

Exercise 3–18

Adjusting entry for accrued fees
Objective 3 - Text page 104

At the end of the current year, $3,390 of fees have been earned but have not been billed to clients.

a. Journalize the adjusting entry to record the accrued fees.

Date	Description	Debit	Credit

b. If the cash basis rather than the accrual basis had been used, would an adjusting entry have been necessary? Explain.

Exercise 3–19

Adjusting entries for unearned and accrued fees
Objective 3 - Text page 103

The balance in the unearned fees account, before adjustment at the end of the year, is $31,700. Of these fees, $21,500 have been earned. In addition, $9,100 of fees have been earned but have not been billed. Journalize the adjusting entries (a) to adjust the unearned fees account and (b) to record the accrued fees.

Date	Description	Debit	Credit

Exercise 3–20

Effect on financial statements of omitting adjusting entry
Objective 3 - Text page 101

The adjusting entry for accrued fees was omitted at December 31, the end of the current year. Indicate which items will be in error, because of the omission, on:

(a) the income statement for the current year;

(b) the balance sheet as of December 31.

Also indicate whether the items in error will be overstated or understated.

Adjusting entry for depreciation
Objective 3 - Text page 107

The estimated amount of depreciation on equipment for the current year
is $4,400. Journalize the adjusting entry to record the depreciation.

Date	Description	Debit	Credit

Exercise 3–22

Determine fixed asset's book value
Objective 3 - Text page 107   ✔ a. $263,800

The balance in the equipment
account is $379,200, and the balance
in the accumulated depreciation—
equipment account is $115,400.

a. What is the book value of the
   equipment?

b. Does the balance in
   the accumulated
   depreciation
   account mean that
   the equipment's
   loss of value is
   $115,400? Explain.

Exercise 3–23

Book value of fixed assets
Objective 3 - Text page 107

Microsoft Corporation reported *Property, Plant, and Equipment* of $2,777
million and *Accumulated Depreciation* of $1,312 million at June 30, 1997.

a. What was the book value of the
   fixed assets at June 30, 1997?

b. Would the book value of
   Microsoft Corporation's fixed
   assets normally approximate
   their fair market values?

**Adjusting entries for depreciation;
effect of error**
Objective 3 - Text page 107

On December 31, a business estimates depreciation on equipment
used during the first year of operations to be $4,300.
(a) Journalize the adjusting entry required as of December 31.

Date	Description	Debit	Credit

(b) If the adjusting entry in (a) were omitted,
    which items would be erroneously stated on:

   (1) the income
       statement for
       the year?

   (2) the balance
       sheet as of
       December 31?

Adjusting entries from trial balances
Objectives 3, 4 - Text pages 101 and 108

The unadjusted and adjusted trial balances for Surgical Services Co. on December 31, 1999, are shown below.

Surgical Services Co.
Trial Balance
December 31, 1999

Account Title	Unadjusted Debit	Unadjusted Credit	Adjusted Debit	Adjusted Credit
Cash	6		6	
Accounts Receivable	18		21	
Supplies	6		2	
Prepaid Insurance	10		6	
Land	12		12	
Equipment	20		20	
Accum. Depr. - Equipment		3		5
Accounts Payable		13		13
Wages Payable		0		1
Randy Reese, Capital		44		44
Randy Reese, Drawing	4		4	
Fees Earned		36		39
Wages Expense	12		13	
Rent Expense	4		4	
Insurance Expense	0		4	
Utilities Expense	2		2	
Depreciation Expense	0		2	
Supplies Expense	0		4	
Miscellaneous Expense	2		2	
Totals	96	96	102	102

Journalize the five entries that adjusted the accounts at December 31, 1999. None of the accounts were affected by more than one adjusting entry.

Date	Description	Debit	Credit

Exercise 3–26

Adjusting entries from trial balances
Objectives 3, 4 - Text pages 101 and 108 ✔ Corrected trial balance totals: $177,520

The accountant for Homestead Laundry prepared the following unadjusted and adjusted trial balances. Assume that all balances in the unadjusted trial balance and the amounts of the adjustments are correct. How many errors can you find in the accountant's work?

Homestead Laundry
Trial Balance
August 31, 1999

Account Title	Unadjusted		Adjusted	
	Debit	Credit	Debit	Credit
Cash	7,790		7,790	
Accounts Receivable	10,000		12,500	
Laundry Supplies	4,750		8,660	
Prepaid Insurance*	2,825		1,325	
Laundry Equipment	85,600		79,880	
Accum. Depreciation		55,700		55,700
Accounts Payable		4,950		5,800
Wages Payable				850
Kim Momin, Capital		30,900		30,900
Kim Momin, Drawing	8,000		8,000	
Laundry Revenue		76,900		76,900
Wages Expense	24,500		24,500	
Rent Expense	15,575		15,575	
Utilities Expense	8,500		8,500	
Depreciation Expense			5,720	
Laundry Supplies Expense			3,910	
Insurance Expense			500	
Miscellaneous Expense	910		910	
Totals	168,450	168,450	177,770	170,150

*$1,500 of insurance expired during the year.

Financial Analysis and Interpretation

Objective: Use vertical analysis to compare financial statement items with each other and with industry averages.

Comparative Income Statements
For the Years Ended December 31, 2000 and 2001

	2001 Amount	2001 Percent	2000 Amount	2000 Percent
Fees earned	$ 187,500	100.0%	$ 150,000	100.0%
Operating expenses:				
Wages expense	$ 60,000	32.0%	$ 45,000	30.0%

Vertical Analysis:

$$\frac{\text{Wages expense}}{\text{Fees earned}} = \frac{\$ 60,000}{\$ 187,500} = 32.0\%$$

Exercise 3–27

Vertical analysis of income statement
Objective 5 - Text page 112

The financial statements for **Hershey Foods Corporation** are presented in Appendix G at the end of the text.

a. Determine for Hershey Foods Corporation:

1. The amount of the change and percent of change in net income for the year ended December 31, 1996.

2. The percentage relationship between net income and net sales (net income divided by net sales) for the years ended December 31, 1996 and 1995.

b. What conclusions can you draw from your analysis?

Blank Page

Adjusting entries
Objective 3 - Text page 101

On December 31, the end of the current year, the following data were accumulated to assist the accountant in preparing the adjusting entries for Lakeview Realty:

a. Fees accrued but unbilled at December 31 are $3,750.

b. The supplies account balance on December 31 is $3,100. The supplies on hand at December 31 are $720.

c. Wages accrued but not paid at December 31 are $1,100.

d. The unearned rent account balance on December 31 is $4,800, representing the receipt of an advance payment on December 1 of four months' rent from tenants.

e. Depreciation of office equipment for the year is $2,100.

Instructions

1. Journalize the adjusting entries required at December 31.

DATE	DESCRIPTION	DEBIT	CREDIT

2. Briefly explain the difference between adjusting entries and entries that would be made to correct errors.

Blank Page

Problem 3–2A Claremont Realty

Name:

Adjusting entries
Objective 3 - Text page 101

Selected account balances before adjustment for Claremont Realty at October 31, the end of the current year, are shown.

Elizabeth Roland
Real Estate Broker

Instructions

Journalize the six adjusting entries required at October 31, based upon the data presented.

	Debits	Credits
Accounts Receivable	$ 9,250	
Supplies	2,700	
Prepaid Rent	21,000	
Equipment	50,500	
Accum. Depreciation		$ 16,900
Wages Payable		0
Unearned Fees		6,500
Fees Earned		99,850
Wages Expense	40,750	
Rent Expense	0	
Depreciation Expense	0	
Supplies Expense	0	

Data needed for year-end adjustments are as follows:

a. Supplies on hand at October 31, $1,030.
b. Depreciation of equipment during year, $1,800.
c. Rent expired during year, $18,000.
d. Wages accrued but not paid at October 31, $990.
e. Unearned fees at October 31, $2,500.
f. Unbilled fees at October 31, $6,790.

DATE	DESCRIPTION	DEBIT	CREDIT

Blank Page

Adjusting entries and adjusted trial balances
Objectives 3, 4 - Text pages 101 and 108 ✔ 2. Total of Debit Column: $469,900

Atwater Service Co., which specializes in appliance repair services, is owned and operated by Carri Atwater. Atwater Service Co.'s accounting clerk prepared the following trial balance at December 31, the end of the current year:

ACCOUNT TITLE	TRIAL BALANCE DEBIT	TRIAL BALANCE CREDIT	ADJUSTMENTS DEBIT	ADJUSTMENTS CREDIT	ADJ. TRIAL BALANCE DEBIT	ADJ. TRIAL BALANCE CREDIT
Cash	3,200					
Accounts Receivable	17,200					
Prepaid Insurance	3,900					
Supplies	2,450					
Land	50,000					
Building	141,500					
Accum Depr. - Building		95,700				
Equipment	90,100					
Accum. Depr. - Equipment		65,300				
Accounts Payable		7,500				
Unearned Rent		4,000				
Carrie Atwater, Capital		65,900				
Carrie Atwater, Drawing	5,000					
Fees Earned		218,400				
Salaries and Wages Expense	78,700					
Utilities Expense	28,200					
Advertising Expense	19,000					
Repairs Expense	13,500					
Miscellaneous Expense	4,050					
	456,800	456,800				

Instructions

1. Using a blank **FORM GJ**, journalize the adjusting entries. Add additional accounts as needed.
2. Using the form above, determine the balances of the accounts affected by the adjusting entries and complete the adjusted trial balance.

The data needed to determine year-end adjustments are as follows:

a. Depreciation of building for the year, $1,500.
b. Depreciation of equipment for the year, $5,500.
c. Accrued salaries and wages at December 31, $1,150.
d. Unexpired insurance at December 31, $1,100.
e. Fees earned but unbilled on December 31, $4,950.
b. Supplies on hand at December 31, $500.
e. Rent unearned at December 31, $1,500.

Blank Page

Adjusting entries
Objective 3 - Text page 101

On December 31, the end of the current year, the following data were accumulated to assist the accountant in preparing the adjusting entries for Simkin Realty:

a. The supplies account balance on December 31 is $1,450. The supplies on hand on December 31 are $315.

b. The unearned rent account balance on December 31 is $3,600, representing the receipt of an advance payment on December 1 of three months' rent from tenants.

c. Wages accrued but not paid at December 31 are $850.

d. Fees accrued but unbilled at December 31 are $11,500.

e. Depreciation on office equipment for the year is $1,500.

Instructions

1. Journalize the adjusting entries required at December 31.

DATE	DESCRIPTION	DEBIT	CREDIT

2. Briefly explain the difference between adjusting entries and entries that would be made to correct errors.

Blank Page

Adjusting entries
Objective 3 - Text page 101

Selected account balances before adjustment for Ocean City Realty at December 31, the end of the current year, are shown.

Stan Yasuda
Real Estate Broker

	Debits	Credits
Accounts Receivable	$ 11,250	
Supplies	4,750	
Prepaid Rent	27,000	
Equipment	42,500	
Accum. Depreciation		$ 10,900
Wages Payable		0
Unearned Fees		5,000
Fees Earned		87,950
Wages Expense	29,400	
Rent Expense	0	
Depreciation Expense....................	0	
Supplies Expense	0	

Data needed for year-end adjustments are as follows:

a. Unbilled fees at December 31, $4,150.
b. Supplies on hand at December 31, $980.
c. Rent expired during year, $24,000.
d. Depreciation of equipment during year, $3,050.
e. Unearned fees at December 31, $3,750.
f. Wages accrued but not paid at December 31, $920.

Instructions

Journalize the six adjusting entries required at December 31, based upon the data presented.

DATE	DESCRIPTION	DEBIT	CREDIT

Blank Page

Problem 3–5B Zornes Company   Name: _____

Adjusting entries and adjusted trial balances

Objectives 3, 4 - Text pages 101 and 108 ✔ 2. Total of Debit Column: $482,570

Zornes Company is a small editorial services company owned and operated by Valerie Spann. The following trial balance has been prepared on December 31, the end of the current year:

ACCOUNT TITLE	TRIAL BALANCE DEBIT	TRIAL BALANCE CREDIT	ADJUSTMENTS DEBIT	ADJUSTMENTS CREDIT	ADJ. TRIAL BALANCE DEBIT	ADJ. TRIAL BALANCE CREDIT
Cash	6,700					
Accounts Receivable	23,800					
Prepaid Insurance	3,400					
Supplies	1,950					
Land	50,000					
Building	141,500					
Accum Depr. - Building		91,700				
Equipment	90,100					
Accum. Depr. - Equipment		65,300				
Accounts Payable		7,500				
Unearned Rent		6,000				
Valarie Spann, Capital		81,500				
Valarie Spann, Drawing	10,000					
Fees Earned		218,400				
Salaries and Wages Expense	80,200					
Utilities Expense	28,200					
Advertising Expense	19,000					
Repairs Expense	11,500					
Miscellaneous Expense	4,050					
	470,400	470,400				

Instructions

1. Using a blank **FORM GJ**, journalize the adjusting entries. Add additional accounts as needed.
2. Using the form above, determine the balances of the accounts affected by the adjusting entries and complete the adjusted trial balance.

The data needed to determine year-end adjustments are as follows:

a. Unexpired insurance at December 31, $1,200.
b. Supplies on hand at December 31, $500.
c. Depreciation of building for the year, $1,620.
d. Depreciation of equipment for the year, $5,500.
e. Rent unearned at December 31, $2,000.
f. Accrued salaries and wages at December 31, $1,300.
g. Fees earned but unbilled on December 31, $3,750.

Blank Page

Chapter 4

Completing the Accounting Cycle

The matching concept and the adjusting process were described and illustrated in Chapter 3. In this chapter, the flow of the adjustment data into the accounts and into the financial statements is discussed. This process is accomplished by using a work sheet. In addition, journalizing and posting the adjusting entries is illustrated. Finally, the chapter concludes with a discussion of procedures for preparing the accounting records for the next accounting period.

Learning objectives are listed for the exercises and problems that follow. Use the information to the right to determine the nature of the objective and the page number to refer to your textbook for a discussion of the topic.

Objective 1 — Work Sheet 136
Prepare a work sheet.

Objective 2 — Financial Statements 136D
Prepare financial statements from a work sheet.

Objective 3 — Adjusting and Closing Entries 139
Prepare the adjusting and closing entries from a work sheet.

Objective 4 — Fiscal Year 146
Explain what is meant by the fiscal year and the natural business year.

Objective 5 — Accounting Cycle 147
Review the seven basic steps of the accounting cycle.

Objective 6 — Financial Analysis and Interpretation 148
Analyze and interpret the financial solvency of a business by computing the working capital and the current ratio.

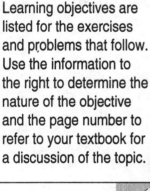

Accounting Information Systems

" An accounting information system is part of a larger business information system. Like most business systems, the accounting system processes raw data and produces information which can be analyzed and interpreted to make decisions. Business transactions are supported by source documents and represent the raw data. Information is produced in the form of financial reports. "

" Data can be processed either manually or electronically. Your textbook lists seven steps used in the manual accounting cycle. Let's take a different view of the basic processing steps used for both manual and computer systems and compare the two systems. "

Robert Lynch
Accounting Instructor

Processing Steps	Manual System	Computer System
1. Record Data. Business transactions and adjustments are analyzed and recorded.	Transactions and adjustments are recorded in paper journals.	Transactions and adjustments are recorded and stored on magnetic disks.
2. Classify Transactions. Classifying data means to rearrange or sort it by some attribute other than date. Data can be rearranged either physically or logically.	Data is physically rearranged using a process called posting. This process is inefficient and subject to errors.	Data is logically rearranged without physically moving data. Logical processing is extremely fast, and many logical views can be produced on demand.
3. Summarize Accounts. All entries in each account are totaled. A listing of each account and its balance are prepared.	This process is time consuming and subject to errors.	This process is simply a logical view of the transaction database.
4. Categorize Accounts. Financial statements are produced.	This clerical process is time consuming and also subject to error.	This process is simply a logical view of the transaction database.
5. Analyze and Interpret Reports. Financial statements are analyzed.		

Exercise 4–1

Place account balances in a work sheet
Objective 1 - Text page136

The balances for the accounts listed below appear in the Adjusted Trial
Balance columns of the work sheet. Indicate whether each balance should
be extended to:

a. the Income Statement (IS) column, or

b. the Balance Sheet (BS) column.

Working
Papers
Plus

Chapter 4

—— 1. Accounts Payable   —— 6. Unearned Fees

—— 2. Wages Expense   —— 7. Utilities Expense

—— 3. Pete Parham, Capital   —— 8. Pete Parham, Drawing

—— 4. Fees Earned   —— 9. Wages Payable

—— 5. Supplies   ——10. Accounts Receivable

Exercise 4–2

Classify accounts
Objective 1 - Text page136

Balances for each of the following accounts appear in the Adjusted
Trial Balance columns of the work sheet. Identify each as (a) asset ,
(b) liability, (c) revenue, or (d) expense.

—— 1. Prepaid Advertising   —— 7. Accounts Receivable

—— 2. Supplies   —— 8. Land

—— 3. Unearned Rent   —— 9. Salary Payable

—— 4. Rent Revenue   ——10. Fees Earned

—— 5. Salary Expense   ——11. Supplies Expense

—— 6. Insurance Expense   ——12. Prepaid Insurance

Exercise 4-3

Steps in completing a work sheet
Objective 1 - Text page136

The steps performed in completing a work sheet are listed below in random order.

a. Add the Debit and Credit columns of the Balance Sheet and Income Statement columns of the work sheet to determine the amount of net income or net loss for the period.

b. Enter the unadjusted account balances from the general ledger into the unadjusted Trial Balance columns of the work sheet.

c. Enter the amount of net income or net loss for the period in the proper Income Statement column and Balance Sheet column.

d. Add the Debit and Credit columns of the Balance Sheet and Income Statement columns of the work sheet to verify that the totals are equal.

e. Extend the adjusted trial balance amounts to the Income Statement columns and the Balance Sheet columns.

f. Add the Debit and Credit columns of the Adjusted Trial Balance columns of the work sheet to verify that the totals are equal.

g. Add or deduct adjusting entry data to trial balance amounts and extend amounts to the Adjusted Trial Balance columns.

h. Add the Debit and Credit columns of the unadjusted Trial Balance columns of the work sheet to verify that the totals are equal.

i. Add the Debit and Credit columns of the Adjustments columns of the work sheet to verify that the totals are equal.

j. Enter the adjusting entries into the work sheet, based upon the adjustment data.

Indicate the order in which the preceding steps would be performed in preparing and completing a work sheet.

Exercise 4–4   Name: _____

Adjustments data on work sheet

Objective 1 - Text page136   ✔ Total debits of Adjustments column: $14

Betty's Sanitize Services Co. offers cleaning services to business
clients. The trial balance for Betty's Sanitize Services Co. had been
prepared on the following work sheet for the year ended
December 31, 1999:

Betty's Sanitize Services Co.
Work Sheet
For the Year Ended December 31, 1999

Account Title	Trial Balance		Adjustments		Adj. Trial Balance	
	Debit	Credit	Debit	Credit	Debit	Credit
Cash	6					
Accounts Receivable	25					
Supplies	4					
Prepaid Insurance	6					
Land	10					
Equipment	14					
Accum. Depr. - Equip.		1				
Accounts Payable		13				
Wages Payable		0				
Betty Ratcliff, Capital		41				
Betty Ratcliff, Drawing	4					
Fees Earned		30				
Wages Expense	8					
Rent Expense	4					
Insurance Expense	0					
Utilities Expense	2					
Depreciation Expense	0					
Supplies Expense	0					
Miscellaneous Expense	2					
Totals	85	85				

The data for year-end adjustments are as follows:

    a. Fees earned, but not yet billed, $4.
    b. Supplies on hand, $2.
    c. Insurance premiums expired, $4.
    d. Depreciation expense, $2.
    e. Wages accrued, but not paid, $2.

Enter the adjustments data, and place the
balances in the Adjusted Trial Balance columns.

Exercise 4–5

Complete a work sheet

Objective 1 - Text page136   ✔ Net income: $8

Betty's Sanitize Services Co. offers cleaning services to business clients. The following is a partially completed work sheet for Betty's Sanitize Services Co.

Betty's Sanitize Services Co.
Work Sheet
For the Year Ended December 31, 1999

Account Title	Adj. Trial Balance		Income Statement		Balance Sheet	
	Debit	Credit	Debit	Credit	Debit	Credit
Cash	6					
Accounts Receivable	29					
Supplies	2					
Prepaid Insurance	2					
Land	10					
Equipment	14					
Accum. Depr. - Equip.		3				
Accounts Payable		13				
Wages Payable		2				
Betty Ratcliff, Capital		41				
Betty Ratcliff, Drawing	4					
Fees Earned		34				
Wages Expense	10					
Rent Expense	4					
Insurance Expense	4					
Utilities Expense	2					
Depreciation Expense	2					
Supplies Expense	2					
Miscellaneous Expense	2					
Totals	93	93				
Net income (Loss)						

Complete the work sheet.

Financial statements

Objective 2 - Text page136D

✔ Betty Ratcliff, capital, Dec. 31, 1999: $45

Based upon the data in Exercise 4-5, prepare an income statement, statement of owner's equity, and balance sheet for Betty's Sanitize Services Co.

Betty's Sanitize Services Co.
Income Statement
For the Year Ended December 31, 1999

Betty's Sanitize Services Co.
Statement of Owner's Equity
For the Year Ended December 31, 1999

Betty's Sanitize Services Co.
Balance Sheet
December 31, 1999

Exercise 4–7

Adjusting entries
Objective 3 - Text page139

Based upon the data in Exercise 4-4, prepare the adjusting entries for Betty's Sanitize Services Co.

Date	Description	Debit	Credit

Exercise 4–8

Closing entries
Objective 3 - Text page139

Based upon the data in Exercise 4-5, prepare the closing entries for Betty's Sanitize Services Co.

Date	Description	Debit	Credit

Name: _____

Income statement

Objective 2 - Text page136D   ✔ Net Income: $99,950

The following account balances were taken from the Adjusted Trial Balance columns of the work sheet for The Messenger Co., a delivery service firm, for the current fiscal year ended June 30:

The Messenger Co.
Income Statement
For Year Ended June 30, 20__

Fees Earned $183,700
Salaries Expense 47,100
Rent Expense 18,000
Utilities Expense 7,500
Supplies Expense 3,100
Miscellaneous Expense ... 1,350
Insurance Expense 1,500
Depreciation Expense...... 5,200

Prepare an income statement.

Exercise 4–10

Income statement; net loss

Objective 2 - Text page136D   ✔ Net loss: $(4,150)

The following revenue and expense account balances were taken from the ledger of Reimer Services Co. after the accounts had been adjusted on March 31, the end of the current fiscal year:

Reimer Services Co.
Income Statement
For Year Ended March 31, 20__

Depreciation Expense.... $ 7,500
Insurance Expense 3,900
Miscellaneous Expense 2,250
Rent Expense ....,..... 36,000
Service Revenue 113,900
Supplies Expense 3,100
Utilities Expense 8,500
Wages Expense................ 56,800

Prepare an income statement.

Exercise 4–11

Statement of owner's equity
Objective 2 - Text page137   ✔ Marion Weaver, capital, Dec. 31: $167,000

Neophyte Services Co. offers its services to new arrivals in the Evanston area. Selected accounts from the ledger of Neophyte Services Co., for the current fiscal year ended December 31, are shown below. Prepare a statement of owner's equity for the year.

Marion Weaver, Capital

Dec. 31	10,000	Jan. 1	143,750
		Dec. 31	33,250

Income Summary

Dec. 31	578,150	Dec. 31	611,400
Dec. 31	33,250		

Marion Weaver, Drawing

Mar. 31	2,500	Dec. 31	10,000
Jun. 30	2,500		
Sep. 30	2,500		
Dec. 31	2,500		

Exercise 4–12

Statement of owner's equity; net loss
Objective 2 - Text page137   ✔ Casey Martin, capital, July 31: $309,800

Selected accounts from the ledger of Casey Sports Services Co., for the current fiscal year ended July 31, are shown below. Prepare a statement of owner's equity for the year.

Casey Martin, Capital

July 31	40,000	Aug. 1	410,300
31	60,500		

Income Summary

July 31	723,400	July 31	662,900
		July 31	60,500

Casey Martin, Drawing

Oct. 31	10,000	July 31	40,000
Jan. 31	10,000		
Apr. 30	10,000		
July 31	10,000		

Exercise 4–14

Name:

Balance sheet classification
Objective 2 - Text page137

At the balance sheet date, a business owes a mortgage note payable of $450,000, the terms of which provide for monthly payments of $15,000. Explain how the liability should be classified on the balance sheet.

Exercise 4–15

Balance sheet
Objective 2 - Text page137   ✔ Total Assets: $116,820

Looking Good Co. offers personal weight reduction consulting services to individuals. After all of the accounts have been closed on April 30, the end of the current fiscal year, the balances of selected accounts from the ledger of Looking Good Co. are as follows:

Accounts Payable	$ 12,750	Prepaid Rent	$ 2,400
Accounts Receivable	28,920	Salaries Payable	3,750
Accum. Depr.—Equipment	21,100	Supplies	4,750
Cash	7,150	Unearned Fees	2,500
Equipment	90,600		
M. Monroe, Capital	97,820		
Prepaid Insurance	4,100		

Looking Good Co.
Balance Sheet
April 30, 20__

Prepare a classified balance sheet.

Exercise 4–16

Balance sheet
Objective 2 - Text page137   ✔ Corrected balance sheet, total assets: $132,500

List the errors you can find in the following balance sheet.
Prepare a corrected balance sheet.

SPA Services Co.
Balance Sheet
For the Year Ended August 31, 1999

Assets			Liabilities	
Current assets:			Current liabilities:	
Cash	$ 5,170		Accounts receivable	$ 5,390
Accounts payable	4,390		Accum. depr. - building	23,000
Supplies	590		Accum. depr. - equipment	16,000
Prepaid insurance	1,600		Net loss	15,500
Land	75,000		Total liabilities	$ 59,890
Total current assets		$ 86,750		
			Owner's Equity	
Property, plant and equipment:			Wages payable	$ 975
Building	$ 55,500		S. Elby, capital	127,135
Equipment	28,250		Total owner's equity	$128,110
Total prop., plant, and equ.	$101,250		Total liabilities and	
Total assets	$188,000		owner's equity	$188,000

Errors

Adjusting entries from work sheet
Objective 3 - Text page139

Air Clean Purifier Co. is a consulting firm specializing in pollution control. The entries in the Adjustments columns of the work sheet for Air Clean Purifier Co. are shown below.

	Adjustments	
	Dr.	Cr.
Accounts Receivable	2,100	
Supplies		1,025
Prepaid Insurance		1,100
Accum. Depr. - Equip.		800
Wages Payable		636
Unearned Rent	3,500	
Fees Earned		2,100
Wages Expense	636	
Supplies Expense	1,025	
Rent Revenue		3,500
Insurance Expense	1,100	
Depreciation Expense	800	

Prepare the adjusting journal entries.

Date	Description	Debit	Credit

Exercise 4–18

Identify accounts to be closed
Objective 3 - Text page140

From the following list, circle the letter of the accounts that should be closed to Income Summary at the end of the fiscal year:

a. Accounts Payable

b. Accum. Depr. - Buildings

c. Depr. Exp. - Buildings

d. Donna Taff, Capital

e. Donna Taff, Drawing

f. Equipment

g. Fees Earned

h. Land

i. Supplies Expense

j. Salaries Payable

k. Supplies

l. Supplies Expense

Exercise 4–19

Closing entries
Objective 3 - Text page140

Prior to its closing, Income Summary had total debits of $417,500 and total credits of $520,000. Briefly explain the purpose served by the income summary account and the nature of the entries that resulted in the $417,500 and the $520,000.

Exercise 4–20

Closing entries
Objective 3 - Text page140 ✔ b. $438,000

After all revenue and expense accounts have been closed at the end of the fiscal year, Income Summary has a debit of $695,500 and a credit of $839,000. At the same date, Shawn Marsh, Capital has a credit balance of $319,500, and Shawn Marsh, Drawing has a balance of $25,000.

(a) Journalize the entries required to complete the closing of the accounts.

Date	Description	Debit	Credit

(b) Determine the amount of Shawn Marsh, Capital at the end of the period. $_____

Closing entries
Objective 3 - Text page140

Minish Services Co. offers its services to individuals desiring to improve their personal images. After the accounts have been adjusted at October 31, the end of the fiscal year, the following balances were taken from the ledger of Minish Services Co.:

B. J. Galis, Capital .... $298,500   Rent Expense .... $ 74,000
B. J. Galis, Drawing.......... 30,000   Supplies Expense 15,500
Fees Earned 355,000   Miscellaneous Expense 5,500
Wages Expense.............. 197,300

Journalize the four entries required to close the accounts.

Date	Description	Debit	Credit

Exercise 4–22

Identify permanent accounts
Objective 3 - Text page146

Circle the letter of the following accounts that usually appear in the post-closing trial balance.

a. Accounts Receivable   g. Erik Geering, Drawing
b. Accumulated Depreciation   h. Fees Earned
c. Cash   i. Supplies
d. Depreciation Expense   j. Wages Expense
e. Equipment   k. Wages Payable
f. Erik Geering, Capital

Exercise 4–23

Post-closing trial balance
Objective 3 - Text page146   ✔ Correct column totals, $67,000

An accountant prepared the following post-closing trial balance:

Uptown Repairs Co.
Post-Closing Trial Balance
March 31, 20___

			Corrected Trial Balance	
Cash	7,400			
Accounts Receivable	18,500			
Supplies		1,100		
Equipment		40,000		
Accum. Depr.- Equip.	11,100			
Accounts Payable	7,250			
Salaries Payable		1,500		
Unearned Rent	4,000			
Lorraine Penn, Capital	43,150			
	91,400	42,600		

Prepare a corrected post-closing trial balance on the form above. Assume that all accounts have normal balances and that the amounts shown are correct.

Exercise 4–24

Steps in the accounting cycle
Objective 5 - Text page147

Rearrange the following steps in the accounting cycle in proper sequence:

a. Adjusting entries are journalized and posted to ledger.
b. Closing entries are journalized and posted to ledger.
c. Financial statements are prepared.
d. A post-closing trial balance is prepared.
e. Transactions are analyzed and recorded in the journal.
f. Transactions are posted to the ledger.
g. A trial balance is prepared, adjustment data are assembled, and the work sheet is completed.

Financial Analysis and Interpretation

Working Capital and Current Ratio

Objective: Analyze and interpret the financial solvency of a business by computing the working capital and the current ratio.

Working Capital (WC)

Current Assets minus Current Liabilities

Current Ratio (CR)

$$\frac{\text{Current Assets}}{\text{Current Liabilities}}$$

Example

Computer King

WC = $7,845 - $1,390 = $6,455

CR = $7,845 / $1,390 = 5.6

Exercise 4–25

Working capital and current ratio
Objective 6 - Text page148

The financial statements for **Hershey Foods Corporation** are presented in Appendix G at the end of the text.

a. Determine the working capital and the current ratio for Hershey Foods Corporation as of December 31, 1996 and 1995.

b. What conclusions concerning the company's ability to meet its financial obligations can you draw from these data?

Appendix Exercise 4–26

Adjusting and reversing entries
Text page150

On the basis of the following data, (a) journalize the adjusting entries at December 31, 1999, the end of the current fiscal year, and (b) journalize the reversing entries on January 1, 2000, the first day of the following year.

1. Sales salaries are uniformly $7,500 for a five-day workweek, ending on Friday. The last payday of the year was Friday, December 26.

Date	Description	Debit	Credit

2. Accrued fees earned but not recorded at December 31, $13,200.

Date	Description	Debit	Credit

Appendix Exercise 4–27

Entries posted to the wages expense account
Text page150

Using the account information shown in the text on page 164:

a. Indicate the nature of the entry (payment, adjusting, closing, reversing) from which each numbered posting was made.

(1)_____

(2)_____

(3)_____

(4)_____

(5)_____

b. Journalize the complete entry from which each numbered posting was made.

Work sheet and related items
Objectives 1, 2, 3 ✔ 2. Net income: $21,340

Note: The working papers that follow this problem may be used with either Problem 4-1A or 4-1B.

The trial balance of Wonder Wash Laundry at August 31, 2000, the end of the current fiscal year, and the data needed to determine year-end adjustments are as follows:

Louis Krupman - Owner

" Being in your own business is working 80 hours a week so that you can avoid working 40 hours a week for someone else—I love it! "

Wonder Wash Laundry
Trial Balance
August 31, 2000

Cash	13,100	
Laundry Supplies	6,560	
Prepaid Insurance	4,490	
Laundry Equipment	95,100	
Accumulated Depreciation		40,200
Accounts Payable		6,100
Louis Krupman, Capital		37,800
Louis Krupman, Drawing	2,000	
Laundry Revenue		140,900
Wages Expense	51,400	
Rent Expense	36,000	
Utilities Expense	13,650	
Miscellaneous Expense	2,700	
	225,000	225,000

a. Wages accrued but not paid at August 31 are $1,350.
b. Depreciation of equipment during the year is $6,600.
c. Laundry supplies on hand at August 31 are $1,500.
d. Insurance premiums expired during the year are $2,800.

Instructions

1. Enter the trial balance on a ten-column work sheet and complete the work sheet. Add accounts as needed.

2. Prepare an income statement, a statement of owner's equity (no additional investments were made during the year), and a balance sheet.

3. On the basis of the adjustment data in the work sheet, journalize the adjusting entries.

4. On the basis of the data in the work sheet, journalize the closing entries.

Blank page

PROBLEM 4-1 _____

1. Record the trial balance on a ten-column work sheet and complete the work sheet.

Note: This work sheet may be used with either Problem 4-1A or Problem 4-1B.

Work Sheet

Account Title	Trial Balance		Adjustments		Adjusted Trial Balance		Income Statement		Balance Sheet	
	Debit	Credit	Debit	Credit	Debit	Credit	Debit	Credit	Debit	Credit
Cash										
Laundry Supplies										
Prepaid Insurance										
Laundry Equipment										
Accum. Depreciation										
Accounts Payable										
_____, Capital										
_____, Drawing										
Laundry Revenue										
Wages Expense										
Rent Expense										
Utilities Expense										
Misc. Expense										

Blank page

2. Prepare an income statement.
2. Prepare a statement of owner's equity.

Income Statement

Statement of Owner's Equity

2. Prepare a balance sheet.

Balance Sheet

Wonder Wash Laundry
Net Income, $21,340

The Wash and Dry Laundromat
Net Income, $7,630

3. Record adjusting entries.
4. Record closing entries.

GENERAL JOURNAL

Page

Date		Description	Post. Ref.	Debit		Credit	
		Adjusting Entries					
		Closing Entries					

Blank page

Note: The working papers that follow Problem 4-1A may be used with either Problem 4-1A or Problem 4-1B.

The trial balance of The Wash and Dry Laundromat at July 31, 2000, the end of the current fiscal year, and the data needed to determine year-end adjustments are as follows:

Nikki Weiss - Owner

" To open a business like this is relative easy— keeping it open, well .... that's another story. "

The Wash and Dry Laundromat
Trial Balance
July 31, 2000

Cash	6,290	
Laundry Supplies	5,850	
Prepaid Insurance	2,400	
Laundry Equipment	99,750	
Accumulated Depreciation		52,700
Accounts Payable		6,950
Nikki Weiss, Capital		37,450
Nikki Weiss, Drawing	4,000	
Laundry Revenue		67,900
Wages Expense	22,900	
Rent Expense	14,400	
Utilities Expense	8,500	
Miscellaneous Expense	910	
	165,000	165,000

a. Laundry supplies on hand at March 31 are $1,240.
b. Insurance premiums expired during the year are $1,700.
c. Depreciation of equipment during the year is $6,200.
d. Wages accrued but not paid at March 31 are $1,050.

Instructions

1. Enter the trial balance on a ten-column work sheet and complete the work sheet. Add accounts as needed.

2. Prepare an income statement, a statement of owner's equity (no additional investments were made during the year), and a balance sheet.

3. On the basis of the adjustment data in the work sheet, journalize the adjusting entries.

4. On the basis of the data in the work sheet, journalize the closing entries.

Blank page

COMPREHENSIVE PROBLEM 1 - Interactive Consulting
Accounting Cycle for a Service Company

✔ 4. Net income: $6,775

Typically, when a person starts a business from scratch, the service or product is developed in the home. As the business grows, the owner may need to expand into commericial office space.

Company Profile:
For the past several years, Angie Mills has operated a part-time consulting business from her home. As of September 1, 2000, Angie decided to move to rented quarters and to operate the business, which was to be known as Interactive Consulting, on a full-time basis. Mrs. Mills has asked you to prepare all of the accounting records for the month of September, including the financial statements. Mrs. Mills has persuaded you to negotiate your accounting fee after she reviews the quality of your work.

Interactive Consulting entered into the following transactions during September:

Sept. 1. The following assets were received from Angie Mills: cash, $7,050; accounts receivable, $1,500; supplies, $1,250; and office equipment, $7,200. There were no liabilties received.

   2. Paid three months' rent on a lease rental contract, $3,600.

   2. Paid the premiums on property and casualty insurance policies, $1,500.

   4. Received cash from clients as an advance payment for services to be provided and recorded it as unearned fees, $3,500.

   5. Purchased additional office equipment on account from Payne Company, $1,800.

   6. Received cash from clients on account, $800.

   10. Paid cash for a newspaper advertisement, $120.

   12. Paid Payne Company for part of the debt incurred on September 5, $800.

   12. Recorded services provided on account for the period September 1-12, $1,200.

   13. Paid part-time receptionist for two weeks' salary, $400.

   17. Recorded cash from cash clients for fees earned during the first half of September, $2,100.

   18. Paid cash for supplies, $750.

   20. Recorded services provided on account for the period September 13-20, $1,100.

   24. Recorded cash from cash clients for fees earned for the period September 17-24, $1,850.

   25. Received cash from clients on account, $1,300.

   27. Paid part-time receptionist for two weeks' salary, $400.

   29. Paid telephone bill for September, $130.

   30. Paid electricity bill for September, $200.

   30. Recorded cash from cash clients for fees earned for the period September 25-30, $1,050.

   30. Recorded services provided on account for the remainder of September, $500.

   30. Angie withdrew $1,500 for personal use.

Instructions

1. Journalize each transaction in a two-column journal, referring to the following chart of accounts in selecting the accounts to be debited and credited. (Do not insert the account numbers in the journal at this time.)

11 Cash	21 Accounts Payable	41 Fees Earned
12 Accounts Receivable	22 Salaries Payable	51 Salary Expense
14 Supplies	23 Unearned Fees	52 Rent Expense
15 Prepaid Rent	31 Angie Mills, Capital	53 Supplies Expense
16 Prepaid Insurance	32 Angie Mills, Drawing	54 Depreciation Expense
18 Office Equipment	33 Income Summary	55 Insurance Expense
19 Accumulated Depreciation		59 Miscellaneous Expense

2. Post the journal to a ledger of four-column accounts.

Continued

3. Prepare a trial balance as of September 30, 2000, on a ten-column work sheet, listing all the accounts in the order given in the ledger. Complete the work sheet, using the following adjustment data:

   a. Insurance expired during September is $125.

   b. Supplies on hand on September 30 are $1,220.

   c. Depreciation of office equipment for September is $250.

   d. Accrued receptionist salary on September 30 is $120.

   e. Rent expired during September is $800.

   f. Unearned fees on September 30 are $1,200.

4. Prepare an income statement, a statement of owner's equity, and a balance sheet.

5. Journalize and post the adjusting entries.

6. Journalize and post the closing entries. (Income Summary is account #33 in the chart of accounts.) Indicate closed accounts by inserting a line in both Balance columns opposite the closing entry.

7. Prepare a post-closing trial balance.

Suggestions

This problem uses a number of forms. Removing each form as it is needed will reduce paper shuffling.
Remove the following pages, place them side by side, and complete instruction 1.

   C4 - 30 (transactions, accounts)
   C4 - 33, 34 (general journal)

When completing instruction 2, you may want to staple the general ledger pages together.

Forms

General Journal **C4 - 33, 34, 45, 46**
General Ledger **C4 - 35, 36, 37, 38, 39**
Work Sheet **C4 - 41**
Financial Statements **C4 - 43, 44**
Post-Closing Trial Balance **C4 - 47**

Blank page

1. Journalize monthly transactions.

GENERAL JOURNAL

Page 1

Date		Description	Post. Ref.	Debit		Credit	

GENERAL JOURNAL

Date	Description	Post. Ref.	Debit	Credit

COMPREHENSIVE PROBLEM 1

Name: _____

2. Post monthly transactions.
5. Post adjusting entries.
6. Post closing entries.

GENERAL LEDGER

ACCOUNT Cash   NO. 11

Date	Description	Post. Ref.	Debit	Credit	Balance Debit	Balance Credit

ACCOUNT Accounts Receivable   NO. 12

Date	Description	Post. Ref.	Debit	Credit	Balance Debit	Balance Credit

ACCOUNT Supplies   NO. 14

Date	Description	Post. Ref.	Debit	Credit	Balance Debit	Balance Credit

ACCOUNT Prepaid Rent   NO. 15

Date	Description	Post. Ref.	Debit	Credit	Balance Debit	Balance Credit

ACCOUNT Prepaid Insurance   NO. 16

Date	Description	Post. Ref.	Debit	Credit	Balance Debit	Balance Credit

ACCOUNT Office Equipment   NO. 18

Date	Description	Post. Ref.	Debit	Credit	Balance Debit	Balance Credit

ACCOUNT Accumulated Depreciation   NO. 19

Date	Description	Post. Ref.	Debit	Credit	Balance Debit	Balance Credit

ACCOUNT Accounts Payable NO. 21

Date	Description	Post. Ref.	Debit	Credit	Balance Debit	Balance Credit

ACCOUNT Salaries Payable NO. 22

Date	Description	Post. Ref.	Debit	Credit	Balance Debit	Balance Credit

ACCOUNT Unearned Fees NO. 23

Date	Description	Post. Ref.	Debit	Credit	Balance Debit	Balance Credit

ACCOUNT Angie Mills, Capital NO. 31

Date	Description	Post. Ref.	Debit	Credit	Balance Debit	Balance Credit

ACCOUNT Angie Mills, Drawing NO. 32

Date	Description	Post. Ref.	Debit	Credit	Balance Debit	Balance Credit

COMPREHENSIVE PROBLEM 1

continued

ACCOUNT Income Summary   NO. 33

Date	Description	Post. Ref.	Debit	Credit	Balance Debit	Balance Credit

ACCOUNT Fees Earned   NO. 41

Date	Description	Post. Ref.	Debit	Credit	Balance Debit	Balance Credit

ACCOUNT Salary Expense   NO. 51

Date	Description	Post. Ref.	Debit	Credit	Balance Debit	Balance Credit

ACCOUNT Rent Expense   NO. 52

Date	Description	Post. Ref.	Debit	Credit	Balance Debit	Balance Credit

ACCOUNT Supplies Expense   NO. 53

Date	Description	Post. Ref.	Debit	Credit	Balance Debit	Balance Credit

ACCOUNT Depreciation Expense   NO. 54

Date	Description	Post. Ref.	Debit	Credit	Balance Debit	Balance Credit

ACCOUNT Insurance Expense   NO. 55

Date	Description	Post. Ref.	Debit	Credit	Balance Debit	Balance Credit

ACCOUNT Miscellaneous Expense   NO. 59

Date	Description	Post. Ref.	Debit	Credit	Balance Debit	Balance Credit

Blank page

COMPREHENSIVE PROBLEM 1

3. Prepare trial balance and work sheet.

Interactive Consulting
Work Sheet
For Month Ended September 30, 2000

Acct	Account Title	Trial Balance		Adjustments		Adjusted Trial Balance		Income Statement		Balance Sheet	
		Debit	Credit	Debit	Credit	Debit	Credit	Debit	Credit	Debit	Credit
11	Cash										
12	Accounts Receivable										
14	Supplies										
15	Prepaid Rent										
16	Prepaid Insurance										
18	Office Equipment										
19	Accumulated Depreciation										
21	Accounts Payable										
22	Salaries Payable										
23	Unearned Fees										
31	Angie Mills, Capital										
32	Angie Mills, Drawing										
41	Fees Earned										
51	Salary Expense										
52	Rent Expense										
53	Supplies Expense										
54	Depreciation Expense										
55	Insurance Expense										
59	Miscellaneous Expense										
	Totals										
	Net income										

Blank page

4. Prepare financial statements.

Interactive Consulting
Income Statement
For Month Ended September 30, 2000

Interactive Consulting
Statement of Owner's Equity
For Month Ended September 30, 2000

Net Income
$6,775

Interactive Consulting
Balance Sheet
September 30, 2000

5. Journalize adjusting entries.

GENERAL JOURNAL

Page 3

Date		Description	Post. Ref.	Debit		Credit	
		Adjusting Entries					

6. Journalize closing entries.

GENERAL JOURNAL

Page 4

Date		Description	Post. Ref.	Debit		Credit	
		Closing Entries					

7. Prepare post-closing trial balance.

Interactive Consulting
Post-Closing Trial Balance
September 30, 2000

No.	Account	Debit	Credit

Blank page

Chapter 5

Accounting Systems and Internal Controls

Just as there are many examples of controls throughout society, businesses must also implement controls to help guide the behavior of their employees toward enterprise objectives. This chapter discusses controls that can be used to provide assurance about the reliability of the financial statements.

Learning objectives are listed for the exercises and problems that follow. Use the information to the right to determine the nature of the objective and the page number to refer to your textbook for a discussion of the topic.

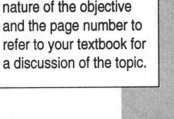

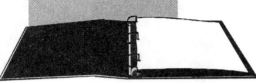

Blank page

Internal controls
Objective 2 - Text page 179

Debbie Byers has recently been hired as the manager of Long Island Deli. Long Island Deli is a national chain of franchised delicatessens. During her first month as store manager, Debbie encountered the following internal control situations. State whether you agree or disagree with Debbie's handling of each situation and explain your answer in the space provided.

Debbie Byers
Deli Manager

Working
Papers
Plus
―――
Chapter 5

a. Long Island Deli has one cash register. Prior to Debbie's joining the deli, each employee working on a shift would take a customer order, accept payment, and then prepare the order. Debbie made one employee on each shift responsible for taking orders and accepting the customer's payment. Other employees prepare the orders.

b. Since only one employee uses the cash register, that employee is responsible for counting the cash at the end of the shift and verifying that the cash in the drawer matches the amount of cash sales recorded by the cash register. Debbie expects each cashier to balance the drawer to the penny *every* time—no exceptions.

c. Debbie caught an employee putting a box of 100 single-serving bags of potato chips in his car. Not wanting to create a scene, Debbie smiled and said, "I don't think you're putting those chips on the right shelf. Don't they belong inside the deli?" The employee returned the chips to the stockroom.

Exercise 5–2

Internal controls
Objective 2 - Text page 179

Gypsy Fashions is a retail store specializing in women's clothing. The store has established a liberal return policy for the holiday season in order to encourage gift purchases. Any item purchased during November and December may be returned through January 31, with a receipt, for cash or exchange. If the customer does not have a receipt, cash will still be refunded for any item under $25. If the item is more than $25, a check is mailed to the customer.

Whenever an item is returned, a store clerk completes a return slip, which the customer signs. The return slip is placed in a special box. The store manager visits the return counter approximately once every two hours to authorize the return slips. Clerks are instructed to place the returned merchandise on the proper rack on the selling floor as soon as possible.

This year, returns at Gypsy Fashions have reached an all-time high. There are a large number of returns under $25 without receipts.

a. How can sales clerks employed at Gypsy Fashions use the store's return policy to steal money from the cash register?

b. 1. What internal control weaknesses do you see in the return policy that make cash thefts easier?

2. Would issuing a store credit in place of a cash refund for all merchandise returned without a receipt reduce the possibility of theft? List some advantages and disadvantages of issuing a store credit in place of a cash refund.

3. Assume that Gypsy Fashions is committed to the current policy of issuing cash refunds without a receipt. What changes could be made in the store's procedures regarding customer refunds in order to improve internal control?

Internal controls for bank lending
Objective 2 - Text page 179

Las Cruz Bank provides loans to businesses in the community through its
Commercial Lending Department. Small loans (less than $100,000) may be
approved by an individual loan officer, while larger loans (greater than
$100,000) must be approved by a board of loan officers. Once a loan is
approved, the funds are made available to the loan applicant under agreed
terms. The president of Las Cruz Bank has instituted a policy whereby she
has the individual authority to approve loans up to $5,000,000. The
president believes that this policy will allow flexibility to approve loans to
valued clients much quicker than under the previous policy.

As an internal auditor of Las
Cruz Bank, how would you
respond to this change in
policy?

Exercise 5–4

Identify postings from revenue journal
Objective 3 - Text page 184

Using the following revenue journal for J. A. Bach Co., identify each of the posting references, indicated by a letter, as representing:
(1) a posting to a general ledger account,
(2) a posting to a subsidiary ledger account, or
(3) a posting to two general ledger accounts.

Revenue Journal

Date	Invoice No.	Account Debited	Post. Ref.	
Nov. 1	772	Environmental Safety Co.	(a)____	$2,465
10	773	Greenberg Co.	(b)____	580
20	774	Smith and Smith	(c)____	1,520
27	775	Envirolab	(d)____	965
30				$5,530

Place your answer in the space provided to the right of each letter (a-e).
(e)____

Exercise 5–5

Accounts receivable ledger
Objective 3 - Text page 184 ✔ d. Total accounts receivable, $5,965

Based upon the data presented in Exercise 5-4, assume that the beginning balances for the customer accounts were zero, except for Envirolab, which had a $435 beginning balance. In addition, there were no collections during the period.

General Ledger

Accounts Receivable

Accounts Receivable Subsidiary Ledger

Environmental Safety Co.

Smith and Smith

Greenberg Co.

Envirolab

J. A. Bach Co.
Schedule of Accounts Receivable
November 30, 20__

Instructions: (a) the T account for Accounts Receivable and T accounts for the four accounts needed in the customer ledger have been set up, (b) post to the T accounts, (c) determine the balance in the accounts, if necessary, and (d) prepare a schedule of accounts receivable at November 30.

Exercise 5–6 _____   **Name:** _____

Identify journals

Objective 3 - Text page 184

Assuming the use of a two-column (all-purpose) general journal (G), a revenue journal (R), and a cash receipts journal (CR) as illustrated in this chapter, indicate the journal in which each of the following transactions should be recorded:

_____ (a) Receipt of cash for rent.

_____ (b) Closing of drawing account at the end of the year.

_____ (c) Adjustment to record accrued salaries at the end of the year.

_____ (d) Sale of office supplies on account, at cost, to a neighboring business.

_____ (e) Receipt of cash on account from a customer.

_____ (f) Receipt of cash from sale of office equipment.

_____ (g) Providing services on account.

_____ (h) Providing services for cash.

_____ (i) Investment of additional cash in the business by the owner.

_____ (j) Receipt of cash refund from overpayment of taxes.

Exercise 5–7 _____

Identify journals

Objective 3 - Text page 184

Assuming the use of a two-column (all-purpose) general journal (G), a purchases journal (P), and a cash payments journal (CP) as illustrated in this chapter, indicate the journal in which each of the following transactions should be recorded:

_____ (a) Purchase of office equipment for cash.

_____ (b) Purchase of services on account.

_____ (c) Adjustment to prepaid insurance at the end of the month.

_____ (d) Adjustment to record depreciation at the end of the month.

_____ (e) Adjustment to prepaid rent at the end of the month.

_____ (f) Adjustment to record accrued salaries at the end of the period.

_____ (g) Purchase of office supplies for cash.

_____ (h) Advance payment of a one-year fire insurance policy on the office.

_____ (i) Purchase of office supplies on account.

_____ (j) Purchase of an office computer on account.

_____ (k) Payment of six months' rent in advance.

Exercise 5–8

Identify transactions in accounts receivable ledger
Objective 3 - Text page 184

The debits and credits from three related transactions are presented in the following customer's account taken from the accounts receivable subsidiary ledger.

NAME: Good Times Catering
ADDRESS: 1319 Maple Street

Date	Item	Post. Ref.	Debit	Credit	Balance
2000					
Sep. 3		R50	450		450
9		J9		60	390
13		CR38		390	—

Describe each transaction and identify the source of each posting.

Sep. 3 _____

Sep. 9 _____

Sep. 13 _____

Exercise 5–9, 10

Use textbook and blank paper for these exercises.

Exercise 5–11

Identify transactions in accounts payable ledger account
Objective 3 - Text page 184

The debits and credits from three related transactions are presented in the following creditor's account taken from the accounts payable ledger:

NAME: Echo Co.
ADDRESS: 1717 Kirby Street

Date	Item	Post. Ref.	Debit	Credit	Balance
2000					
July 6		P34		10,500	10,500
10		J10	500		10,000
16		CP37	10,000		—

Describe each transaction and identify the source of each posting.

July 6 _____

July 10 _____

July 16 _____

Exercise 5–12

Refer to textbook for this
exercise.

Exercise 5–13

Identify postings from special journals
Objective 3 - Text page 184

Albright Consulting Company makes most of its sales and purchases on credit. It uses the five
journals described in this chapter and shown below. Identify the journal most likely used in
recording the postings for selected transactions indicated by letter in the following T accounts.
Place the appropriate transaction letters on the line following each journal.

	Cash		
a.	10,000	b.	8,750

	Accounts Receivable		
c.	10,950	d.	9,200

	Office Supplies	
e.	6,500	

	Rent Expense	
j.	400	

	Prepaid Rent	
		f.	400

	Accounts Payable		
g.	7,600	h.	7,790

	Fees Earned	
		i.	10,950

Revenue journal _____
Cash receipts journal _____
Purchases journal _____
Cash payments journal _____
General journal _____

Exercise 5–14

Refer to textbook for this
exercise.

Exercise 5–15

Modified special journals
Objectives 3, 4 - Text pages 184 and 195

Wellguard Health Clinic was established on June 15 of the current year. The clients for whom Wellguard provided health services during the remainder of June are listed below. These clients pay Wellguard the amount indicated plus a 5% sales tax.

June 16. A. Sommerfeld on account, Invoice No. 1, $200 plus tax.
     19. B. Lin, Invoice No. 2, $80 plus tax.
     21. J. Koss, Invoice No. 3, $60 plus tax.
     22. D. Jeffries, Invoice No. 4, $100 plus tax.
     24. K. Sallinger, in exchange for medical supplies having a value of $160 plus tax.
     26. J. Koss, Invoice No. 5, $120 plus tax.
     28. B. Lin, Invoice No. 6, $40 plus tax.
     30. D. Finnigan, Invoice No. 7, $260 plus tax.

a. Journalize the transactions for June, using the three-column revenue journal and the two-column general journal shown below. Post the customer accounts in the accounts receivable subsidiary ledger on the next page, and insert the balance immediately after recording each entry.

Revenue Journal

Date	Inv. No.	Account Debited	Post. Ref.	Accts. Rec. Debit	Fees Earned Credit	Sales Tax Payable Credit

General Journal

Date	Description	Post. Ref.	Debit	Credit

Continued on next page

Accounts Receivable Subsidiary Ledger

D. Finnigan

Date		Description	Post. Ref.	Debit	Credit	Balance

D. Jeffries

Date		Description	Post. Ref.	Debit	Credit	Balance

J. Koss

Date		Description	Post. Ref.	Debit	Credit	Balance

B. Lin

Date		Description	Post. Ref.	Debit	Credit	Balance

A. Sommerfeld

Date		Description	Post. Ref.	Debit	Credit	Balance

Continued on next page

b. Post the general journal and the revenue journal to the following general ledger accounts, inserting account balances only after the last postings.

General Ledger

Accounts Receivable   Acct. No. 12

Date	Description	Post. Ref.	Debit	Credit	Balance Debit	Balance Credit

Medical Supplies   Acct. No. 14

Date	Description	Post. Ref.	Debit	Credit	Balance Debit	Balance Credit

Sales Tax Payable   Acct. No. 22

Date	Description	Post. Ref.	Debit	Credit	Balance Debit	Balance Credit

Fees Earned   Acct. No. 41

Date	Description	Post. Ref.	Debit	Credit	Balance Debit	Balance Credit

c. 1. What is the sum of the balances in the accounts receivable subsidiary ledger at June 30?

2. What is the balance of the controlling account at June 30?

Exercise 5–16

Computer components
Objective 5 - Text page 196

Which of the following items are used for computer data input or output?

	Input	Output
a. Keyboard	_____	_____
b. Monitor	_____	_____
c. Operating system	_____	_____
d. RAM	_____	_____
e. Modem	_____	_____
f. CD Drive	_____	_____
g. Hard Drive	_____	_____
h. Network	_____	_____
i. Application	_____	_____
j. Printer	_____	_____

Exercise 5–17

Computerized accounting systems
Objective 5 - Text page 196

Most computerized accounting systems use electronic forms to record transaction information, as illustrated in textbook Exhibit 11.

a. Identify the key input fields (spaces) to an electronic invoice form.

b. What accounts are posted from an electronic invoice form?

c. Why aren't special journal totals posted to control accounts at the end of the month in an electronic accounting system?

Obtain a copy of a recent computer magazine (such as *PC Week*) from the library or magazine stard. In this magazine, select an ad by a company that offers a variety of microcomputer systems—from a basic system to a top-of-the-line system. Some good examples would be **Dell, Micron, Compaq,** or **Gateway 2000.** Alternatively, go to the web page of one of the computer companies to obtain product information. Divide responsibilities among your team so that you can accomplish the following tasks:

1. Bring to class one of the ads or a printout of web pages with product specifications. The Internet sites of the companies mentioned above are:

   www.dell.com

   www.micron.com

   www.compaq.com

   www.gateway.com

2. List and briefly explain each feature of the top-of-the-line computer identified in the ad or web page. Compare the features of the top-of-the-line system and the basic entry-level system. How do they differ? How do the prices differ?

3. Try to discover the purpose of the features that are not familiar to you by talking to others in your group or to friends.

Revenue and cash receipts journals;
accounts receivable and general ledgers
Objective 3   ✔ 3. Total cash receipts, $98,880

Note: The working papers that follow this problem may be used with either Problem 5–2A or 5–2B.

Transactions related to revenue and cash receipts completed by Elite Engineering Services during the period November 15–30 of the current year are as follows:

Nov. 15. Issued Invoice No. 717 to Yamura Co., $9,450.
16. Received cash from AGI Co. for the balance owed on its account.
17. Issued Invoice No. 718 to Hardy Co., $2,400.
18. Issued Invoice No. 719 to Ross and Son, $9,600.
        Post all journals to the accounts receivable ledger.

21. Received cash from Hardy Co. for the balance owed on November 15.
24. Issued Invoice No. 720 to Hardy Co., $11,400.
        Post all journals to the accounts receivable ledger.

25. Received cash from Yamura Co. for the balance due on invoice of November 15.
26. Received cash from Hardy Co. for invoice of November 17.
27. Issued Invoice No. 721 to AGI Co., $9,540.
29. Recorded fees earned for the second half of the month, $14,300.
30. Received office equipment in settlement of balance due on the Ross and Son account.
        Post all journals to the accounts receivable ledger.

Michael Gough
General Manager

Instructions

1. Set up the following accounts and balances in the general ledger as of November 1:

11 Cash.................................. $ 9,450
12 Accounts Receivable 14,750
18 Office Equipment 4,500
41 Fees Earned 0

2. Insert the following balances in the accounts receivable ledger as of November 15:

AGI Co. $8,700
Hardy Co. 5,400
Ross and Son 0
Yamura Co. 0

3. Insert *November 15 Total(s) Forwarded* on the left side of the first line of the revenue journal and the cash receipts journal. Insert a check mark (✓) in the Post. Ref. column and the following dollar figures in the respective amount columns: **Revenue journal**: amount column, $38,750. **Cash receipts journal**: Other Accounts, $6,780; Fees Earned, $12,450; Accounts Receivable, $39,400; Cash, $58,630. These amounts have not been posted, but represent the totals of the November 1-15 transactions.

4. Using the two special journals and the two-column general journal, journalize the transactions for the remainder of November. Post to the accounts receivable ledger, and insert the balances at the points indicated in the narrative of transactions. Determine the balance in the customer's account before recording a cash receipt.

5. Total each of the columns of the special journals, and post the individual entries and totals to the general ledger. Insert account balances after the last posting.

6. Determine that the subsidiary ledger agrees with the controlling account in the general ledger. Complete the schedule of accounts receivable on the next page.

Continued

Suggestions

This problem has been designed to minimize the turning of pages. The pages are shown below.

Accounts Receivable Ledger

B

P5–2 Transactions

A

Three Journals

D

C

General Ledger

(A) Place the transactions page next to the journal page. Analyze and record each transaction in the appropriate journal.

(B) Place the journal page next to the accounts receivable ledger page and post as indicated in step 4 of the instructions.

(C) Place the journal page next to the general ledger page and post as indicated in step 5 of the instructions.

(D) Complete the schedule of accounts receivable below to determine that the subsidiary ledger agrees with the controlling account in the general ledger.

"If the total of this schedule agrees with the general ledger accounts receivable account and the auditor's figures, you're hired."

Elite Engineering Services
Schedule of Accounts Receivable
November 30, 20__

Customer Name	Balance

3. Insert Total Forwarded amounts.
4. Journalize transactions.
5. Post from the journals to the general ledger.

Revenue Journal

Page 40

Date	Invoice Number	Account Debited	Post. Ref.	Accts. Rec. Dr Fees Earned Cr.

Cash Receipts Journal

Page 36

Date	Account Credited	Post. Ref.	Other Accts. Credit	Fees Earned Credit	Accts. Rec. Credit	Cash Debit

General Journal

Page 1

Date	Description	Post. Ref.	Debit	Credit

Blank Page

2. Insert beginning balances
4. Post transactions.

Accounts Receivable Subsidiary Ledger

AGI Co.

Date		Description	P.R.	Debit	Credit	Balance

Hardy Co.

Date		Description	P.R.	Debit	Credit	Balance

Ross and Son

Date		Description	P.R.	Debit	Credit	Balance

Yamura Co.

Date		Description	P.R.	Debit	Credit	Balance

1. Insert beginning balances.
5. Post transactions.

General Ledger

Account: No.

Date	Description	P.R.	Debit	Credit	Balance Debit	Balance Credit

Account: No.

Date	Description	P.R.	Debit	Credit	Balance Debit	Balance Credit

Elite Engineering Services
Balance $20,940
___
Continental Architects Co.
Balance $5,890

Account: No.

Date	Description	P.R.	Debit	Credit	Balance Debit	Balance Credit

Account: No.

Date	Description	P.R.	Debit	Credit	Balance Debit	Balance Credit

Purchases and cash payments journals;
accounts payable and general ledgers
Objective 3 ✔ 1. Total cash payments, $60,150

Note: The working papers that follow this problem
may be used with either Problem 5–4A or 5–4B.

Black Gold Exploration Co. was established on March 15, 2000, to provide oil-drilling services. Black Gold uses field equipment (rigs and pipe) and field supplies (drill bits and lubricants) in its operations. Transactions related to purchases and cash payments during the remainder of March are as follows:

March 16. Issued Check No. 1 in payment of rent for the remainder of March, $1,000.
   16. Purchased field equipment on account from Harper Equipment Co., $20,000.
   17. Purchased field supplies on account from Culver Supply Co., $6,200.
   18. Issued Check No. 2 in payment of field supplies, $1,200, and office supplies, $120.
   19. Purchased office equipment on account from Lacy Co., $12,400.
   20. Purchased office supplies on account from Ange Supply Co., $230.
        Post the journals to the accounts payable ledger.

   24. Issued Check No. 3 to Harper Equipment Co. in payment of invoice, $20,000.
   26. Issued Check No. 4 to Culver Supply Co. in payment of invoice, $6,200.
   28. Issued Check No. 5 to purchase land from the owner, $10,000.
   28. Issued Check No. 6 to Lacy Co. in payment of the balance owed.
   28. Purchased office supplies on account from Ange Supply Co., $630.
        Post the journals to the accounts payable ledger.

   30. Purchased the following from Harper Equipment Co. on account: field supplies, $2,300; and office equipment, $4,400.
   30. Issued Check No. 7 to Ange Supply Co. in payment of invoice, $230.
   30. Purchased field supplies on account from Culver Supply Co., $1,900.
   31. Issued Check No. 8 in payment of salaries, $9,000.
   31. Acquired land in exchange for field equipment having a cost of $6,000.
        Post the journals to the accounts payable ledger.

Instructions

1. Using the purchases journal, cash payments journal, and two-column general journal on the following pages, journalize the transactions for March. Refer to the following partial chart of accounts:

   11 Cash   19 Land
   14 Field Supplies   21 Accounts Payable
   15 Office Supplies   61 Salary Expense
   17 Field Equipment   71 Rent Expense
   18 Office Equipment

   At the points indicated in the narrative of transactions, post to the following accounts in the accounts payable ledger:

   Ange Supply Co.
   Culver Supply Co.
   Harper Equipment Co.
   Lacy Co.

Continued

2. Post the individual entries (Other Accounts columns of the purchases journal and the cash payments journal; both columns of the general journal) to the appropriate general ledger accounts.

3. Total each of the columns of the purchases journal and the cash payments journal, and post the appropriate totals to the general ledger. (Because the problem does not include transactions related to cash receipts, the cash account in the ledger will have a credit balance.)

4. Using the form below. prepare a schedule of accounts payable.

Helen Waite
Accounts Payable
Supervisor
_____
It's not easy
getting paid — you
have to go to
Helen Waite!

Black Gold Exploration Co.
Schedule of Accounts Payable
March 31, 20__

Supplier Name	Balance

Name:

Note: These working papers may be used with either Problem 5–4A or 5–4B.

Cash Payments Journal

Page 1

Date	Ck. No.	Account Debited	Post. Ref.	Other Accounts Debit	Accounts Payable Debit	Cash Credit

General Journal

Page 1

Date	Description	Post. Ref.	Debit	Credit

Continued

PROBLEM 5-4

1., 2., and 3.

Purchases Journal

Page 1

Date	Account Credited	Post. Ref.	Accounts Payable Credit	Field Supplies Debit	Office Supplies Debit	Other Accounts Debit		
						Account	Post. Ref.	Amount

1.

Accounts Payable Subsidiary Ledger

Name:

Date	Description	P.R.	Debit	Credit	Balance

Name:

Date	Description	P.R.	Debit	Credit	Balance

Name:

Date	Description	P.R.	Debit	Credit	Balance

Name:

Date	Description	P.R.	Debit	Credit	Balance

2. and 3.

General Ledger

Cash   No. 11

Date	Description	P.R.	Debit	Credit	Balance Debit	Balance Credit

Field Supplies   No. 14

Date	Description	P.R.	Debit	Credit	Balance Debit	Balance Credit

2. and 3.

General Ledger

Office Supplies   No. 15

Date		Description	P.R.	Debit	Credit	Balance	
						Debit	Credit

Field Equipment   No. 17

Date		Description	P.R.	Debit	Credit	Balance	
						Debit	Credit

Office Equipment   No. 18

Date		Description	P.R.	Debit	Credit	Balance	
						Debit	Credit

Land   No. 19

Date		Description	P.R.	Debit	Credit	Balance	
						Debit	Credit

Accounts Payable   No. 21

Date		Description	P.R.	Debit	Credit	Balance	
						Debit	Credit

Salary Expense   No. 61

Date		Description	P.R.	Debit	Credit	Balance	
						Debit	Credit

Rent Expense   No. 71

Date		Description	P.R.	Debit	Credit	Balance	
						Debit	Credit

Revenue and cash receipts journals;
accounts receivable and general ledgers
Objective 3   ✔ 3. Total cash receipts, $83,990

Note: The working papers that follow Problem 5–2A
may be used with either Problem 5-2A or 5-2B.

Transactions related to revenue and cash receipts completed by Continental
Architects Co. during the period June 15–30, 2000, are as follows:

Letha JeanPierre
Sales Manager

June   15. Issued Invoice No. 793 to Ping Co., $6,500.
16. Received cash from Morton Co. for the balance owed on its account.
19. Issued Invoice No. 794 to Quest Co., $5,570.
20. Issued Invoice No. 795 to Mendez Co., $6,780.
Post all journals to the accounts receivable ledger.

23. Received cash from Quest Co. for the balance owed on June 15.
24. Issued Invoice No. 796 to Quest Co., $2,430.
Post all journals to the accounts receivable ledger.

25. Received cash from Ping Co. for the balance due on invoice of June 15.
28. Received cash from Quest Co. for invoice of June 19.
28. Issued Invoice No. 797 to Morton Co., $3,460.
30. Received $6,780 notes receivable in settlement of the balance due on the Mendez Co. account.
30. Recorded cash fees received for the second half of the month, $8,500.
Post all journals to the accounts receivable ledger.

Instructions

1. Insert the following balances in the general ledger as of June 1:

   11 Cash $10,550
   12 Accounts Receivable 12,650
   14 Notes Receivable 4,000
   41 Fees Earned 0

2. Insert the following balances in the accounts receivable ledger as of June 15:

   Mendez Co. ..... $ 0
   Morton Co. 14,500
   Ping Co. 0
   Quest Co. 8,350

3. Insert *June 15 Total(s) Forwarded* on the left side of the first line of the revenue journal and the cash receipts journal. Insert a check mark (✓) in the Post. Ref. column and the following dollar figures in the respective amount columns: **Revenue journal**: amount column, $32,650. **Cash receipts journal**: Other Accounts, $4,560; Fees Earned, $13,560; Accounts Receivable, $22,450; Cash, $40,570. These amounts have not been posted, but represent the totals of the June 1-15 transactions.

4. Using the two special journals and the two-column general journal, journalize the transactions for the remainder of June. Post to the accounts receivable ledger, and insert the balances at the points indicated in the narrative of transactions. Determine the balance in the customer's account before recording a cash receipt.

5. Total each of the columns of the special journals, and post the individual entries and totals to the general ledger. Insert account balances after the last posting.

6. Determine that the subsidiary ledger agrees with the controlling account in the general ledger. Complete the schedule of accounts receivable on the next page.

Continued

Letha JeanPierre
Sales Manager

" We need a list of the balances owed by each of our customers. Please complete the schedule below and compare the total with the accounts receivable account in the general ledger. If you can get these to agree, I'm sure we'll use your services next month. Thanks. "

Continental Architects Co.
Schedule of Accounts Receivable
June 30, 20__

Customer Name	Balance

Purchases and cash payments journals;
accounts payable and general ledgers

Note: The working papers that follow Problem 5–4A may be used with with either Problem 5-4A or 5-4B.

Objective 3 ✔ 1. Total cash payments, $57,030

Purity Water Testing Service was established on June 16, 2000. Purity uses field equipment and field supplies (chemicals and other supplies) to analyze water for unsafe contaminants in streams, lakes, and ponds. Transactions related to purchases and cash payments during the remainder of June are as follows:

June   16. Issued Check No. 1 in payment of rent for the remainder of June, $900.
       16. Purchased field supplies on account from Heath Supply Co., $4,200.
       16. Purchased field equipment on account from Juan Equipment Co., $13,000.
       17. Purchased office supplies on account from Aztec Supply Co., $530.
       18. Purchased office equipment on account from Chavez Co., $3,800.
       19. Issued Check No. 2 in payment of field supplies, $2,200, and office supplies, $400.
            Post the journals to the accounts payable ledger.

       23. Purchased office supplies on account from Aztec Supply Co., $900.
       23. Issued Check No. 3 to purchase land from the owner, $20,000.
       24. Issued Check No. 4 to Heath Supply Co. in payment of invoice, $4,200.
       25. Issued Check No. 5 to Chavez Co. in payment of the balance owed.
       26. Issued Check No. 6 to Juan Equipment Co. in payment of invoice, $13,000.
            Post the journals to the accounts payable ledger.

       30. Acquired land in exchange for field equipment having a cost of $8,000.
       30. Purchased field supplies on account from Heath Supply Co., $6,400.
       30. Issued Check No. 7 to Aztec Supply Co. in payment of invoice, $530.
       30. Purchased the following from Juan Equipment Co. on account: field supplies, $3,400; and field equipment, $5,000.
       30. Issued Check No. 8 in payment of salaries, $12,000.
            Post the journals to the accounts payable ledger.

Instructions

1. Using the purchases journal, cash payments journal, and two-column general journal that follow Problem 5–4A, journalize the transactions for June. Refer to the following partial chart of accounts:

    11 Cash   19 Land
    14 Field Supplies   21 Accounts Payable
    15 Office Supplies   61 Salary Expense
    17 Field Equipment   71 Rent Expense
    18 Office Equipment

   At the points indicated in the narrative of transactions, post to the following accounts in the accounts payable ledger:

   Aztec Supply Co.
   Chavez Co.
   Heath Supply Co.
   Juan Equipment Co.

Continued

2. Post the individual entries (Other Accounts columns of the purchases journal and the cash payments journal; both columns of the general journal) to the appropriate general ledger accounts.

3. Total each of the columns of the purchases journal and the cash payments journal, and post the appropriate totals to the general ledger. (Because the problem does not include transactions related to cash receipts, the cash account in the ledger will have a credit balance.)

4. Using the form below, prepare a schedule of accounts payable.

Frank Lawton
Accounts Payable
Supervisor

"If you think that
nobody cares if
you're alive, try
missing a couple of
payments."

Purity Water Testing Service
Schedule of Accounts Payable
June 30, 20__

Supplier Name	Balance

Chapter 6

Accounting for Merchandising Businesses

This chapter focuses on the accounting principles and concepts for merchandising businesses. Differences in the activities of such businesses and service businesses will be highlighted, and purchases and sales transactions for merchandising businesses will be illustrated. Financial statements for merchandisers will be prepared.

Learning objectives are listed for the exercises and problems that follow. Use the information to the right to determine the nature of the objective and the page number to refer to your textbook for a discussion of the topic.

Blank Page

Determining gross profit
Objective 1 - Text page 225 ✔ a. $280,000

During the current year, merchandise is sold for $180,000 cash and for $520,000 on account. The cost of the merchandise sold is $420,000.

a. What is the amount of the gross profit?

$_____

Working
Papers
Plus

Chapter 6

b. Will the income statement necessarily report a net income? Explain.

Exercise 6–2

Determining cost of merchandise sold
Objective 1 - Text page 225 ✔ $330,000

Sales were $415,000, and the gross profit was $85,000. What was the amount of the cost of merchandise sold?

Exercise 6–3

Purchase-related transaction
Objective 2 - Text page 226 ✔ a. $2,940

Gupta Company purchased merchandise on account from a supplier for $4,000, terms 2/10, n/30. Gupta Company returned $1,000 of the merchandise and received full credit.

a. If Gupta company pays the invoice within the discount period, what is the amount of cash required for the payment?

b. Under a perpetual inventory system, what account is credited by Gupta Company to record the return?

Exercise 6–4

Determining amounts to be paid on invoices
Objective 2 - Text page 223 ✔ a. $3,762

Determine the amount to be paid in full settlement of each of the following invoices, assuming that credit for returns and allowances was received prior to payment and that all invoices were paid within the discount period.

	Merchandise	Transportation Paid by Seller	Terms	Returns and Allowances	Amount to be Paid in Full
a.	$5,000	—	FOB shipping point, 1/10, n/30	$1,200	$_____
b.	1,000	$50	FOB shipping point, 2/10, n/30	600	$_____
c.	9,500	—	FOB destination, n/30	400	$_____
d.	3,000	75	FOB shipping point, 1/10, n/30	500	$_____
e.	5,000	—	FOB destination, 2/10, n/30	—	$_____

Exercise 6–5

Purchase-related transactions
Objective 2 - Text page 226 ✔ B. $7,227

A retailer is considering the purchase of ten units of a specific item from either of two suppliers. Their offers are as follows:

A: $700 a unit, total of $7,000, 2/10, n/30, plus transportation costs of $375.
B: $730 a unit, total of $7,300, 1/10, n/30, no charge for transportation.

Which of the two offers, A or B, yields the lower price?

Purchase-related transactions
Objective 2 - Text page 226

Name: _____

The debits and credits from four related transactions are presented in the following T accounts.

Describe each transaction.

Cash

| | (2) .... 150 |
| | (4) .... 5,445 |

(1)

Merchandise Inventory

| (1) .... 6,000 | (3) .... 500 |
| (2) .... 150 | (4) .... 55 |

(2)

(3)

Accounts Payable

| (3) .... 500 | (1) .... 6,000 |
| (4) .... 5,500 | |

(4)

Exercise 6–7

Purchase-related transactions
Objective 2 - Text page 226 ✔ (c) Cash, cr. $11,270

Elissa Co., a women's clothing store, purchased $14,000 of merchandise from a supplier on account, terms FOB destination, 2/10, n/30. Elissa Co. returned $2,500 of the merchandise, receiving a credit memorandum, and then paid the amount due within the discount period. Journalize Elissa Co.'s entries to record (a) the purchase, (b) the merchandise return, and (c) the payment.

Date	Description	Debit	Credit

Exercise 6–8

Purchase-related transactions

Objective 2 - Text page 226 ✔ (e) Cash, dr. $920

Journalize entries for the following related transactions of Restoration Company:

a. Purchased $10,000 of merchandise from Veneer Co. on account, terms 2/10, n/30.
b. Paid the amount owed on the invoice within the discount period.
c. Discovered that $4,000 of the merchandise was defective and returned items, receiving credit.
d. Purchased $3,000 of merchandise from Veneer Co. on account, terms n/30.
e. Received a check for the balance owed from the return in (c), after deducting for the purchase in (d).

Date	Description	Debit	Credit

**Sales-related transactions,
including the use of credit cards**
Objective 2 - Text page 230

Journalize the entries for the following transactions:

a. Sold merchandise for cash, $12,800. The cost of the merchandise sold was $7,500.
b. Sold merchandise on account, $9,500. The cost of the merchandise sold was $6,000.
c. Sold merchandise to customers who used MasterCard and VISA, $6,750. The cost of the merchandise sold was $3,850.
d. Sold merchandise to customers who used American Express, $5,100. The cost of merchandise sold was $2,860.
e. Paid an invoice from First National Bank for $350, representing a service fee for processing MasterCard and VISA sales.
f. Received $4,845 from American Express Company after a $255 collection fee had been deducted.

Date	Description	Debit	Credit

Exercise 6–10

Sales returns and allowances
Objective 2 - Text page 230

During the year, sales returns and allowances totaled $212,150. The cost of the merchandise returned was $167,300. The accountant recorded all the returns and allowances by debiting the sales account and crediting Cost of Merchandise Sold for $212,150.

Was the accountant's method of recording returns acceptable? Explain. In your explanation, include the advantages of using a sales returns and allowances account.

Exercise 6–11

Sales-related transactions
Objective 2 - Text page 230 ✔ a. $7,350

After the amount due on a sale of $7,500, terms 2/10, n/eom, is received from a customer within the discount period, the seller consents to the return of the entire shipment. The cost of the merchandise returned was $4,380

a) What is the amount of the refund owed to the customer?

(b) Journalize the entries made by the seller to record the return and the refund.

Date	Description	Debit	Credit

Sales-related transactions
Objective 2 - Text page 230

The debits and credits for three related transactions
are presented in the following T accounts.

Cash	**Describe each transaction.**

Cash

(5) .... 7,920 |

(1)

Accounts Receivable

(1) .... 9,000 | (3) 1,000
                  | (5) 8,000

(2)

Merchandise Inventory

(4) .... 550 | (2) 6,000

(3)

Sales

| (1) 9,000

Sales Discounts   (4)

(5) .... 80 |

Sales Returns and Allowances
                                   (5)
(3) .... 1,000 |

Cost of Merchandise Sold

(2) .... 6,000 | (4) 550

Exercise 6–13

Sales-related transactions
Objective 2 - Text page 230 ✔ d. $10,225

Merchandise is sold on account to a customer for $10,000, terms FOB shipping
point, 3/10, n/30. The seller paid the transportation costs of $525.
Determine the following:

(a) amount of the sale.

(b) amount debited to
    Accounts Receivable.

(c) amount of the discount
    for early payment.

(d) amount due within the
    discount period.

Exercise 6–14

Sales tax
Objective 2 - Text page 233 ✔ c. $1,365

A sale of merchandise on account for $1,300 is subject to a 5% sales tax.

(a) Should the sales tax be recorded at the time of sale or when payment is received?

(b) What is the amount of the sale?

(c) What is the amount debited to Accounts Receivable?

(d) What is the title of the account to which the $65 is credited?

Exercise 6–15

Sales tax transactions
Objective 2 - Text page 233

Journalize the entries to record the following selected transactions:
a. Sold $12,000 of merchandise on account, subject to a sales tax of 4%. The cost of the merchandise sold was $7,000.
b. Paid $2,380 to the state sales tax department for taxes collected.

Date	Description	Debit	Credit

Exercise 6–16   Name:

Sales-related transactions
Objectives 2 - Text page 230

Sauls Co., a furniture wholesaler, sells merchandise to Bayer Co. on account, $7,000, terms 2/15, n/30. The cost of the merchandise sold is $3,900. Sauls Co. issues a credit memorandum for $800 for merchandise returned and subsequently receives the amount due within the discount period. The cost of the merchandise returned is $410. Journalize Sauls Co.'s entries for (a) the sale, including the cost of the merchandise sold, (b) the credit memorandum, including the cost of the returned merchandise, and (c) the receipt of the check for the amount due from Bayer Co.

Date	Description	Debit	Credit

Exercise 6–17

Purchase-related transactions
Objectives 2 - Text page 226

Based on the data presented in Exercise 6-16 , journalize Bayer Co.'s entries for (a) the purchase, (b) the return of the merchandise for credit, and (c) the payment of the invoice within the discount period.

Date	Description	Debit	Credit

Exercise 6–18

Normal balances of merchandise accounts
Objective 2 - Text page 230

What is the normal balance of the following accounts?

	Debit	Credit
(a) Sales Returns and Allowances	_____	_____
(b) Merchandise Inventory	_____	_____
(c) Sales Discounts	_____	_____
(d) Transportation Out	_____	_____
(e) Sales	_____	_____
(f) Cost of Merchandise Sold	_____	_____

Exercise 6–19

Chart of accounts
Objective 3 - Text page 237

Hurley Co. is a newly organized business with the following
list of accounts, arranged in alphabetical order:

Accounts Payable
Accounts Receivable
Accumulated Depreciation - Office Equipment
Accumulated Depreciation - Store Equipment
Advertising Expense
Cash
Cost of Merchandise Sold
Derpreciation Expense - Office Equipment
Depreciation Expense - Store Equipment
Income Summary
Insurance Expense
Interest Expense
Interest Receivable
Interest Revenue
J. Hurley, Capital
J. Hurley, Drawing
Land
Merchandise Inventory

Miscellaneous Administrative Expense
Miscellaneous Selling Expense
Notes Payable (short-term)
Notes Receivable (short-term)
Office Equipment
Office Salaries Expense
Office Supplies
Office Supplies Expense
Prepaid Insurance
Rent Expense
Salaries Payable
Sales
Sales Discounts
Sales Returns and Allowances
Sales Salaries Expense
Store Equipment
Store Supplies
Store Supplies Expense
Transportation Out

Using a blank sheet of paper, construct a chart of accounts, assigning account
numbers and arranging the accounts in balance sheet and income statement order,
as illustrated in Exhibit 6 of your textbook.

Each account number is three digits: the first digit is to indicate the major
classification ("1" for assets, and so on); the second digit is to indicate the
subclassification ("11" for current assets, and so on); and the third digit is to identify
the specific account ("110" for Cash, and so on).

Income statement for merchandiser
Objective 4 - Text page 238 ✔ Gross profit: $1,130,000

For the fiscal year, sales were $3,230,000, sales discounts were $120,000, sales returns and allowances were $280,000, and the cost of merchandise sold was $1,700,000.

What was the
amount of net
sales and gross
profit?

Exercise 6–21

Income statement for merchandiser
Objective 4 - Text page 238

The following expenses were incurred by a merchandising business during the year. In which expense section of the income statement should each be reported: (a) selling, (b) administrative, or (c) other?

____ 1.   Interest expense on notes payable.
____ 2.   Salaries of office personnel.
____ 3.   Advertising expense.
____ 4.   Insurance expense on store equipment.
____ 5.   Rent expense on office building.
____ 6.   Depreciation expense on office equipment.
____ 7.   Office supplies used.
____ 8.   Salary of sales manager.

Exercise 6–22

**Determining amounts for items
omitted from income statement**
Objective 4 - Text page 238 ✔ a. $298,000, h. $690,000

Two items are omitted in each of the following four independent lists of income statement data. Determine the amounts of the missing items. Enter your answer next to the appropriate letter.

Sales	(a)_____	$600,000	$800,000	$757,500
Sales returns and allowances	10,000	10,000	(e)_____	30,500
Sales discounts	8,000	5,000	10,000	(g)_____
Net sales	280,000	(c)_____	765,000	(h)_____
Cost of merchandise sold	150,000	345,000	(f)_____	540,000
Gross profit	(b)_____	(d)_____	300,000	150,000

Multiple-step income statement
Objective 4 - Text page 239

Use textbook and paper to solve this exercise.

Exercise 6–24

Single-step income statement
Objective 4 - Text page 241 ✔ Net income: $412,500

Summary operating data for McNeely Company during the current year ended June 30, 2000, are as follows: cost of merchandise sold, $900,000; administrative expenses, $125,000; interest expense, $17,500; rent revenue, $30,000; net sales, $1,600,000; and selling expenses, $175,000. Prepare a single-step income statement.

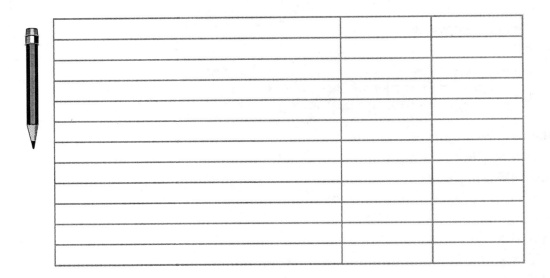

Exercise 6–25

Multiple-step income statement
Objective 4 - Text page 239 ✔ Net income: $57,500

At the end of the year, the balances of the accounts appearing in the ledger of Satellite Company, a furniture wholesaler, are as follows:

Administrative Expenses	$ 70,000	Salaries Payable	3,220
Building	512,500	Sales	975,000
Cash	48,500	Sales Discounts	10,000
Cost of Merchandise Sold	650,000	Sales Returns and Allowances	45,000
Interest Expense	7,500	Selling Expenses	135,000
Merchandise Inventory	130,000	Store Supplies	7,700
Notes Payable	25,000	T. Turner, Capital	638,580
Office Supplies	10,600	T. Turner, Drawing	15,000

All selling expenses have been recorded in the account entitled *Selling Expenses,* and all administrative expenses have been recorded in the account entitled *Administrative Expenses.*

a. Using the form below, prepare a multiple-step income statement for the year ended December 31.

b. Compare the major advantages and disadvantages of the multiple-step and single-step forms of income statements.

Exercise 6–26

Adjusting entry for merchandise inventory shrinkage
Objective 5 - Text page 241

Widmer Inc. perpetual inventory records indicate that $317,200 of merchandise should be on hand on December 31, 2000. The physical inventory indicates that $298,700 of merchandise is actually on hand.

Journalize the adjusting entry for the inventory shrinkage for Widmer Inc. for the year ended December 31, 2000.

Date	Description	Debit	Credit

Exercise 6–27

Closing the accounts of a merchandiser
Objective 5 - Text page 241

From the following list, circle the accounts that should be closed to Income Summary at the end of the fiscal year:

(a) Accounts Receivable

(b) Cost of Merchandise Sold

(c) Merchandise Inventory

(d) Sales

(e) Sales Discounts

(f) Sales Returns and Allowances

(g) Supplies

(h) Supplies Expense

(i) Salaries Expense

(j) Salaries Payable

Financial Analysis and Interpretation

Profitability Analysis

> **Profitability** is the ability of an entity to earn profits.
>
> This ability to earn profits depends on the effectiveness and efficiency of <u>operations</u> as well as <u>resources</u> available.
>
> <u>Profitability analysis</u> focuses primarily on the relationship between operating results reported in the <u>income statement</u> and resources reported in the <u>balance sheet.</u>

Profitability Measures — Effective Use of Assets

Ratio of Net Sales to Assets

	2000	1999
Net sales	$1,498,000	$1,200,000
Total assets:		
Beginning of year	$1,053,000	$1,010,000
End of year	1,044,500	1,053,000
Total	$2,097,500	$2,063,000
Average	$1,048,750	$1,031,500
Ratio of net sales to assets	1.4 to 1	1.2 to 1

Use: To assess the effectiveness in the use of assets

Is this ratio also called the **Asset Turnover** ratio?

Exercise 6–28

Ratio of net sales to total assets
Objective 6 - Text page 244

The financial statements for **Hershey Foods Corporation** are presented in Appendix G at the end of the text.

a. Determine the ratio of net sales to average total assets for Hershey Foods Corporation for the years ended December 31, 1996 and 1995.

b. What conclusions can be drawn from these ratios concerning the trend in the ability of Hershey to effectively use its assets to generate sales?

Note: Hershey's total assets at the end of 1994 were $2,890,981,000.

Blank Page

**Sales-related and purchase-related
transactions for seller and buyer**
Objective 2

The following selected transactions were completed during November between
Singh Company and Bristol Company. Journalize the November transactions
for both Singh Company and Bristol Company in the journals below.

Nov. 3. Singh Company sold merchandise on account to Bristol Company, $11,200, terms
FOB shipping point, 2/10, n/30. Singh Company paid transportation costs of $600,
which were added to the invoice. The cost of the merchandise sold was $7,500.

Singh Company – Seller

Date	Description	Debit	Credit

Bristol Company – Buyer

Date	Description	Debit	Credit

Nov. 8. Singh Company sold merchandise on account to Bristol Company, $13,500, terms
FOB destination, 1/15, n/eom. The cost of the merchandise sold was $9,500.

Singh Company – Seller

Date	Description	Debit	Credit

Bristol Company – Buyer

Date	Description	Debit	Credit

Continued

Nov. 8. Singh Company paid transportation costs of $750 for delivery of merchandise sold to Bristol Company on November 8.

Singh Company – Seller

Date	Description	Debit	Credit

Nov. 12. Bristol Company returned $3,000 of merchandise purchased on account on November 8 from Singh Company. The cost of the merchandise returned was $1,600.

Singh Company – Seller

Date	Description	Debit	Credit

Bristol Company – Buyer

Date	Description	Debit	Credit

Nov. 13. Bristol Company paid Singh Company for purchase of November 3, less discount.

Singh Company – Seller

Date	Description	Debit	Credit

Bristol Company – Buyer

Date	Description	Debit	Credit

Continued

Nov. 23. Bristol Company paid Singh Company for purchase of November 8, less discount and less return of November 12.

Singh Company – Seller

Date	Description	Debit	Credit

Bristol Company – Buyer

Date	Description	Debit	Credit

Nov. 24. Singh Company sold merchandise on account to Bristol Company, $7,100, terms FOB shipping point, n/eom. The cost of the merchandise sold was $4,000.

Singh Company – Seller

Date	Description	Debit	Credit

Bristol Company – Buyer

Date	Description	Debit	Credit

Nov. 27. Bristol Company paid transportation charges of $150 on November 24 purchase from Singh Company

Bristol Company – Buyer

Date	Description	Debit	Credit

Continued

Nov. 30. Bristol Company paid Singh Company on account for purchase of November 24.

Singh Company – Seller

Date	Description	Debit	Credit

Bristol Company – Buyer

Date	Description	Debit	Credit

Problem 6–7A The Wash Co.

Name: _____

Work sheet, financial statements, and adjusting and closing entries
Appendix 2 ✔ 2. Net income: $153,865

Note: The work sheet that follows this problem may be used with either Problem 6–7A or 6–7B. If you are working both the A and B problems, make a copy of the work sheet.

" The accounts and their balances in the ledger of The Wash Co. on December 31 of the current year are shown below. My accountant is missing and I need the financial reports as soon as possible. "

M. Tag, Owner

Cash	$ 51,165	Sales	$1,007,500
Accounts Receivable	116,100	Sales Returns and Allowances	15,500
Merchandise Inventory	235,000	Sales Discounts	6,000
Prepaid Insurance	10,600	Cost of Merchandise Sold	571,200
Store Supplies	3,750	Sales Salaries Expense	86,400
Office Supplies	1,700	Advertising Expense	29,450
Store Equipment	125,000	Depr. Expense – Store Equip.	0
Accum. Depr. – Store Equip.	40,300	Store Supplies Expense	0
Office Equipment	62,000	Miscellaneous Selling Expense	1,885
Accum. Depr. – Office Equip.	17,200	Office Salaries Expense	60,000
Accounts Payable	66,700	Rent Expense	30,000
Salaries Payable	0	Insurance Expense	0
Unearned Rent	1,200	Depr. Expense – Office Equip.	0
Note Payable	105,000	Office Supplies Expense	0
(final payment due 2010)		Miscellaneous Admin. Expense	1,650
M. Tag, Capital	222,100	Rent Revenue	0
M. Tag, Drawing	40,000	Interest Expense	12,600
Income Summary	0		

Instructions

1. Using the form following this problem, prepare a work sheet for the fiscal year ended December 31.

2. Prepare a multiple-step income statement.

3. Prepare a statement of owner's equity.

4. Prepare a report form of balance sheet, assuming that the current portion of the note payable is $15,000.

5. Journalize the adjusting entries.

6. Journalize the closing entries.

The data needed for year-end adjustments on December 31 are as follows:	
Physical merchandise inventory on December 31	$225,000
Insurance expired during the year	7,100
Supplies on hand on December 31:	
Store supplies	1,050
Office supplies	750
Depreciation for the year:	
Store equipment	8,500
Office equipment	4,500
Salaries payable on December 31:	
Sales salaries	$3,450
Office salaries	2,550 6,000
Unearned rent on December 31	400

Note: For steps 2-6, use the appropriate blank forms at the back of the working papers.

Blank Page

PROBLEM 6-7 _____

Account Title	Trial Balance		Adjustments		Income Statement		Balance Sheet	
	Debit	Credit	Debit	Credit	Debit	Credit	Debit	Credit
Cash								
Accounts Receivable								
Merchandise Inventory								
Prepaid Insurance								
Store Supplies								
Office Supplies								
Store Equipment								
Accum. Depr. – Store Equip.								
Office Equipment								
Accum. Depr. – Office Equip.								
Accounts Payable								
Salaries Payable								
Unearned Rent								
Note Payable								
_____ , Capital								
_____ , Drawing								
Sales								
Sales Returns and Allowances								
Sales Discounts								
Cost of Merchandise Sold								
Sales Salaries Expense								
Advertising Expense								
Depr. Expense – Store Equip.								
Store Supplies Expense								
Miscellaneous Selling Expense								
Office Salaries Expense								
Rent Expense								
Insurance Expense								
Depr. Expense – Office Equip.								
Office Supplies Expense								
Miscellaneous Admin. Expense								
Rent Revenue								
Interest Expense								

Blank Page

Problem 6–4B Servco Company and Barkey Co.   Name: _____

Sales-related and purchase-related
transactions for seller and buyer
Objective 2

The following selected transactions were completed during July between
Servco Company and Barkey Co. Journalize the July transactions for both
Servco Company and Barkey Co. in the journals below.

July 3. Servco Company sold merchandise on account to Barkey Co., $10,500, terms FOB
destination, 2/15, n/eom. The cost of the merchandise sold was $6,000.

Servco Company – Seller

Date	Description	Debit	Credit

Barkey Co. – Buyer

Date	Description	Debit	Credit

July 3. Servco Company paid transportation costs of $450 for delivery of merchandise
sold to Barkey Co. on July 3.

Servco Company – Seller

Date	Description	Debit	Credit

July 10. Servco Company sold merchandise on account to Barkey Co., $12,000, terms FOB
shipping point, n/eom. The cost of the merchandise sold was $9,000.

Servco Company – Seller

Date	Description	Debit	Credit

Barkey Co. – Buyer

Date	Description	Debit	Credit

Continued

July 11. Barkey Co. returned $2,000 of merchandise purchased on account on July 3 from Servco Company. The cost of the merchandise returned was $1,200.

Servco Company – Seller

Date	Description	Debit	Credit

Barkey Co. – Buyer

Date	Description	Debit	Credit

July 14. Barkey Co. paid transportation charges of $200 on July 10 purchase from Servco Company.

Barkey Co. – Buyer

Date	Description	Debit	Credit

July 17. Servco Company sold merchandise on account to Barkey Co., $20,000, terms FOB shipping point, 1/10, n/30. Servco Company paid transportation costs of $1,750, which were added to the invoice. The cost of the merchandise sold was $12,000.

Servco Company – Seller

Date	Description	Debit	Credit

Barkey Co. – Buyer

Date	Description	Debit	Credit

Continued

July 18. Barkey Co. paid Servco Company for purchase of July 3, less discount and
less return of July 11.

Servco Company – Seller

Date	Description	Debit	Credit

Barkey Co. – Buyer

Date	Description	Debit	Credit

July 27. Barkey Co. paid Servco Company on account for purchase of July 17, less
discount.

Servco Company – Seller

Date	Description	Debit	Credit

Barkey Co. – Buyer

Date	Description	Debit	Credit

July 31. Barkey Co. paid Servco Company on account for purchase of July 10.

Servco Company – Seller

Date	Description	Debit	Credit

Barkey Co. – Buyer

Date	Description	Debit	Credit

Blank Page

Problem 6–7B The Shoe Co.

Name:

Work sheet, financial statements, and adjusting and closing entries
Appendix 2 ✔ 2. Net income: $169,250

Note: The work sheet that follows Problem 6–7A may be used with either Problem 6–7A or 6–7B. If you are working both the A and B problems, make a copy of the work sheet.

" The accounts and their balances in the ledger of The Shoe Co. on December 31 of the current year are shown below. My accountant is missing and I need the financial reports as soon as possible. "

J. Oxford, Owner

Cash	$ 38,000	Sales	$895,000
Accounts Receivable...................	112,500	Sales Returns and Allowances	11,900
Merchandise Inventory..............	230,000	Sales Discounts	7,100
Prepaid Insurance	9,700	Cost of Merchandise Sold	476,200
Store Supplies	4,250	Sales Salaries Expense	76,400
Office Supplies	2,100	Advertising Expense	25,000
Store Equipment	132,000	Depr. Expense – Store Equip.	0
Accum. Depr. – Store Equip.	40,300	Store Supplies Expense	0
Office Equipment	50,000	Miscellaneous Selling Expense	1,600
Accum. Depr. – Office Equip.	17,200	Office Salaries Expense	44,000
Accounts Payable	66,700	Rent Expense	26,000
Salaries Payable	0	Insurance Expense	0
Unearned Rent	1,200	Depr. Expense – Office Equip.	0
Note Payable	105,000	Office Supplies Expense	0
(final payment due 2010)		Miscellaneous Admin. Expense	1,650
J. Oxford, Capital	174,600	Rent Revenue..	0
J. Oxford, Drawing	40,000	Interest Expense	11,600
Income Summary	0		

Instructions

1. Using the form following Problem 6–7A, prepare a work sheet for the fiscal year ended December 31.

2. Prepare a multiple-step income statement.

3. Prepare a statement of owner's equity.

4. Prepare a report form of balance sheet, assuming that the current portion of the note payable is $15,000.

5. Journalize the adjusting entries.

6. Journalize the closing entries.

The data needed for year-end adjustments on December 31 are as follows:

Physical merchandise inventory on December 31	$212,000
Insurance expired during the year	6,500
Supplies on hand on December 31:	
Store supplies	1,300
Office supplies	750
Depreciation for the year:	
Store equipment	7,500
Office equipment	3,800
Salaries payable on December 31:	
Sales salaries $3,850	
Office salaries 1,150	5,000
Unearned rent on December 31	400

Note: For steps 2-6, use the appropriate blank forms at the back of the working papers.

Blank Page

COMPREHENSIVE PROBLEM 2 - The Cycle Co.

Accounting Cycle for a Merchandising Company
Perpetual Inventory System

✔ 5. Net income: $67,415

For many entrepreneurs, starting a business is only part of the dream. Even more important is making it grow.

Company Profile:

Florence Schwinn is one of four children of a Detroit steelworker. From that rather humble start in life, Florence has bootstrapped herself into a fast-growing company, designing state-of-the-art bicycles. Florence established her company with a dream of providing a wide range of products at an affordable price using high-quality materials. The Cycle Co. designs and markets superior products and maintains contracts with two manufacturing companies which provide quality products. The Cycle Co. plans to gradually develop their own manufacturing capability.

COMPREHENSIVE PROBLEM 2

The Cycle Co. is a merchandising business. The account balances for The Cycle Co. as of May 1, 2000 (unless otherwise indicated) are as follows:

110	Cash .... $ 29,160	410	Sales 731,600
111	Notes Receivable 0	411	Sales Returns and Allowances 13,600
112	Accounts Receivable 56,220	412	Sales Discounts 5,200
113	Interest Receivable 0	510	Cost of Merchandise Sold 497,540
115	Merchandise Inventory 123,900	520	Sales Salaries Expense 74,400
116	Prepaid Insurance 3,750	521	Advertising Expense 18,000
117	Store Supplies 2,550	522	Depreciation Expense 0
123	Store Equipment 54,300	523	Store Supplies Expense 0
124	Accum. Dep.-Store Equip. .. 12,600	529	Misc. Selling Expense 2,800
210	Accounts Payable 38,500	530	Office Salaries Expense 29,400
211	Salaries Payable 0	531	Rent Expense 24,500
310	F. R. Schwinn, Capital,	532	Insurance Expense 0
	June 1, 1999 179,270	539	Misc. Admin. Expense 1,650
311	F. R. Schwinn, Drawing 25,000	611	Interest Revenue 0
312	Income Summary 0		

During May, the last month of the fiscal year, the following transactions were completed:

May 1. Paid rent for May, $2,400.

1. Received a $7,500 note receivable from Holmes Co. on account.

2. Purchased merchandise on account from Lindsey Co., terms 2/10, n/30, FOB shipping point, $25,000.

3. Paid transportation charges on purchase of May 2, $750.

5. Sold merchandise on account to Richards Co., terms 2/10, n/30, FOB shipping point, $8,500. The cost of the merchandise sold was $5,000.

7. Received $16,900 cash from Vasquez Co. on account, no discount.

10. Sold merchandise for cash, $18,300. The cost of the merchandise sold was $11,000.

12. Paid for merchandise purchased on May 2, less discount.

13. Received merchandise returned on sale of May 5, $1,500. The cost of the merchandise returned was $900.

14. Paid advertising expense for last half of May, $2,500.

15. Received cash from sale of May 5, less return of May 13 and discount.

19. Purchased merchandise for cash, $7,400.

19. Paid $25,950 to Chang Co. on account, no discount.

20. Sold merchandise on account to Petroski Co., terms 1/10, n/30, FOB shipping point, $16,000. The cost of the merchandise sold was $9,600.

21. For the convenience of the customer, paid shipping charges on sale of May 20, $600.

21. Received $31,000 cash from Sinnett Co. on account, no discounts.

21. Purchased merchandise on account from Hummer Co., terms 1/10, n/30, FOB destination, $15,000.

24. Returned $2,500 of damaged merchandise purchased on May 21, receiving credit from the seller.

25. Refunded cash on sales made for cash, $750. The cost of the merchandise returned was $480.

27. Paid sales salaries of $2,700 and office salaries of $900.

Continued

May transactions continued.

29. Purchased store supplies for cash, $350.
30. Sold merchandise on account to Brown Co., terms 2/10, n/30, FOB shipping point, $43,100. The cost of the merchandise sold was $25,000.
30. Received cash from sale of May 20, less discount, plus transportation paid on May 21.
31. Paid for purchase of May 21, less return of May 24 and discount.

Instructions

(**Note:** If the work sheet described in the appendix is used, follow the alternative instructions on the next page.)

1. Enter the balances of each of the accounts in the appropriate balance column of the four-column accounts that follow. Write *Balance* in the item section, and place a check mark (✓) in the Posting Reference column.

2. Journalize the transactions for May.

3. Post the journal to the general ledger, extending the month-end balances to the appropriate balance columns after all posting is completed. In this problem, you are not required to update or post to the accounts receivable and accounts payable subsidiary ledgers.

4. Journalize and post the adjusting entries, using the following adjustment data:
   a. Interest accrued on notes receivable on May 31 ..... $　　100
   b. Merchandise inventory on May 31 110,000
   c. Insurance expired during the year 1,250
   d. Store supplies on hand on May 31 1,050
   e. Depreciation for the current year 8,860
   f. Accrued salaries on May 31:
      Sales salaries $400
      Office salaries 140 540

5. Prepare a multiple-step income statement, a statement of owner's equity, and a report form of balance sheet.

6. Journalize and post the closing entries. Indicate closed accounts by inserting a line in both balance columns opposite the closing entry. Insert the new balance in the owner's capital account.

7. Prepare a post-closing trial balance.

Continued

COMPREHENSIVE PROBLEM 2

Continued

Alternative Instructions

1. Enter the balances of each of the accounts in the appropriate balance column of the four-column accounts that follow. Write *Balance* in the item section, and place a check mark (✓) in the Posting Reference column.

2. Journalize the transactions for May.

3. Post the journal to the general ledger, extending the month-end balances to the appropriate balance columns after all posting is completed. In this problem, you are not required to update or post to the accounts receivable and accounts payable subsidiary ledgers.

4. Prepare a trial balance as of May 31 on the work sheet which is provided. Complete the work sheet for the fiscal year ended May 31, using the following adjustment data:

   a. Interest accrued on notes receivable on May 31 ..... $ 100
   b. Merchandise inventory on May 31 110,000
   c. Insurance expired during the year 1,250
   d. Store supplies on hand on May 31 1,050
   e. Depreciation for the current year..................................... 8,860
   f. Accrued salaries on May 31:
      Sales salaries.. $400
      Office salaries 140 540

5. Prepare a multiple-step income statement, a statement of owner's equity, and a report form of balance sheet.

6. Journalize and post the adjusting entries.

7. Journalize and post the closing entries. Indicate closed accounts by inserting a line in both balance columns opposite the closing entry. Insert the new balance in the owner's capital account.

8. Prepare a post-closing trial balance.

GENERAL JOURNAL

Page 20

Date		Description	Post. Ref.	Debit		Credit	

GENERAL JOURNAL

Page 21

Date	Description	Post. Ref.	Debit	Credit

Name:

GENERAL JOURNAL

Page 22

Date		Description	Post. Ref.	Debit		Credit	

GENERAL JOURNAL

Date	Description	Post. Ref.	Debit	Credit

Journalize adjusting entries.

GENERAL JOURNAL

Date	Description	Post. Ref.	Debit	Credit
	Adjusting Entries			

Journalize closing entries.

GENERAL JOURNAL

Date	Description	Post. Ref.	Debit	Credit
	Closing Entries			

Post Journal to the Ledger.

GENERAL LEDGER

ACCOUNT Cash   NO. 110

Date		Description	Post. Ref.	Debit	Credit	Balance Debit	Balance Credit

ACCOUNT Notes Receivable   NO. 111

Date		Description	Post. Ref.	Debit	Credit	Balance Debit	Balance Credit

ACCOUNT Accounts Receivable   NO. 112

Date	Description	Post. Ref.	Debit	Credit	Balance Debit	Credit

ACCOUNT Interest Receivable   NO. 113

Date	Description	Post. Ref.	Debit	Credit	Balance Debit	Credit

ACCOUNT Merchandise Inventory   NO. 115

Date	Description	Post. Ref.	Debit	Credit	Balance Debit	Balance Credit

ACCOUNT Prepaid Insurance   NO. 116

Date	Description	Post. Ref.	Debit	Credit	Balance Debit	Balance Credit

ACCOUNT Store Supplies   NO. 117

Date	Description	Post. Ref.	Debit	Credit	Balance Debit	Balance Credit

ACCOUNT Store Equipment   NO. 123

Date	Description	Post. Ref.	Debit	Credit	Balance Debit	Balance Credit

ACCOUNT Accumulated Depreciation – Store Equipment   NO. 124

Date	Description	Post. Ref.	Debit	Credit	Balance Debit	Balance Credit

ACCOUNT Accounts Payable   NO. 210

Date	Description	Post. Ref.	Debit	Credit	Balance Debit	Balance Credit

ACCOUNT Salaries Payable   NO. 211

Date	Description	Post. Ref.	Debit	Credit	Balance Debit	Balance Credit

ACCOUNT F. R. Schwinn, Capital   NO. 310

Date	Description	Post. Ref.	Debit	Credit	Balance Debit	Balance Credit

ACCOUNT F. R. Schwinn, Drawing   NO. 311

Date	Description	Post. Ref.	Debit	Credit	Balance Debit	Balance Credit

ACCOUNT Income Summary   NO. 312

Date	Description	Post. Ref.	Debit	Credit	Balance Debit	Balance Credit

ACCOUNT Sales   NO. 410

Date	Description	Post. Ref.	Debit	Credit	Balance Debit	Balance Credit

ACCOUNT Sales Returns and Allowances   NO. 411

Date	Description	Post. Ref.	Debit	Credit	Balance Debit	Balance Credit

ACCOUNT Sales Discounts   NO. 412

Date	Description	Post. Ref.	Debit	Credit	Balance Debit	Balance Credit

ACCOUNT Cost of Merchandise Sold   NO. 510

Date	Description	Post. Ref.	Debit	Credit	Balance Debit	Balance Credit

ACCOUNT Sales Salaries Expense　　　　　　　　　　　NO. 520

Date		Description	Post. Ref.	Debit	Credit	Balance Debit	Credit

ACCOUNT Advertising Expense　　　　　　　　　　　NO. 521

Date		Description	Post. Ref.	Debit	Credit	Balance Debit	Credit

ACCOUNT Depreciation Expense　　　　　　　　　　　NO. 522

Date		Description	Post. Ref.	Debit	Credit	Balance Debit	Credit

ACCOUNT Store Supplies Expense　　　　　　　　　　　NO. 523

Date		Description	Post. Ref.	Debit	Credit	Balance Debit	Credit

ACCOUNT Miscellaneous Selling Expense　　　　　　　　　　　NO. 529

Date		Description	Post. Ref.	Debit	Credit	Balance Debit	Credit

ACCOUNT Office Salaries Expense   NO. 530

Date	Description	Post. Ref.	Debit	Credit	Balance Debit	Balance Credit

ACCOUNT Rent Expense   NO. 531

Date	Description	Post. Ref.	Debit	Credit	Balance Debit	Balance Credit

ACCOUNT Insurance Expense   NO. 532

Date	Description	Post. Ref.	Debit	Credit	Balance Debit	Balance Credit

ACCOUNT Miscellaneous Administrative Expense   NO. 539

Date	Description	Post. Ref.	Debit	Credit	Balance Debit	Balance Credit

ACCOUNT Interest Revenue   NO. 611

Date	Description	Post. Ref.	Debit	Credit	Balance Debit	Balance Credit

COMPREHENSIVE PROBLEM 2 The Cycle Co. (Use for Alternative Instructions)

Act#	Account Title	Trial Balance		Adjustments		Income Statement		Balance Sheet	
		Debit	Credit	Debit	Credit	Debit	Credit	Debit	Credit
110	Cash								
111	Notes Receivable								
112	Accounts Receivable								
113	Interest Receivable								
115	Merchandise Inventory								
116	Prepaid Insurance								
117	Store Supplies								
123	Store Equipment								
124	Accum. Depr.-Store Equip.								
210	Accounts Payable								
211	Salaries Payable								
310	F. R. Schwinn, Capital								
311	F. R. Schwinn, Drawing								
410	Sales								
411	Sales Returns and Allowances								
412	Sales Discounts								
510	Cost of Merchandise Sold								
520	Sales Salaries Expense								
521	Advertising Expense								
522	Depreciation Expense								
523	Store Supplies Expense								
529	Misc. Selling Expense								
530	Office Salaries Expense								
531	Rent Revenue								
532	Insurance Expense								
539	Misc. Admin. Expense								
611	Interest Revenue								

Blank Page

COMPREHENSIVE PROBLEM 2

Name: _____

Prepare financial statements.

The Cycle Co.
Income Statement
For Year Ended May 31, 2000

The Cycle Co.
Statement of Owner's Equity
For the Year Ended May 31, 2000

Net Income
$67,415

The Cycle Co.
Balance Sheet
May 31, 2000

Prepare post-closing trial balance.

The Cycle Co.
Post-Closing Trial Balance
May 31, 2000

No.	Account	Debit	Credit

Blank Page

Chapter 7
Cash

The qualities of a properly designed accounting system and the principles of internal control for directing operations have been discussed in preceding chapters. This chapter applies these principles to the design of systems for controlling cash and the accounting for cash transactions.

Learning objectives are listed for the exercises and problems that follow. Use the information to the right to determine the nature of the objective and the page number to refer to your textbook for a discussion of the topic.

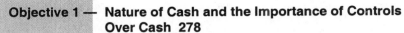

Objective 1 — **Nature of Cash and the Importance of Controls Over Cash 278**
Describe the nature of cash and the importance of internal control over cash.

Objective 2 — **Control of Cash Receipts 278**
Summarize basic procedures for achieving internal control over cash receipts.

Objective 3 — **Internal Control of Cash Payments 280**
Summarize basic procedures for achieving internal control over cash payments, including the use of a voucher system.

Objective 4 — **Bank Accounts: Their Nature and Use as a Control Over Cash 282**
Describe the nature of a bank account and its use in controlling cash.

Objective 5 — **Bank Reconciliation 286**
Prepare a bank reconciliation and journalize any necessary entries.

Objective 6 — **Petty Cash 289**
Account for small cash transactions, using a petty cash fund.

Objective 7 — **Presentation of Cash on the Balance Sheet 291**
Summarize how cash is presented on the balance sheet.

Objective 8 — **Financial Analysis and Interpretation 291**
Compute and interpret the ratio of cash to current liabilities.

Blank Page

Exercise 7–1

Name: _____

Internal control of cash receipts
Objective 2 - Text page 278

The procedures used for over-the-counter receipts are as follows. At the close of each day's business, the sales clerks count the cash in their respective cash drawers, after which they determine the amount recorded by the cash register and prepare the memorandum cash form, noting any descrepancies. An employee from the cashier's office counts the cash, compares the total with the memorandum, and takes the cash to the cashier's office.

Working
Papers
Plus
_____
Chapter 7

a. Indicate the weak link in internal control.

b. How can the weakness be corrected?

Exercise 7–2

Internal control of cash receipts
Objective 2 - Text page 278

Don Carey works at the drive-through window of Bob's Burgers. Occasionally, when a drive-through customer orders, Don fills the order and pockets the customer's money. He does not ring up the order on the cash register.

Identify the internal control weaknesses that exist at Bob's Burgers, and discuss what can be done to prevent this theft.

Exercise 7–3

Internal control of cash receipts
Objective 2 - Text page 278

The mailroom employees send all remittances and remittance advices to the cashier. The cashier deposits the cash in the bank and forwards the remittance advices and duplicate deposit slips to the Accounting Department.

a. Indicate the
   weak link in
   internal control
   in the handling
   of cash receipts.

b. How can the
   weakness be
   corrected?

Exercise 7–4

Entry for cash sales; cash short
Objective 2 - Text page 278

The actual cash received from cash sales was $11,940.50, and the amount indicated by the cash register total was $11,965.75. Journalize the entry to record the cash receipts and cash sales.

Date	Description	Debit	Credit

Exercise 7–5   **Name:** _____

Entry for cash sales; cash over
Objective 2 - Text page 278

The actual cash received from cash sales was $13,189.20, and the amount
indicated by the cash register total was $13,180.70. Journalize the entry to
record the cash receipts and cash sales.

Date	Description	Debit		Credit	

Exercise 7–6

Internal control of cash payments
Objective 3 - Text page 280

Panatone Co. is a medium-size merchandising company. An investigation revealed
that in spite of a sufficient bank balance, a significant amount of available cash
discounts had been lost because of failure to make timely payments. In addition, it was
discovered that several purchases invoices had been paid twice.

Outline procedures
for the payment of
vendors' invoices, so
that the possibilities
of losing available
cash discounts and
of paying an invoice
a second time will be
minimized.

Internal control of cash payments
Objective 3 - Text page 280

Comm3 Company, a communications equipment manufacturer, recently fell victim to an embezzlement scheme masterminded by one of its employees. To understand the scheme, it is necessary to review Comm3's procedures for the purchase of services.

The purchasing agent is responsible for ordering services (such as repairs to a photocopy machine or office cleaning) after receiving a service requisition from an authorized manager. However, since no tangible goods are delivered, a receiving report is not prepared. When the Accounting Department receives an invoice billing Comm3 for a service call, the accounts payable clerk calls the manager who requested the service in order to verify that it was performed.

The embezzlement scheme involves Kim Mira, the manager of plant and facilities. Kim arranged for her uncle's company, Gear Industrial Supply and Service, to be placed on Comm3's approved vendor list. Kim did not disclose the family relationship.

On several occasions, Kim would submit a requisition for services to be provided by Gear's Industrial Supply and Service. However, the service requested was really not needed, and it was never performed. Gear would bill Comm3 for the service and then split the cash payment with Kim.

Explain what
changes should be
made to Comm3's
procedures for
ordering and paying
for services in order
to prevent such
occurrences in the
future.

Exercise 7–8   Name: _____

Bank reconciliation
Objective 5 - Text page 286

Identify each of the following reconciling items as:

(a) an addition to the cash balance according to the bank statement,

(b) a deduction from the cash balance according to the bank statement,

(c) an addition to the cash balance according to the depositor's records, or

(d) a deduction from the cash balance according to the depositor's records.

(None of the transactions reported by bank debit and credit
memorandums have been recorded by the depositor.)

_____ 1. Check for $37 charged by bank as $73.

_____ 2. Check drawn by depositor for $150 but recorded as $1,500.

_____ 3. Outstanding checks, $8,512.30.

_____ 4. Deposit in transit, $12,300.

_____ 5. Note collected by bank, $5,200.00.

_____ 6. Check of a customer returned by bank to depositor because
of insufficient funds, $650.

_____ 7. Bank service charges, $30.

Exercise 7–9

Entries based on bank reconciliation
Objective 5 - Text page 286

Which of the reconciling items listed in Exercise 7–8 require an entry in
the depositor's accounts?

Exercise 7–10

Bank reconciliation
Objective 5 - Text page 286 ✔ Adjusted balance: $12,604.70

The following data were accumulated for use in reconciling the bank account of The Skin Saver Co. for October:

a. Cash balance according to the depositor's records at October 31, $12,530.20.
b. Cash balance according to the bank statement at October 31, $11,100.50.
c. Checks outstanding, $3,276.20.
d. Deposit in transit, not recorded by bank, $4,780.40.
e. A check for $340 in payment of an account was erroneously recorded in the check register as $430.
f. Bank debit memorandum for service charges, $15.50.

Prepare a bank reconciliation.

The Skin Saver Co.
Bank Reconciliation
October 31, 20__

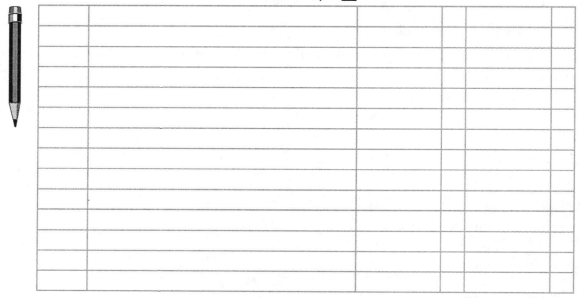

Exercise 7–11

Entries for bank reconciliation
Objective 5 - Text page 286

Using the data presented in Exercise 7–10, journalize the entry or entries that should be made by the depositor.

Date	Description	Debit	Credit

Entries for note collected by bank
Objective 5 - Text page 286

Accompanying a bank statement for Profumeria Company is a credit memorandum for $13,900, representing the principal ($13,000) and interest ($900) on a note that had been collected by the bank. The depositor had been notified by the bank at the time of the collection, but had made no entries. In general journal form, journalize the entry that should be made by the depositor to bring the accounting records up to date.

Date	Description	Debit	Credit

Bank reconciliation
Objective 5 - Text page 286 ✔ Adjusted balance: $13,055.15

An accounting clerk for The Zhanay Co. prepared the following bank reconciliation:

The Zhanay Co.
Bank Reconciliation
January 31, 2000

Cash balance according to depositor's records		$11,100.75
Add: Outstanding checks	$5,557.12	
Error by The Zhanay Co. in recording Check No. 345 as $2,510 instead of $2,150	360.00	
Note for $1,500 collected by bank, including interest	1,620.00	7,537.12
		$18,637.87
Deduct: Deposit in transit on January 31	$1,150.00	
Bank service charges	25.60	1,175.60
Cash balance according to bank statement		$17,462.27

a. Using the data in the above bank reconciliation, prepare a new bank reconciliation for The Zhanay Co. in the format shown in the illustrative problem.

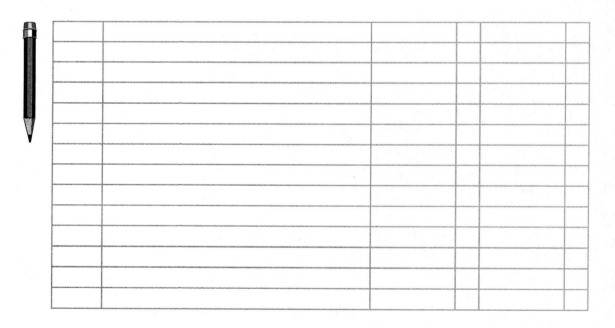

b. If a balance sheet were prepared for The Zhanay Co. on January 31, 2000, what amount should be reported for cash?

**Using bank reconciliation to
determine cash receipts stolen**
Objective 5 - Text page 286 ✔ a. $238.36

" Monarch Co. records all cash receipts on the basis of its cash register tapes. I discovered during June 2000 that one of our sales clerks had stolen an undetermined amount of cash receipts when he took the daily deposits to the bank. We have gathered the following data for June. No deposits were in transit on June 30, which fell on a Sunday. We desperately need your help to determine the amount stolen. Also, please advise us so this won't happen again. "

Dan Ness, Treasurer

Cash in bank according to the general ledger .... $ 9,573.22
Cash according to the June 30, 2000 bank statement 12,271.14
Outstanding checks as of June 30, 2000 .... 1,901.38
Bank service charge for June 25.10
Note receivable, including interest collected by bank in June 1,060.00

a. Determine the
   amount of
   cash receipts
   stolen by the
   sales clerk.

b. What accounting
   controls would have
   prevented or
   detected this theft?

Exercise 7–15

Bank reconciliation

Objective 5 - Text page 286 ✔ Corrected adjusted balance: $11,998.02

How many errors can you find in the following bank reconciliation prepared as of the end of the current month?

Enrico Co.
Bank Reconciliation
For the Month Ended June 30, 20—

Cash balance according to bank statement			$12,767.76
Add outstanding checks			
No. 3721		$ 545.95	
3739		172.75	
3743		459.60	
3744		601.50	1,779.80
			$14,547.56
Deduct deposit of June 30, not recorded by bank			1,010.06
Adjusted balance			$12,537.50
Cash balance according to depositor's records			$ 9,048.72
Add: Proceeds of note collected by bank:			
Principal	$3,000.00		
Interest	150.00	$3,150.00	
Service charges		19.50	3,169.50
			$12,218.22
Deduct: Check returned because of			
insufficient funds		$ 451.20	
Error in recording May 15			
deposit of $1,859 as $1,589		270.00	721.20
Adjusted balance			$11,497.02

Petty cash fund entries
Objective 6 - Text page 289

Journalize the entries to record the following:

a. Check No. 2511 is issued to establish a petty cash fund of $500.

b. The amount of cash in the petty cash fund is now $79.30. Check No. 2555 is issued to
    replenish the fund, based on the following summary of petty cash receipts: office supplies,
    $215.83; miscellaneous selling expense, $125.60; miscellaneous administrative expense,
    $68.10. (Since the amount of the check to replenish the fund plus the balance in the fund do
    not equal $500, record the discrepancy in the cash short and over account.)

Date	Description	Debit	Credit

" I told the boss that we needed a $600 petty cash
fund to cover miscellaneous items that we
needed to buy from time-to-time. He said,
'That's a lot of miscellaneous stuff.' He was
willing to try a fund of $500 and asked me to
watch it closely. What do you think he'll say
when he finds out I'm short by $11.17? "

Joyce Dame
Petty Cash Custodian
With Second Thoughts

Solvency Analysis

Solvency is the ability of a business to meet its financial obligations (debts) as they are due.

Solvency analysis focuses on the ability of a business to pay or otherwise satisfy its current and noncurrent liabilities.

This ability is normally assessed by examining balance sheet relationships.

Solvency Measures — The Short-Term Creditor

Doomsday Ratio

	Laettner Co.	Oakley Co.
A. Cash and equivalents	$100,000	$ 120,000
B. Current liabilities	400,000	1,500,000
Doomsday Ratio A / B	0.25	0.08

Use: To indicate the worst case assumption that the business ceases to exist and only the cash on hand is available to meet creditor obligations.

Exercise 7–17

Doomsday ratio
Objective 8 - Text page 291

The financial statements for **Hershey Foods Corporation** are presented in Appendix G at the end of the text.

a. Compute the doomsday ratio for Hershey Foods Corporation for 1996 and 1995.

b. What conclusions can be drawn from comparing the ratios for 1996 and 1995?

Evaluating internal control of cash
Objectives 1, 2, 3

The following procedures were recently installed by Sixto Company.
Indicate whether each of the procedures of internal control over cash represents:

(1) a strength, or

(2) a weakness.

Place your answer to the left of each letter.

_____a. Each cashier is assigned a separate cash register drawer to which no other cashier has access.

_____b. All sales are rung up on the cash register, and a receipt is given to the customer. All sales are recorded on a tape locked inside the cash register.

_____c. At the end of a shift, each cashier counts the cash in his or her cash register, unlocks the tape, and compares the amount of cash with the amount on the tape to determine cash shortages and overages.

_____d. Checks received through the mail are given daily to the accounts receivable clerk for recording collections on account and for depositing in the bank.

_____e. The bank reconciliation is prepared by the accountant.

_____f. Disbursements are made from the petty cash fund only after a petty cash receipt has been completed and signed by the payee.

_____g. Vouchers and all supporting documents are perforated with a PAID designation after being paid by the treasurer.

For each weakness, indicate why it exists.

Blank page

Bank reconciliation and entries
Objective 5 - Text page 286 ✔ 1. Adjusted balance: $29,393.00

The cash account for Universal Systems at March 31 of the current year indicated a balance of $26,740.50. The bank statement indicated a balance of $33,391.40 on March 31. Comparing the bank statement and the accompanying canceled checks and memorandums with the records revealed the following reconciling items:

a. Checks outstanding totaled $4,943.90.

b. A deposit of $1,215.50, representing receipts of March 31, had been made too late to appear on the bank statement.

c. The bank had collected $2,600 on a note left for collection. The face of the note was $2,500.

d. A check for $675 returned with the statement had been incorrectly recorded by Universal Systems as $765. The check was for the payment of an obligation to Jones Co. for the purchase of office supplies on account.

e. A check drawn for $1,300 had been incorrectly charged by the bank as $1,030.

f. Bank service charges for March amounted to $37.50.

Amanda Janiece
Bookkeeper

Instructions

1. Prepare a bank reconciliation.

Universal Systems
Bank Reconciliation
March 31, 20___

Continued

2. Journalize the necessary entries. The accounts have not been closed.

Date	Description	Debit		Credit	

" The bank reconciliation is an important part of our system of internal control. Because our company is small, and because I personally handle cash receipts and cash payments, we have our accountant prepare the reconciliation and the related journal entries. Occasionally, the accountant finds errors that I have made. Although this is embarrassing when it happens, I realize that this is an important part of a good internal control system. "

Amanda Janiece
Bookkeeper

Evaluating internal control of cash
Objectives 1, 2, 3

The following procedures were recently installed by Epic Company.
Indicate whether each of the procedures of internal control over cash represents:

(1) a strength, or

(2) a weakness.

Place your answer to the left of each letter.

_____a. All mail is opened by the mail clerk, who forwards all cash remittances to the cashier. The cashier prepares a listing of the cash receipts and forwards a copy of the list to the accounts receivable clerk for recording in the accounts.

_____b. At the end of each day, an accounting clerk compares the duplicate copy of the daily cash deposit slip with the deposit receipt obtained from the bank.

_____c. The bank reconciliation is prepared by the cashier, who works under the supervision of the treasurer.

_____d. At the end of each day, any deposited cash receipts are placed in the bank's night depository.

_____e. At the end of the day, cash register clerks are required to use their own funds to make up any cash shortages in their registers.

_____f. The accounts payable clerk prepares a voucher for each disbursement. The voucher along with the supporting documentation is forwarded to the treasurer's office for approval.

_____g. After necessary approvals have been obtained for the payment of a voucher, the treasurer signs and mails the check. The treasurer then stamps the voucher and supporting documentation as paid and returns the voucher and supporting documentation to the accounts payable clerk for filing.

_____h. Along with petty cash expense receipts for postage, office supplies, etc., several post-dated employee checks are in the petty cash fund.

For each weakness, indicate why it exists.

Blank page

Bank reconciliation and entries

Objective 5 - Text page 286 ✔ 1. Adjusted balance: $27,854.30

The cash account for Astoria Carpets at November 30 of the current year indicated a balance of $25,640.30. The bank statement indicated a balance of $31,016.30 on November 30. Comparing the bank statement and the accompanying canceled checks and memorandums with the records revealed the following reconciling items:

a. Checks outstanding totaled $6,169.75.

b. A deposit of $2,917.75, representing receipts of November 30, had been made too late to appear on the bank statement.

c. The bank had collected $3,150 on a note left for collection. The face of the note was $3,000.

d. A check for $2,100 returned with the statement had been incorrectly recorded by Astoria Carpets as $1,200. The check was for the payment of an obligation to Ace Co. for the purchase of office equipment on account.

e. A check drawn for $1,780 had been erroneously charged by the bank as $1,870.

f. Bank service charges for November amounted to $36.00.

Instructions

1. Prepare a bank reconciliation.

Astoria Carpets
Bank Reconciliation
November 30, 20___

Continued

2. Journalize the necessary entries. The accounts have not been closed.

Date	Description	Debit		Credit	

Bank reconciliation and entries
Objective 5 - Text page 286 ✔ 1. Adjusted balance: $15,119.87

The cash account for Ambos Co. at August 1 of the current year indicated a balance of $12,705.37. During August, the total cash deposited was $30,650.75, and checks written totaled $31,770.25. The bank statement indicated a balance of $16,465.50 on August 31. Comparing the bank statement, the canceled checks, and the accompanying memorandums with the records revealed the following reconciling items:

a. Checks outstanding totaled $8,003.84.

b. A deposit of $3,148.21, representing receipts of August 31, had been made too late to appear on the bank statement.

c. The bank had collected for Ambos Co. $3,650 on a note left for collection. The face of the note was $3,500.

d. A check for $390 returned with the statement had been incorrectly charged by the bank as $3,900.

e. A check for $210 returned with the statement had been recorded by Ambos Co. as $120. The check was for the payment of an obligation to Bartles Co. on account.

f. Bank service charges for August amounted to $26.

Instructions

1. Prepare a bank reconciliation as of August 31.

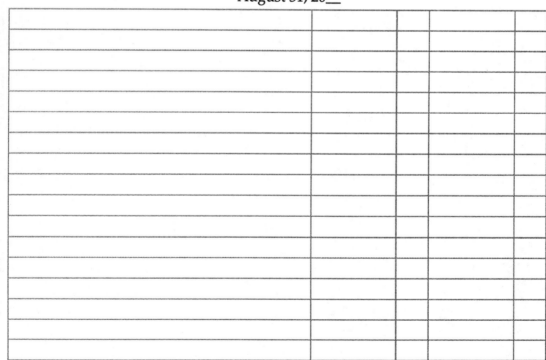

Ambos Co.
Bank Reconciliation
August 31, 20__

Continued

2. Journalize the necessary entries. The accounts have not been closed.

Date	Description	Debit	Credit

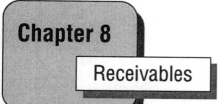

Chapter 8

Receivables

For many businesses, the revenue from sales on account is one of the largest factors influencing the amount of net income. As credit is granted, the resulting receivables may represent a significant portion of the total current assets. This chapter discusses the accounting for such receivables as well as the accounting for notes receivable.

Learning objectives are listed for the exercises and problems that follow. Use the information to the right to determine the nature of the objective and the page number to refer to your textbook for a discussion of the topic.

Blank Page

Internal control procedures
Objective 2 - Text page 312

Cardinal Company sells carpeting. Over 75% of all carpet sales are on credit. The following procedures are used by Cardinal to process this large number of credit sales and the subsequent collections. State whether each of these procedures is appropriate or inappropriate, considering the principles of internal control. If inappropriate, state which internal control procedure is violated.

a. All credit sales to a first-time customer must be approved by the Credit Department. Salespersons will assist the customer in filling out a credit application, but an employee in the Credit Department is responsible for verifying employment and checking the customer's credit history before granting credit.

b. Cardinal's standard credit period is 45 days. The Credit Department may approve an extension of this repayment period of up to one year. Whenever an extension is granted, the customer signs a promissory note. Up to 30% of the credit sales in any one year are for repayment periods exceeding 45 days.

c. A formal ledger is not maintained for customers who sign promissory notes. Cardinal simply keeps a copy of each signed note in a file cabinet. These unpaid notes are filed by due date.

d. Cardinal employs an accounts receivable clerk. The clerk is responsible for recording customer credit sales (based on sales tickets), receiving cash from customers, giving customers credit for their payments, and handling all customer billing complaints.

e. The general ledger control account for Accounts Receivable is maintained by the General Accounting Department at Cardinal. This department records total credit sales, based on credit sale information from the store's electronic cash register, and total customer receipts, based on the bank deposit slip.

Exercise 8–2

Nature of uncollectible accounts
Objective 3 - Text page 313 ✔ a. 4.3% b. 25.3%

Hilton Hotels Corporation owns and operates casinos at several of its hotels, located primarily in Nevada. At the end of a recent fiscal year, the following accounts and notes receivable were reported (in thousands):

Hotel accounts and notes receivable $75,796
    Less: Allowance for doubtful accounts 3,256

                                             $72,540

Casino accounts receivable $26,334
    Less: Allowance for doubtful accounts 6,654

                                             19,680

a. Compute the percentage of allowance for doubtful accounts to the gross hotel accounts and notes receivable for the end of the fiscal year.

b. Compute the percentage of the allowance for doubtful accounts to the gross casino accounts receivable for the end of the fiscal year.

c. Discuss possible reasons for the difference in the two ratios computed in (a) and (b).

Exercise 8–3

Estimating doubtful accounts
Objective 4 - Text page 314 ✔ $20,685

Swenson Co. is a wholesaler of office supplies. An aging of
the company's accounts receivable on December 31, 2000,
and a historical analysis of the percentage of uncollectible
accounts in each age category are as follows:

Age Interval	Balance	Percent Uncollectible
Not past due	$325,000	2 %
1-30 days past due	86,000	4
31-60 days past due	17,000	9
61-90 days past due	12,000	15
91-180 days past due	7,400	60
Over 180 days past due	3,500	85
	$450,900	

Estimate what the proper balance of the allowance for
doubtful accounts should be as of December 31, 2000.

Age Interval	Balance	Estimated Uncollectible Accounts Percent	Amount
Not past due	$325,000	2%	
1-30 days past due	86,000	4	
31-60 days past due	17,000	9	
61-90 days past due	12,000	15	
91-180 days past due	7,400	60	
Over 180 days past due	3,500	85	
Total	$450,900		

Exercise 8–4

Entry for uncollectible accounts
Objective 4 - Text page 314

Using the data in Exercise 8–3, assume that the allowance for doubtful accounts
for Swenson Co. had a debit balance of $3,050 as of December 31, 2000.

Journalize the adjusting entry for uncollectible accounts as of December 31, 2000.

Date	Description	Debit	Credit

Exercise 8–5

Providing for doubtful accounts
Objective 4 - Text page 314 ✔ a. $10,000 b. $35,600

At the end of the current year, the accounts receivable account has a debit balance of $575,000, and net sales for the year total $4,000,000. Determine the amount of the adjusting entry to provide for doubtful accounts under each of the following assumptions:

(a) The allowance account before adjustment has a credit balance of $2,750. Uncollectible accounts expense is estimated at 1/4 of 1% of net sales.

(b) The allowance account before adjustment has a credit balance of $2,750. Analysis of the accounts in the customer's ledger indicates doubtful accounts of $38,350.

(c) The allowance account before adjustment has a debit balance of $1,050. Uncollectible accounts expense is estimated at 1/2 of 1% of net sales.

(d) The allowance account before adjustment has a debit balance of $1,050. Analysis of the accounts in the customer's ledger indicates doubtful accounts of $31,400.

Exercise 8–6

Entries to write off accounts receivable
Objectives 4, 5 - Text pages 314 and 318

Aspen Company, a computer consulting firm, has decided to write off the $2,800 balance of an account owed by a customer. Journalize the entry to record the write-off, (a) assuming that the allowance method is used, and (b) assuming that the direct write-off method is used.

Date	Description	Debit	Credit

**Entries for uncollectible receivables,
using allowance method**
Objective 4 - Text page 314

Journalize the following transactions in the accounts of Alpine Company, a restaurant supply company that uses the allowance method of accounting for uncollectible receivables:

Feb. 20.   Sold merchandise on account to J. Renner, $5,500. The cost of the merchandise sold was $3,400.

May 19.   Received $3,000 from J. Renner and wrote off the remainder owed on the sale of February 20 as uncollectible.

Sept.30.   Reinstated the account of J. Renner that had been written off on May 19 and received $2,500 cash in full payment.

Date	Description	Debit	Credit

Exercise 8–8

**Entries for uncollectible accounts,
using direct write-off method**
Objective 5 - Text page 318

Journalize the following transactions in the accounts of MedCo Co., a hospital supply company that uses the direct write-off method of accounting for uncollectible receivables:

Mar. 11.   Sold merchandise on account to E. Hayes, $6,200. The cost of the merchandise sold was $4,250.

May 1.   Received $1,800 from E. Hayes and wrote off the remainder owed on the sale of March 11 as uncollectible.

Aug. 15.   Reinstated the account of E. Hayes that had been written off on May 1 and received $4,400 cash in full payment.

Date	Description	Debit	Credit

Effect of doubtful accounts on net income
Objectives 4, 5 - Text pages 314 and 318 ✔ $53,400

" During our first year of operations, Klondike Automotive Supply Co. had net sales of $1,050,000, wrote off $32,800 of accounts as uncollectible, using the direct write-off method, and reported net income of $62,600. If the allowance method of accounting for uncollectibles had been used, 4% of net sales would have been estimated as uncollectible. Please help us determine what the net income would have been if the allowance method had been used. We're trying to decide which method is better. What do you think? "

Lee Tomasello
President

Exercise 8–10

Effect of doubtful accounts on net income
Objectives 4, 5 - Text pages 314 and 318 ✔ a. $94,800 b. $26,700

Using the data in Exercise 8–9, assume that during the second year of operations Klondike Automotive Supply Co. had net sales of $1,800,000, wrote off $54,500 of accounts as uncollectible, using the direct write-off method, and reported net income of $112,300.

a. Determine what net income would have been in the second year if the allowance method (using 4% of net sales) had been used in both the first and second years.

b. Determine what the balance of the allowance for doubtful accounts would have been at the end of the second year if the allowance method had been used in both the first and second years.

Exercise 8–11

Determine due date and interest on notes
Objective 6 - Text page 319 ✔ a. May 18; $100

Determine the due date and the amount of interest due at maturity on the following notes:

Date of Note	Face Amount	Term of Note	Interest Rate	Due Date	Interest Due
a. April 3	$10,000	45 days	8%	_____	_____
b. May 20	6,000	60 days	10%	_____	_____
c. August 31	8,000	90 days	14%	_____	_____
d. June 9	15,000	90 days	10%	_____	_____
e. October 1	12,500	120 days	12%	_____	_____

Exercise 8–12

Entries for notes receivable
Objectives 6, 7 - Text pages 319 and 321 ✔ b. $15,450

Gier Interior Decorators issued a 120-day, 9% note for $15,000, dated March 3, to Everson Furniture Company on account.

a. Determine the due date of the note.

b. Determine the maturity value of the note.

c. Journalize the entries to record the following: (1) receipt of the note by the payee, and (2) receipt by the payee of payment of the note at maturity.

Date	Description	Debit	Credit

Exercise 8–13   Name: _____

Entries for notes receivable
Objective 7 - Text page 321

The series of seven transactions recorded in the T accounts shown on the right were related to a sale to a customer on account and the receipt of the amount owed. Briefly describe each transaction.

Cash			
(7)	28,300	(7)	28,000

Sales			
		(1)	30,000

Merchandise Inventory			
(4)	1,500	(2)	18,000

Sales Returns and Allowances			
(3)	2,500		

Notes Receivable			
(5)	27,500	(6)	27,500

Cost of Merchandise Sold			
(2)	18,000	(4)	1,500

Accounts Receivable			
(1)	30,000	(3)	2,500
(6)	28,000	(5)	27,500
		(7)	28,000

Interest Revenue			
		(6)	500
		(7)	300

1. _____

2. _____

3. _____

4. _____

5. _____

6. _____

7. _____

Exercise 8–14

**Entries for notes receivable,
including year-end entries**
Objective 7 - Text page 321

The following selected transactions were completed by Frith Co., a
supplier of elastic bands for clothing:

1999
Dec. 15. Received from Acker Co., on account, a $27,000, 90-day, 10% note
dated December 15.

31. Recorded an adjusting entry for accrued interest on the note of
December 15.

31. Closed the interest revenue account. The only entry in this account
originated from the December 31 adjustment.

2000
Mar. 14. Received payment of note and interest from Acker Co.

Journalize the transactions.

Date	Description	Debit	Credit

**Entries for receipt and
dishonor of note receivable**
Objective 7 - Text page 321

Journalize the following transactions of Iris Theater Productions:

Aug. 1. Received a $60,000, 90-day, 10% note dated August 1 from
      Broadway Company on account.

Oct. 30. The note is dishonored by Broadway Company.

Nov. 29. Received the amount due on the dishonored note plus interest for
      30 days at 15% on the total amount charged to Broadway Company
      on October 30.

Date	Description	Debit	Credit

Exercise 8–17

Receivables in the balance sheet
Objective 8 - Text page 322

List any errors you can find in the following partial balance sheet.

James Company
Balance Sheet
December 31, 20__

Assets

Current assets:
Cash		$ 95,000
Notes receivable	$250,000	
Less interest receivable	9,000	241,000
Accounts receivable	$445,000	
Plus allowance for doubtful accounts	15,000	460,000

Exercise 8–16

**Entries for receipt and
dishonor of notes receivable**
Objectives 4, 7 - Text pages 314 and 321

Journalize the following transactions in the accounts of Clinton Co., which
operates a riverboat casino:

Mar. 1. Received an $8,000, 30-day, 12% note dated March 1 from Adams Co. on account.

21. Received a $15,000, 60-day, 10% note dated March 21 from Murphy Co. on account.

31. The note dated March 1 from Adams Co. is dishonored, and the customer's account is
charged for the note, including interest.

May 20. The note dated March 21 from Murphy Co. is dishonored, and the customer's account
is charged for the note, including interest.

June 29. Cash is received for the amount due on the dishonored note dated March 1 plus
interest for 90 days at 15% on the total amount debited to Adams Co. on March 31.

Aug. 31. Wrote off against the allowance account the amount charged to Murphy Co. on May
20 for the dishonored note dated March 21.

Date	Description	Debit	Credit

Solvency Measures — The Short-Term Creditor

Accounts Receivable Turnover

	1997	1996
Net sales on account	$1,498,000	$1,200,000
Accounts receivable (net):		
Beginning of year	$ 120,000	$ 140,000
End of year	115,500	120,000
Total	$ 235,000	$ 260,000
Average	$ 117,500	$ 130,000
Accts. receivable turnover	12.7 times	9.2 times
Average collection period	29 days	40 days

Use: To assess the efficiency in collecting receivables and in the management of credit

Exercise 8–18

**Accounts receivable turnover;
number of days' sales in receivables**
Objective 9 - Text page 323

The financial statements for **Hershey Foods Corporation** are presented in Appendix G at the end of the text. Assume that all sales are credit sales and that the accounts receivable were $331,670,000 at December 31, 1994.

a. Compute the accounts receivable turnover for 1995 and 1996.

b. Compute the number of days' sales in receivables at December 31, 1995 and 1996.

c. What conclusions can be drawn from these analyses regarding Hershey's efficiency in collecting receivables?

Appendix Exercise 8–19

Discounting notes receivable
Text page 325

Hathaway Co., a building construction company, holds a 90-day, 8% note for $35,000, dated August 18, which was received from a customer on account. On September 17, the note is discounted at the bank at the rate of 12%.

a. Determine the maturity value of the note.

b. Determine the number of days in the discount period.

c. Determine the amount of the discount.

d. Determine the amount of the proceeds.

e. Journalize the entry to record the discounting of the note on September 17.

Appendix Exercise 8–20

Entries for receipt and discounting of note receivable and dishonored notes
Text page 325

Journalize the following transactions for Big Time Theater Productions:

May 1. Received a $100,000, 90-day, 10% note dated May 1 from Johns Company on account.

June 1. Discounted the note at City National Bank at 12%.

July 30. The note is dishonored by Johns Company; paid the bank the amount due on the note, plus a protest fee of $250.

Aug.29. Received the amount due on the dishonored note plus interest for 30 days at 16% on the total amount charged to Johns Company on July 30.

Date	Description	Debit	Credit

Entries related to uncollectible accounts
Objective 4 - Text page 314 ✔ 3. $572,300

The following transactions, adjusting entries, and closing entries were completed
by Runnels Contractors Co. during the current fiscal year ended December 31:

Feb. 10. Received 75% of the $18,000 balance owed by Sackett Co., a bankrupt business, and
wrote off the remainder as uncollectible.

May 3. Reinstated the account of B. Pilon, which had been written off in the preceding year
as uncollectible. Journalized the receipt of $2,050 cash in full payment of Pilon's
account.

Sept.19. Wrote off the $6,250 balance owed by Larkin Co., which has no assets.

Nov.30. Reinstated the account of Giles Co., which had been written off in the preceding year
as uncollectible. Journalized the receipt of $4,500 cash in full payment of the account.

Dec. 31. Wrote off the following accounts as uncollectible (compound entry): Huang Co.,
$2,950; Nance Co., $1,600; Powell Distributors, $6,500; J. J. Stevens, $3,200.

31. Based on an analysis of the $595,000 of accounts receivable, it was estimated that
$22,700 will be uncollectible. Journalized the adjusting entry.

31. Journalized the entry to close the appropriate account to Income Summary.

Instructions

1. Three general ledger accounts are shown on the next page. The January 1
   credit balance of $20,050 is shown in the Allowance for Doubtful Accounts.

2. Using a blank general journal **Form GJ**, journalize the above transactions and the
   adjusting and closing entries. After it has been journalized, post each entry to the three
   selected accounts (on the next page) and determine the new balances.

3. Determine the
   expected net
   realizable value
   of the accounts
   receivable as of
   December 31.

4. Assuming that instead of basing the provision for uncollectible
   accounts on an analysis of receivables, the adjusting entry on
   December 31 had been based on an estimated expense of 3/4 of 1%
   of the net sales of $4,100,000 for the year, determine the following:

   a. Uncollectible accounts
      expense for the year.

   b. Balance in the allowance
      account after the adjustment
      of December 31.

   c. Expected net realizable value
      of the accounts receivable as
      of December 31.

Continued

General Ledger

ACCOUNT Allowance for Doubtful Accounts   NO. 115

Date		Description	Post. Ref.	Debit	Credit	Balance Debit	Balance Credit
Jan.	1	Balance					20,050

ACCOUNT Income Summary   NO. 313

Date		Description	Post. Ref.	Debit	Credit	Balance Debit	Balance Credit

ACCOUNT Uncollectible Accounts Expense   NO. 718

Date		Description	Post. Ref.	Debit	Credit	Balance Debit	Balance Credit

**Compare two methods of accounting
for uncollectible receivables**
Objectives 4, 5 ✔ 1. Year 4: Balance of allowance account, end of year, $9,650

Telco Company, a telephone service and supply company, has just completed its fourth
year of operations. The direct write-off method of recording uncollectible accounts expense
has been used during the entire period. Because of substantial increases in sales volume and
amount of uncollectible accounts, the firm is considering changing to the allowance method.
Information is requested as to the effect that an annual provision of 1% of sales would have
had on the amount of uncollectible accounts expense reported for each of the past four
years. It is also considered desirable to know what the balance of Allowance for Doubtful
Accounts would have been at the end of each year. The following data have been obtained
from the accounts:

| Year | Sales | Uncollectible Accounts Written Off | Year of Origin of Accounts Receivable Written Off as Uncollectible | | | |
			1st	2nd	3rd	4th
1st	$ 450,000	$2,500	$2,500			
2nd	660,000	3,950	1,900	$2,050		
3rd	850,000	6,700	700	2,600	$3,400	
4th	1,200,000	8,800		2,200	2,550	$4,050

Instructions

1. Assemble the desired data, using the following form.

| | Uncollectible Accounts Expense | | | Balance of |
Year	Expense Actually Reported	Expense Based on Estimate	Increase (Decrease) in Amount of Expense	Allowance Account, End of Year
1st	_____	_____	_____	_____
2nd	_____	_____	_____	_____
3rd	_____	_____	_____	_____
4th	_____	_____	_____	_____

2. Experience during the first four years of operations indicated that the receivables
   were either collected within two years or had to be written off as uncollectible.

   Does the estimate of 1% of
   sales appear to be
   reasonably close to the
   actual experience with
   uncollectible accounts
   originating during the first
   two years? Explain.

Blank Page

Details of notes receivable
and related entries
Objectives 6, 7 ✔ 1. Note 2: Due date, July 11; Interest due at maturity, $150.

During the current fiscal year, Nehls Co. received the following notes. Nehls Co. wholesales bathroom fixtures.

Date	Face Amount	Term	Interest Rate
1. March 11	$24,000	60 days	8%
2. June 11	15,000	30 days	12%
3. Aug. 20	9,200	90 days	7%
4. Oct. 31	12,000	60 days	9%
5. Nov. 28	15,000	60 days	8%
6. Dec. 26	18,000	30 days	12%

Susan Cowgill
Treasurer

Instructions

1. Determine for each note (a) the due date, and
   (b) the amount of interest due at maturity,
   identifying each note by number.

Note	(a) Due Date	(b) Interest Due at Maturity
(1)		
(2)		
(3)		
(4)		
(5)		
(6)		

2. Journalize the entry to record the dishonor of Note (3) on its due date.

Date	Description	Debit	Credit

Continued

Instructions

3. Journalize the adjusting entry to record the accrued interest on Notes (5) and (6) on December 31.

Date	Description	Debit	Credit

Show calculations:

4. Journalize the entries to record the receipt of the amounts due on Notes (5) and (6) in January.

Date	Description	Debit	Credit

Entries related to uncollectible accounts
Objective 4 - Text page 314 ✔ 3. $493,500

The following transactions, adjusting entries, and closing entries were completed
by The Art Gallery during the current fiscal year ended December 31:

Jan.   21. Reinstated the account of Jill Luce, which had been written off in the preceding
             year as uncollectible. Journalized the receipt of $3,025 cash in full payment of
             Luce's account.
        28. Wrote off the $7,500 balance owed by Oasis Co., which is bankrupt.
March   7.   Received 40% of the $8,000 balance owed by Primrose Co., a bankrupt business,
             and wrote off the remainder as uncollectible.
Aug.   29. Reinstated the account of Louis Sabo, which had been written off two years earlier
             as uncollectible. Recorded the receipt of $1,200 cash in full payment.
Dec.   30. Wrote off the following accounts as uncollectible (compound entry): Channel Co.,
             $11,050; Engel Co., $6,260; Loach Furniture, $4,775; Briana Parker, $1,820.
        31. Based on an analysis of the $535,500 of accounts receivable, it was estimated that
             $42,000 will be uncollectible. Journalized the adjusting entry.
        31. Journalized the entry to close the appropriate account to Income Summary.

Instructions

1. Three general ledger accounts are shown on the next page. The January 1
    credit balance of $28,955 is shown in the Allowance for Doubtful Accounts.

2. Using a blank general journal **Form GJ**, journalize the above transactions and the
    adjusting and closing entries. After it has been journalized, post each entry to the three
    selected accounts (on the next page) and determine the new balances.

3. Determine the
    expected net
    realizable value
    of the accounts
    receivable as of
    December 31.

4. Assuming that, instead of basing the provision for uncollectible
    accounts on an analysis of receivables, the adjusting entry on
    December 31 had been based on an estimated expense of 3/4 of 1%
    of the net sales of $5,500,000 for the year, determine the following:

    a. Uncollectible accounts
       expense for the year.

    b. Balance in the allowance
       account after the adjustment
       of December 31.

    c. Expected net realizable value
       of the accounts receivable as
       of December 31.

Continued

General Ledger

ACCOUNT Allowance for Doubtful Accounts   NO. 115

Date		Description	Post. Ref.	Debit	Credit	Balance Debit	Balance Credit
Jan.	1	Balance					$28,955

ACCOUNT Income Summary   NO. 313

Date		Description	Post. Ref.	Debit	Credit	Balance Debit	Balance Credit

ACCOUNT Uncollectible Accounts Expense   NO. 718

Date		Description	Post. Ref.	Debit	Credit	Balance Debit	Balance Credit

**Comparing two methods of accounting
for uncollectible receivables**
Objectives 4, 5 ✔ 1. Year: Balance of allowance account, end of year, $8,450

Baldwin Company, which operates a chain of 30 electronic supply stores, has just completed
its fourth year of operations. The direct write-off method of recording uncollectible accounts
expense has been used during the entire period. Because of substantial increases in sales
volume and amount of uncollectible accounts, the firm is considering changing to the
allowance method. Information is requested as to the effect that an annual provision of 1% of
sales would have had on the amount of uncollectible accounts expense reported for each of
the past four years. It is also considered desirable to know what the balance of Allowance for
Doubtful Accounts would have been at the end of each year. The following data have been
obtained from the accounts:

		Uncollectible Accounts Written	Year of Origin of Accounts Receivable Written Off as Uncollectible			
Year	Sales	Off	1st	2nd	3rd	4th
1st	$ 650,000	$ 2,600	$2,600			
2nd	720,000	3,500	1,950	$1,550		
3rd	950,000	9,600	2,200	3,400	$4,000	
4th	1,250,000	11,550		2,300	2,950	$6,300

Instructions

1. Assemble the desired data, using the following column headings:

	Uncollectible Accounts Expense			Balance of
Year	Expense Actually Reported	Expense Based on Estimate	Increase (Decrease) in Amount of Expense	Allowance Account, End of Year
1st	_____	_____	_____	_____
2nd	_____	_____	_____	_____
3rd	_____	_____	_____	_____
4th	_____	_____	_____	_____

2. Experience during the first four years of operations indicated that the receivables
   were either collected within two years or had to be written off as uncollectible.

   Does the estimate of 1% of
   sales appear to be
   reasonably close to the
   actual experience with
   uncollectible accounts
   originating during the first
   two years? Explain.

Blank Page

**Details of notes receivable
and related entries**
Objectives 6, 7 ✔ 1. Note 2: Due date, Aug. 9; Interest due at maturity, $600.

During the last six months of the current fiscal year, Norby Co. received the following notes.
Norby Co. produces advertising videos.

David Stringer
Treasurer

	Date	Face Amount	Term	Interest Rate
1.	Apr. 1	$15,000	120 days	8%
2.	June 10	30,000	60 days	12%
3.	Aug. 11	18,000	90 days	8%
4.	Sept. 1	20,000	90 days	7%
5.	Nov. 1	24,000	90 days	9%
6.	Dec. 16	36,000	30 days	13%

Instructions

1. Determine for each note (a) the due date, and
   (b) the amount of interest due at maturity,
   identifying each note by number.

Note	(a) Due Date	(b) Interest Due at Maturity
(1)		
(2)		
(3)		
(4)		
(5)		
(6)		

2. Journalize the entry to record the dishonor of Note (3) on its due date.

Date	Description	Debit	Credit

Continued

Instructions

3. Journalize the adjusting entry to record the accrued interest on Notes (5) and (6) on December 31.

Date	Description	Debit	Credit

Show calculations:

4. Journalize the entries to record the receipt of the amounts due on Notes (5) and (6) in January.

Date	Description	Debit	Credit

" If the maker of notes (3) or (4) fails to pay the debt on the due date, the note will be dishonored and is no longer negotiable. Our arrangement with the bank states that if this happens, Norby Co. must pay the note. This potential obligation is called a contingent liability and is a continuing headache for me. "

David Stringer
Treasurer

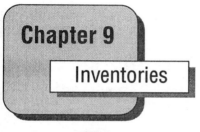

Chapter 9

Inventories

The buying and selling of merchandise is the primary activity in operating a wholesale or retail business. The cost of merchandise sold is often the largest deduction from sales in determining net income. Also, merchandise inventory is usually the largest current asset of such a firm. This chapter describes and illustrates several topics related to merchandise inventory.

Objective 1 — **Internal Control of Inventories 344**
Summarize and provide examples of internal control procedures that apply to inventories.

Objective 2 — **Effect of Inventory Errors on Financial Statements 346**
Describe the effect of inventory errors on the financial statements.

Objective 3 — **Inventory Cost Flow Assumptions 347**
Describe three inventory cost flow assumptions and how they impact the income statement and balance sheet.

Objective 4 — **Inventory Costing Methods Under a Perpetual Inventory System 350**
Compute the cost of inventory under the perpetual inventory system, using the following costing methods: First-in, first-out; Last-in, first-out; Average cost.

Objective 5 — **Inventory Costing Methods Under a Periodic Inventory System 353**
Compute the cost of inventory under the periodic inventory system, using the following costing methods: First-in, first-out; Last-in, first-out; Average cost.

Objective 6 — **Comparing Inventory Costing Methods 356**
Compare and contrast the use of the three inventory costing methods.

Objective 7 — **Valuation of Inventory at Other Than Cost 357**
Compute the proper valuation of inventory at other than cost, using the lower-of-cost-or-market and net realizable value concepts.

Objective 8 — **Presentation of Merchandise Inventory on the Balance Sheet 359**
Prepare a balance sheet presentation of merchandise inventory.

Objective 9 — **Estimating Inventory Cost 359**
Estimate the cost of inventory, using the retail method and the gross profit method.

Objective 10— **Financial Analysis and Interpretation 361**
Compute and interpret the inventory turnover ratio and the number of days' sales in inventory.

Learning objectives are listed for the exercises and problems that follow. Use the information to the right to determine the nature of the objective and the page number to refer to your textbook for a discussion of the topic.

Blank Page

Name:

Internal control of inventories
Objective 1 - Text page 344

Duce Hardware Store currently uses a periodic inventory system. Robin Templin, the owner, is considering the purchase of a computer system that would make it feasible to switch to a perpetual inventory system.

Robin is unhappy with the periodic inventory system because it does not provide timely information on inventory levels. Robin has noticed on several occasions that the store runs out of good-selling items, while too many poor-selling items are on hand.

Robin is also concerned about lost sales while a physical inventory is being taken. Duce Hardware currently takes a physical inventory twice a year. To minimize distractions, the store is closed on the day inventory is taken. Robin believes that closing the store is the only way to get an accurate inventory count.

Will switching to a perpetual inventory system strengthen Duce Hardware's control over inventory items? Will switching to a perpetual inventory system eliminate the need for a physical inventory count? Explain.

Working
Papers
Plus

Chapter 9

Exercise 9–2

Internal control of inventories
Objective 1 - Text page 344

Bryers Luggage Shop is a small retail establishment located in a large shopping mall. This shop has implemented the following procedures regarding inventory items. State whether each of these procedures is appropriate or inappropriate, considering the principles of internal control. If it is inappropriate, state which internal control procedure is violated.

a. Whenever Bryers receives a shipment of new inventory, the items are taken directly to the stockroom. Bryers' accountant uses the vendor's invoice to record the amount of inventory received.

b. Since the display area of the store is limited, only a sample of each piece of luggage is kept on the selling floor. Whenever a customer selects a piece of luggage, the sales clerk gets the appropriate piece from the store's stockroom. Since all sales clerks need access to the stockroom, it is not locked. The stockroom is adjacent to the break room used by all mall employees.

c. Since the shop carries mostly high-quality, designer luggage, all inventory items are tagged with a control device that activates an alarm if a tagged item is removed from the store.

Exercise 9–3

**Identifying items to be
included in inventory**
Objective 1 - Text page 344

Tobiason Co., which is located in Camanche, Iowa, has identified the following items for possible inclusion in its December 31, 1999 year-end inventory. Indicate which items should be included (I) and which should be excluded (E) from the inventory.

_____ a. Tobiason has segregated $15,800 of merchandise ordered by one of its customers for shipment on January 3, 2000.

_____ b. Tobiason has in its warehouse $21,000 of merchandise on consignment from Stovall Co.

_____ c. Merchandise Tobiason shipped FOB shipping point on December 31, 1999, was picked up by the freight company at 11:50 p.m.

_____ d. Merchandise Tobiason shipped to a customer FOB shipping point was picked up by the freight company on December 26, 1999, but had still not arrived at its destination as of December 31, 1999.

_____ e. Tobiason has $35,000 of merchandise on hand, which was sold to customers earlier in the year, but which has been returned by customers to Tobiason for various warranty repairs.

_____ f. Tobiason has sent $100,000 of merchandise to various retailers on a consignment basis.

_____ g. On December 21, 1999, Tobiason ordered $85,000 of merchandise, FOB Camanche. The merchandise was shipped from the supplier on December 28, 1999, but had not been received by December 31, 1999.

_____ h. On December 27, 1999, Tobiason ordered $15,000 of merchandise from a supplier in Des Moines. The merchandise was shipped FOB Des Moines on December 30, 1999, but had not been received by December 31, 1999.

_____ i. On December 31, 1999, Tobiason received $28,000 of merchandise that had been returned by customers because the wrong merchandise had been shipped. The replacement order is to be shipped overnight on January 3, 2000.

Exercise 9–4

Effect of errors in physical inventory
Objective 2 - Text page 346 ✔ a. Owner's equity, $13,800 understated

The River Bottom sells canoes, kayaks, whitewater rafts, and other boating supplies. During the taking of its physical inventory on December 31, 2000, The River Bottom incorrectly counted its inventory as $82,500 instead of the correct amount of $96,300.

a. State the effect of the error on the December 31, 2000 balance sheet of The River Bottom.

Merchandise inventory ...._____

Current assets ...._____

Total assets ...._____

Owner's equity ...._____

b. State the effect of the error on the income statement of The River Bottom for the year ended December 31, 2000.

Cost of merchandise sold ...._____

Gross profit ...._____

Net income ...._____

Effect of errors in physical inventory
Objective 2 - Text page 346 ✔ b. Net income, $6,100 overstated

Thema's Motorcycle Shop sells motorcycles, jet skis, and other related
supplies and accessories. During the taking of its physical inventory
on December 31, 2000, Thema's Motorcycle Shop incorrectly counted
its inventory as $102,800 instead of the correct amount of $96,700.

a. State the effect of the
   error on the December
   31, 2000 balance sheet of
   Thema's Motorcycle
   Shop.

Merchandise inventory .... _____

Current assets .... _____

Total assets .... _____

Owner's equity .... _____

b. State the effect of the
   error on the income
   statement of Thema's
   Motorcycle Shop for the
   year ended December
   31, 2000.

Cost of merchandise sold .... _____

Gross profit .... _____

Net income .... _____

Exercise 9–6

Error in inventory shrinkage
Objective 2 - Text page 346

During 2000, the accountant discovered that the physical inventory at the end of
1999 had been understated by $45,000. Instead of correcting the error, however,
the accountant assumed that a $45,000 overstatement of the physical inventory in
2000 would balance out the error.

Are there any flaws
in the accountant's
assumption?
Explain.

Exercise 9–7

Perpetual inventory using fifo
Objectives 3, 4 ✔ Inventory balance, April 30, $892

Beginning inventory, purchases, and sales data for Commodity MCX are as follows:

Apr. 1   Inventory ...... 25 units at $40
    7   Sale .... 15 units
   12   Purchase .... 18 units at $42
   20   Sale .... 14 units
   22   Sale .... 3 units
   30   Purchase .... 10 units at $43

The business maintains a perpetual inventory system, costing by the first-in, first-out method. Determine the cost of the merchandise sold for each sale and the inventory balance after each sale, presenting the data in the form illustrated in Exhibit 3 and shown below.

Commodity MCX

Date	Purchases Quantity	Purchases Unit Cost	Purchases Total Cost	Cost of Merchandise Sold Quantity	Cost of Merchandise Sold Unit Cost	Cost of Merchandise Sold Total Cost	Inventory Quantity	Inventory Unit Cost	Inventory Total Cost

" In our new perpetual system, all increases and decreases are recorded as they happen. As a result the inventory account constantly (perpetually) shows the balance on hand. This up-to-date information is vital when dealing with customer orders. Our old periodic system was a nightmare. "

Mark Sherby
Inventory Manager

Perpetual inventory using lifo
Objectives 3, 4 ✔ Inventory balance, April 30, $872

Assume that the business in Exercise 9–7 maintains a perpetual inventory
system, costing by the last-in, first-out method. Determine the cost of
merchandise sold for each sale and the inventory balance after each sale,
presenting the data in the form illustrated in Exhibit 4 and shown below.

Commodity MCX

Date	Purchases			Cost of Merchandise Sold			Inventory		
	Quantity	Unit Cost	Total Cost	Quantity	Unit Cost	Total Cost	Quantity	Unit Cost	Total Cost

Exercise 9–9

Perpetual inventory using lifo

Objectives 3, 4 ✔ Inventory balance, March 31, $238

Beginning inventory, purchases, and sales data for Commodity SKM for March are as follows:

Inventory:
Mar. 1 ..... 30 units at $15

Purchases:
Mar. 8 .... 10 units at $18
21 .... 15 units at $19

Sales:
Mar. 11 ..... 9 units
17 ..... 24 units
29 ..... 8 units

Assuming that the perpetual inventory system is used, costing by the lifo method, determine the cost of the inventory balance at March 31, presenting data in the form illustrated in Exhibit 4 and shown below.

Commodity SKM

	Purchases			Cost of Merchandise Sold			Inventory		
Date	Quantity	Unit Cost	Total Cost	Quantity	Unit Cost	Total Cost	Quantity	Unit Cost	Total Cost

Perpetual inventory using fifo
Objectives 3, 4 ✔ Inventory balance, March 31, $266

Assume that the business in Exercise 9–9 maintains a perpetual inventory
system, costing by the first-in, first-out method. Determine the cost of the
inventory balance at March 31, presenting the data in the form illustrated in
Exhibit 3 and shown below.

Commodity SKM

| Date | Purchases | | | Cost of Merchandise Sold | | | Inventory | | |
	Quantity	Unit Cost	Total Cost	Quantity	Unit Cost	Total Cost	Quantity	Unit Cost	Total Cost

Exercise 9–11

**Fifo, lifo costs under perpetual
inventory system**
Objectives 3, 4 ✔ a. $840

The following units of a particular item were available for sale during the year. The firm uses the perpetual inventory system, and there are 15 units of the item on hand at the end of the year.

Beginning inventory .... 20 units at $45
Sale .... 15 units at $90
First purchase .... 30 units at $50
Sale .... 25 units at $90
Second purchase .... 40 units at $56
Sale .... 35 units at $90

What is the total cost of the
ending inventory according to:

(a) fifo

(b) lifo

Exercise 9–12

**Identify items missing in determining
cost of merchandise sold**
Objective 5 - Text page 353

For (a) through (d), identify the items designated by "X."

a. Purchases − (X + X) = Net purchases.

b. Net purchases + X = Cost of merchandise purchased.

c. Merchandise inventory (beginning) + Cost of merchandise purchased = X.

d. Merchandise available for sale − X = Cost of merchandise sold.

**Cost of merchandise sold
and related items**
Objective 5 - Text page 353 ✔ a. Cost of merchandise sold, $536,500

The following data were extracted from the accounting records of C. L. Williams
Company for the year ended April 30, 1999:

Merchandise Inventory, May 1, 1998 .... $115,000
Merchandise Inventory, April 30, 1999 125,000
Purchases 550,000
Purchases Returns and Allowances 4,500
Purchases Discounts 2,950
Sales 670,625
Transportation In 3,950

a. Prepare the cost of merchandise sold
   section of the income statement for the
   year ended April 30, 1999.

b. Determine the gross profit to be reported on
   the income statement for the year ended
   April 30, 1999.

Exercise 9–14

Cost of merchandise sold

Objective 5 - Text page 353 ✔ Correct cost of merchandise sold, $489,700

How many errors can you find in the following schedule of cost of merchandise sold for the current year ended December 31?

Cost of merchandise sold:

Merchandise inventory, December 31			$105,000
Purchases		$500,000	
Plus: Purchases returns and allowances	$12,500		
Purchases discounts	6,500	19,000	
Gross purchases		$519,000	
Less transportation in		2,400	
Cost of merchandise purchased			516,600
Merchandise available for sale			$621,600
Less merchandise inventory, January 1			111,300
Cost of merchandise sold			$510,300

Exercise 9–15

Periodic inventory by three methods

Objectives 3, 5 ✔ b. $1,055

The units of an item available for sale during the year were as shown below. There are 45 units of the item in the physical inventory at December 31. The periodic inventory system is used. Determine the inventory cost by the three methods below.

Jan.	1	Inventory	35 units at $23
Mar.	4	Purchase	10 units at $25
Aug.	20	Purchase	30 units at $28
Nov.	30	Purchase	25 units at $30

(a) first-in, first-out method

(b) last-in, first-out method

(c) average cost method

Exercise 9–16

**Periodic inventory by three methods;
cost of merchandise sold**
Objectives 3, 5 ✔ a. Inventory, $1,390

The units of an item available for sale during the year were as shown below. There are
20 units of the item in the physical inventory at December 31. The periodic inventory
system is used. Determine the inventory cost and the cost of merchandise sold by
three methods, presenting your answers in the form below. Show calculations.

Jan.   1 Inventory   25 units at $60
Mar.   4 Purchase   30 units at $65
Aug.   7 Purchase   10 units at $68
Nov. 15 Purchase   15 units at $70

	Cost	
	Merchandise	Merchandise
Inventory Method	Inventory	Sold
a. First-in, first-out	_____	_____
b. Last-in, first-out	_____	_____
c. Average cost	_____	_____

Exercise 9–17

Lower-of-cost-or-market inventory
Objective 7 - Text page 357 ✔ LCM: $11,715

On the basis of the following data, determine the value of the inventory at the lower of
cost or market. Assemble the data in the form illustrated in Exhibit 7 and shown below.

| | | Unit | Unit | Total | | |
| | Inventory | Cost | Market | | | Lower of |
Commodity	Quantity	Price	Price	Cost	Market	C or M
4HU	10	$325	$320			
153T	17	110	115			
Z10	12	275	260			
SAW1	15	51	45			
SAW2	30	95	100			

Exercise 9–18

Merchandise inventory on the balance sheet
Objective 8 - Text page 359

Based on the data in
Exercise 9–17 and
assuming that cost
was determined by
the fifo method, show
how the merchandise
inventory would
appear on the balance
sheet.

Exercise 9–19

Retail inventory method
Objective 9 - Text page 359 ✔ Inventory: $228,000

A business using the retail method of inventory costing
determines that merchandise inventory at retail is $380,000.

If the ratio of cost to
retail price is 60%,
what is the amount
of inventory to be
reported on the
financial statements?

Retail inventory method
Objective 9 - Text page 359 ✔ Inventory, June 30: $307,200

On the basis of the following data, estimate the cost of the merchandise inventory at June 30 by the retail method:

		Cost	Retail
June 1	Merchandise inventory	$428,300	$ 670,500
June 1-30	Purchases (net)	608,500	949,500
June 1-30	Sales (net)		1,140,000

Exercise 9–21

Gross profit inventory method
Objective 9 - Text page 359 ✔ a. $318,800

The merchandise inventory was destroyed by fire on October 20. The following data were obtained from the accounting records:

Jan. 1	Merchandise inventory	$ 160,000
Jan. 1-Oct. 20	Purchases (net)	850,000
	Sales (net)	1,080,000
	Estimated gross profit rate	36%

a. Estimate the cost of the merchandise destroyed.

b. Briefly describe the situations in which the gross profit method is useful.

Inventory Turnover Ratios

	Supervalu	La-Z-Boy
Cost of goods sold	$15,040,117,000	$ 705,379,000
Inventories:		
Beginning of year	$1,113,937,000	$81,091,000
End of year	1,109,791,000	79,192,000
Total	$2,223,728,000	$ 160,283,000
Average	$1,111,864,000	$80,141,500

Inventory turnover	13.5 times	8.8 times
Average selling period	27 days	41 days

Use: To assess the efficiency in the management of inventory

Exercise 9–22

Inventory turnover and number of days' sales in inventory
Objective 10 - Text page 361

The financial statements for **Hershey Foods Corporation** are presented in Appendix G at the end of the text. Hershey Foods Corporation has inventories of $445,702,000 at December 31, 1994.

a. For the years ended December 31, 1996 and 1995, determine:

(1) the inventory turnover, and

(2) the number of days' sales in inventory.

b. What conclusions can be drawn from these analyses concerning Hershey's efficiency in managing inventory?

Periodic inventory by three methods
Objectives 3, 5 ✔ 1. $10,847

Three Rivers Television uses the periodic inventory system. Details regarding the inventory of television sets at January 1, purchases invoices during the year, and the inventory count at December 31 are summarized as follows:

Model	Inventory, January 1	Purchases Invoices 1st	2nd	3rd	Inventory Count, December 31
B91	4 at $149	6 at $151	8 at $157	7 at $156	6
F10	3 at 208	3 at 212	5 at 213	4 at 225	4
H21	2 at 520	2 at 527	2 at 530	2 at 535	3
J39	6 at 520	8 at 531	4 at 549	6 at 542	7
P80	9 at 213	7 at 215	6 at 222	6 at 225	8
T15	6 at 305	3 at 310	3 at 316	4 at 317	5
V11	—	4 at 222	4 at 232	—	1

Daniel Watkins
Sales Manager

Instructions

1. Determine the cost of the inventory on December 31 by the first-in, first-out method. If the inventory of a particular model comprises one entire purchase plus a portion of another purchase acquired at a different unit cost, use a separate line for each purchase.

2. Determine the cost of the inventory on December 31 by the last-in, first-out method, following the procedures indicated in (1).

FIFO Method

Model	Quan- tity	Unit Cost	Total Cost

LIFO Method

Model	Quan- tity	Unit Cost	Total Cost

Continued

(This table is the same as the one on the previous page. It is repeated for your convenience.)

Model	Inventory, January 1	Purchases Invoices 1st	2nd	3rd	Inventory Count, December 31
B91	4 at $149	6 at $151	8 at $157	7 at $156	6
F10	3 at 208	3 at 212	5 at 213	4 at 225	4
H21	2 at 520	2 at 527	2 at 530	2 at 535	3
J39	6 at 520	8 at 531	4 at 549	6 at 542	7
P80	9 at 213	7 at 215	6 at 222	6 at 225	8
T15	6 at 305	3 at 310	3 at 316	4 at 317	5
V11	—	4 at 222	4 at 232	—	1

3. Determine the cost of the inventory on December 31 by the average cost method, using the table below.

Average Cost Method

Model	Quantity	Unit Cost	Total Cost

Daniel Watkins
Sales Manager

" Our company accountant said that if the cost of units purchased had remained stable, all three methods would have yielded the same results. Although I don't understand why, our accountant also suggested that we use the FIFO method to impress our banker. "

4. Discuss which method (fifo or lifo) would be preferred for income tax purposes in periods of (a) rising prices and (b) declining prices.

Retail method; gross profit method
Objective 9 ✔ 1. $98,800 ✔ 2. a. $246,000

Selected data on merchandise inventory, purchases, and sales
for Bozeman Co. and Gallatin Co. are shown below.

Bozeman Co.	Cost	Retail
Merchandise inventory, February 1	$177,100	$ 227,000
Transactions during February:		
Purchases (net)	903,200	1,435,000
Sales		1,550,000
Sales returns and allowances		40,000

Gallatin Co.	
Merchandise inventory, July 1	$ 317,900
Transactions during July and August:	
Purchases (net)	1,432,100
Sales	2,475,000
Sales returns and allowances	125,000
Estimated gross profit rate	36%

Instructions

1. Determine the estimated
cost of the merchandise
inventory of Bozeman
Co. on February 28 by
the retail method,
presenting details of the
computations.

2. a. Estimate the cost of the
merchandise inventory of
Gallatin Co. on August 31
by the gross profit
method, presenting details
of the computations.

b. Assume that Gallatin Co.
took a physical inventory on
August 31 and discovered
that $212,900 of merchandise
was on hand. What was the
estimated loss of inventory
due to theft or damage
during July and August?

Blank Page

Periodic inventory by three methods
Objectives 3, 5 ✔ 1. $8,951

Martel Television uses the periodic inventory system. Details regarding the
inventory of television sets at July 1, 1999, purchases invoices during the year,
and the inventory count at June 30, 2000, are summarized as follows:

Model	Inventory, July 1	Purchases Invoices 1st	2nd	3rd	Inventory Count, June 30
A37	6 at $240	4 at $250	8 at $260	10 at $262	14
E15	6 at 80	5 at 82	8 at 89	8 at 90	8
L10	2 at 108	2 at 110	3 at 128	3 at 130	3
O18	8 at 88	4 at 79	3 at 85	6 at 92	8
K72	2 at 250	2 at 260	4 at 271	4 at 272	3
S91	5 at 160	4 at 170	4 at 175	7 at 180	8
V17	—	4 at 150	4 at 200	4 at 202	6

Sandy Acebo
General Manager

Instructions

1. Determine the cost of the inventory on
June 30, 2000, by the first-in, first-out
method. If the inventory of a particular
model comprises one entire purchase plus
a portion of another purchase acquired at
a different unit cost, use a separate line for
each purchase.

2. Determine the cost of the inventory on June
30, 2000, by the last-in, first-out method,
following the procedures indicated in (1).

FIFO Method

Model	Quantity	Unit Cost	Total Cost

LIFO Method

Model	Quantity	Unit Cost	Total Cost

Continued

Continued

(This table is the same as the one on the previous page. It is repeated for your convenience.)

Model	Inventory, July 1	Purchases Invoices 1st	2nd	3rd	Inventory Count, June 30
A37	6 at $240	4 at $250	8 at $260	10 at $262	14
E15	6 at 80	5 at 82	8 at 89	8 at 90	8
L10	2 at 108	2 at 110	3 at 128	3 at 130	3
O18	8 at 88	4 at 79	3 at 85	6 at 92	8
K72	2 at 250	2 at 260	4 at 271	4 at 272	3
S91	5 at 160	4 at 170	4 at 175	7 at 180	8
V17	—	4 at 150	4 at 200	4 at 202	6

3. Determine the cost of the inventory on June 30, 2000, by the average cost method, using the table below.

Average Cost Method

Model	Quantity	Unit Cost	Total Cost

Sandy Acebo
General Manager

" The average cost method is also called the weighted average method. In my company the average method approximates the physical flow of goods. I prefer the average method but for some reason the accountants always play with LIFO and FIFO for income tax purposes or for financial reporting purposes. Perhaps you could explain that to me. "

4. Discuss which method (fifo or lifo) would be preferred for income tax purposes in periods of (a) rising prices and (b) declining prices.

Retail method; gross profit method
Objective 9 ✔ 1. $226,300 ✔ 2. a. $128,440

Selected data on merchandise inventory, purchases, and
sales for Hefron Co. and Cummins Co. are shown below.

Hefron Co.	Cost	Retail
Merchandise inventory, August 1	$137,980	$270,000
Transactions during August:		
Purchases (net)	658,450	821,000
Sales		790,000
Sales returns and allowances		9,000

Cummins Co.	
Merchandise inventory, April 1	$ 117,500
Transactions during April and May:	
Purchases (net)	825,000
Sales	1,325,000
Sales returns and allowances	12,000
Estimated gross profit rate	38%

Instructions

1. Determine the estimated
   cost of the merchandise
   inventory of Hefron Co.
   on August 31 by the
   retail method, presenting
   details of the
   computations.

2. a. Estimate the cost of the
      merchandise inventory
      of Cummins Co. on
      May 31 by the gross
      profit method,
      presenting details of
      the computations.

   b. Assume that Cummins Co.
      took a physical inventory on
      May 31 and discovered that
      $118,000 of merchandise was
      on hand. What was the
      estimated loss of inventory due
      to theft or damage during April
      and May?

Blank Page

Chapter 10

Fixed Assets and Intangible Assets

Prior chapters have discussed assets that are classified as current assets. This chapter describes and illustrates accounting principles and concepts for long-term assets of a relatively permanent nature. Such assets include land, buildings, equipment, patents, and copyrights. This chapter discusses the costs of acquiring such assets accounting for their depreciation, depletion, or amortization, and accounting for their disposal.

Learning objectives are listed for the exercises and problems that follow. Use the information to the right to determine the nature of the objective and the page number to refer to your textbook for a discussion of the topic.

Objective 1 — **Nature of Fixed Assets 382**
Define fixed assets and describe the accounting for their cost.

Objective 2 — **Accounting for Depreciation 385**
Compute depreciation, using the following methods: straight-line method, units-of-production method, and declining-balance method.

Objective 3 — **Capital and Revenue Expenditures 390**
Classify fixed asset costs as either capital expenditures or revenue expenditures.

Objective 4 — **Disposal of Fixed Assets 392**
Journalize entries for the disposal of fixed assets.

Objective 5 — **Leasing Fixed Assets 396**
Define a lease and summarize the accounting rules related to the leasing of fixed assets.

Objective 6 — **Internal Control of Fixed Assets 396**
Describe internal controls over fixed assets.

Objective 7 — **Natural Resources 397**
Compute depletion and journalize the entry for depletion.

Objective 8 — **Intangible Assets 398**
Journalize the entries for acquiring and amortizing intangible assets, such as patents, copyrights, and goodwill.

Objective 9 — **Financial Reporting for Fixed Assets and Intangible Assets 399**
Describe how depreciation expense is reported in an income statement and prepare a balance sheet that includes fixed assets and intangible assets.

Objective 10— **Financial Analysis and Interpretation 400**
Compute and interpret the ratio of fixed assets to long-term liabilities.

Blank Page

Cost of acquiring fixed assets
Objective 1 - Text page 382

Working
Papers
Plus
—————
Chapter 10

Eileen Larkin owns and operates First Run Print Co. During July, First Run Print Co. incurred the following costs in acquiring two printing presses. One printing press was new, and the other was used by a business that recently filed for bankruptcy.

Costs related to new printing press:

1. Special foundation
2. Sales tax on purchase price
3. Insurance while in transit
4. Freight
5. New parts to replace those damaged in unloading
6. Fee paid to factory representative for installation

a. Indicate which costs incurred in acquiring the new printing press should be debited to the asset account.

Cost related to secondhand printing press:

7. Freight
8. Installation
9. Repair of vandalism during installation
10. Replacement of worn-out parts
11. Repair of damage incurred in reconditioning the press
12. Fees paid to attorney to review purchase agreement

b. Indicate which costs incurred in acquiring the secondhand printing press should be debited to the asset account.

Exercise 10–2

Determine cost of land
Objective 1 - Text page 382

A company has developed a tract of land into a ski resort. The company has cut the trees, cleared and graded the land and hills, and constructed ski lifts.

a. Should the tree cutting, land clearing, and grading costs of constructing the ski slopes be debited to the land account?

b. If such costs are debited to Land, should they be depreciated?

Exercise 10-3

Determine cost of land
Objective 1 - Text page 382 ✔ $136,200

Langley Delivery Company acquired an adjacent lot to construct a new warehouse, paying $30,000 and giving a short-term note for $90,000. Legal fees paid were $3,500, delinquent taxes assumed were $7,500, and fees paid to remove an old building from the land were $7,200. Materials salvaged from the demolition of the building were sold for $2,000. A contractor was paid $312,500 to construct a new warehouse. Determine the cost of the land to be reported on the balance sheet.

Exercise 10-4

Nature of depreciation
Objective 1 - Text page 382

Sheehan Metal Casting Co. reported $625,000 for equipment and $310,000 for accumulated depreciation - equipment on its balance sheet.

Does this mean (a) that the replacement cost of the equipment is $625,000 and (b) that $310,000 is set aside in a special fund for the replacement of the equipment? Explain.

Exercise 10–5

Straight-line depreciation rates
Objective 2 - Text page 385   ✔ a. 25%

Convert each of the following estimates of useful life to a
straight-line depreciation rate, stated as a percentage, assuming
that the residual value of the fixed asset is to be ignored.

(a)   4 years

(b)   5 years

(c)   10 years

(d) 20 years

(e) 25 years

(f)   40 years

(g) 50 years

Exercise 10–6

Straight-line depreciation
Objective 2 - Text page 385   ✔ $12,800

A refrigerator used by a
meat processor has a cost of
$138,000, an estimated
residual value of $10,000,
and an estimated useful life
of 10 years. What is the
amount of the annual
depreciation computed by
the straight-line method?

Exercise 10–7

Depreciation by units-of-production method
Objective 2 - Text page 385 ✔ $54,750

A diesel-powered generator with a cost of $475,000 and estimated residual
value of $25,000 is expected to have a useful operating life of 60,000 hours.
During July, the generator was operated 7,300 hours.

Determine the
depreciation
for the month.

Exercise 10–8

Depreciation by units-of-production method
Objective 2 - Text page 385 ✔ a. Truck #1, credit Accumulated Depreciation, $4,320

Prior to adjustment at the end of the year, the balance in Trucks is $150,000, and the balance in
Accumulated Depreciation–Trucks is $62,800. Details of the subsidiary ledger are given below.

a. Determine the depreciation rates per mile and the amount to be credited to the accumulated
   depreciation section of each of the subsidiary accounts for the miles operated during the
   current year. Record your answer in the table below.

Truck No.	Cost	Estimated Residual Value	Estimated Useful Life (miles)	Accumulated Depreciation at Beginning of Year	Miles Operated During Year	Depr. Rate Per Mile	Accumulated Depreciation Credit
1	$65,000	$5,000	250,000	$22,500	18,000	$_____	$_____
2	38,600	3,600	200,000	32,000	20,000	$_____	$_____
3	28,000	3,000	100,000	9,300	34,500	$_____	$_____
4	18,400	1,000	120,000	—	12,000	$_____	$_____

b. Journalize the entry to record depreciation for the year.

Date	Description	Debit	Credit

Exercise 10–9

Depreciation by two methods
Objective 2 - Text page 385 ✔ a. $27,500

A backhoe acquired on January 2 at a cost of $220,000 has an estimated
useful life of 8 years. Assuming that it will have no residual value,
determine the depreciation for each of the first two years.

Calculations:

a. by the straight-line method

   Year 1 — $_____

   Year 2 — $_____

b. by the declining-balance method,
   using twice the straight-line rate

   Year 1 — $_____

   Year 2 — $_____

Exercise 10–10

Depreciation by two methods
Objective 2 - Text page 385 ✔ a. $5,200

A dairy storage tank acquired at the beginning of the fiscal year at a
cost of $60,000 has an estimated residual value of $8,000 and an
estimated useful life of 10 years. Determine the following:

a. the amount of
   annual
   depreciation by
   the straight-line
   method.

b. the amount of
   depreciation for
   the first and
   second year
   computed by the
   declining-balance
   method (at twice
   the straight-line
   rate).

Exercise 10–11

Partial-year depreciation
Objective 2 - Text page 385 ✔ a. First year, $18,000; Second year, $24,000

Sandblasting equipment acquired at a cost of $125,000 has an estimated residual value of $5,000 and an estimated useful life of 5 years. It was placed in service on April 1 of the current fiscal year, which ends on December 31. Determine the depreciation for the current fiscal year and for the following fiscal year by:

a. the straight-line
method.

b. the declining-balance
method, at twice the
straight-line rate.

Exercise 10–12

Revision of depreciation
Objective 2 - Text page 385 ✔ a. $8,500

X-ray equipment with a cost of $360,000 has an estimated residual value of $20,000, an estimated useful life of 40 years, and is depreciated by the straight-line method.

a. What is the amount of
the annual
depreciation?

b. What is the book value
at the end of the
twentieth year of use?

c. If at the start of the
twenty-first year it is
estimated that the
remaining life is 15
years and that the
residual value is
$10,000, what is the
depreciation expense
for each of the
remaining 15 years?

Revision of depreciation
Objective 2 - Text page 385 ✔ $10,000

Mobile communications equipment acquired on January 5, 1997, at a cost of $112,500, has an estimated residual value of $11,700 and an estimated useful life of 12 years. Depreciation has been recorded for the first four years ended December 31, 2000, by the straight-line method. Determine the amount of depreciation for the current year ended December 31, 2001, if the revised estimated residual value is $8,900 and the revised estimated remaining useful life (including the current year) is 7 years.

Exercise 10–14

Capital and revenue expenditures
Objective 3 - Text page 390

Absaroka Co. incurred the following costs related to trucks and vans used in operating its delivery service. Classify each of the costs as a capital expenditure or a revenue expenditure. For those costs identified as capital expenditures, classify each as an addition, a betterment, or an extraordinary repair.

1. Overhauled the engine on one of the trucks that had been purchased four years ago.

2. Removed a two-way radio from one of the trucks and installed a new radio with greater range of communication.

3. Installed a hydraulic lift to a van.

4. Changed the oil and greased the joints of all the trucks and vans.

5. Replaced two of the trucks' shock absorbers with new shock absorbers that allow for the delivery of heavier loads.

6. Replaced the brakes and alternator on a truck that had been in service for the past 5 years.

7. Installed security systems on three of the newer trucks.

8. Repaired a flat tire on one of the vans.

9. Rebuilt the transmission on one of the vans that had been driven only 25,000 miles. The van was no longer under warranty.

10. Tinted the back and side windows of one of the vans to discourage theft of contents.

Capital and revenue expenditures
Objective 3 - Text page 390

Mark Lemke Co. owns and operates Second to None Transport Co. During the past year, Mark incurred the following costs related to his 18-wheel truck. Classify each of the costs as a capital expenditure or a revenue expenditure. For those costs identified as capital expenditures, classify each as an addition, a betterment, or an extraordinary repair.

1. Overhauled the engine.

2. Removed the old CB radio and replaced it with a newer model with greater range.

3. Replaced a headlight that had burned out.

4. Replaced the hydraulic brake system that had begun to fail during his latest trip through the Smoky Mountains.

5. Replaced a shock absorber that had worn out.

6. Installed fog lights.

7. Installed a wind deflector on top of the cab to increase fuel mileage.

8. Modified the factory-installed turbo charger with a special-order kit designed to add 30 more horsepower to the engine performance.

9. Replaced the old radar detector with a newer model that detects the KA frequencies now used by many of the state patrol radar guns. The detector is wired directly into the cab, so that it is partially hidden. In addition, Mark fastened the detector to the truck with a locking device that prevents its removal.

10. Installed a television in the sleeping compartment of the truck.

Exercise 10–16

A number of major structural repairs on a building were completed at the beginning of the current fiscal year at a cost of $80,000. The repairs are expected to extend the life of the building 6 years beyond the original estimate. The original cost of the building was $750,000, and it has been depreciated by the straight-line method for 25 years. The residual value is expected to be negligible and has been ignored. The balance of the related accumulated depreciation account after the depreciation adjustment at the end of the preceding year is $330,000.

a. What has the amount of annual depreciation been in past years?

b. To what account should the cost of repairs ($80,000) be debited?

c. What is the book value of the building after the repairs have been recorded?

d. What is the amount of depreciation for the current year using the straight-line method (assuming that the repairs were completed at the very beginning of the year)?

Entries for sale of fixed asset
Objective 4 - Text page 392　✔ a. $46,500

Metal recycling equipment acquired on January 3, 1997, at a cost of $87,500,
has an estimated useful life of 8 years, an estimated residual value of $5,500,
and is depreciated by the straight-line method.

a. What was the book
   value of the equipment
   at December 31, 2000,
   the end of the fiscal
   year?

b. Assuming that the equipment was sold on July 1, 2001, for $40,000,
   journalize the entries to record:

   (1) depreciation for the six months of the current year ending December 31, 2001, and

   (2) the sale of the equipment.

Date	Description	Debit	Credit

Exercise 10–18

Disposal of fixed asset
Objective 4 - Text page 392 ✔ b. $15,500

Equipment acquired on January 3, 1997, at a cost of $51,500, has an
estimated useful life of 4 years and an estimated residual value of $3,500.

a. What was the annual
   amount of depreciation for
   the years 1997, 1998, and
   1999, using the straight-line
   method of depreciation?

b. What was the book
   value of the equipment
   on January 1, 2000?

c. Assuming that the equipment was sold on January 2, 2000,
   for $13,000, journalize the entry to record the sale.

Date	Description	Debit	Credit

d. Assuming that the equipment had been sold on January 2, 2000, for $17,000
   instead of $13,000, journalize the entry to record the sale.

Date	Description	Debit	Credit

Asset traded for similar asset
Objective 4 - Text page 392 ✔ a. $139,000

A printing press priced at $170,000 is acquired by trading in a similar press and paying cash for the difference between the trade-in allowance and the price of the new press.

a. Assuming that the trade-in allowance is $31,000, what is the amount of cash given?

b. Assuming that the book value of the press traded in is $23,800, what is the cost of the new press for financial reporting purposes?

Exercise 10–20

Asset traded for similar asset
Objective 4 - Text page 392 ✔ b. $170,000

Assume the same facts as in Exercise 10–19, except that the book value of the press traded in is $35,000.

a. What is the amount of cash given?

b. What is the cost of the new press for financial reporting purposes?

Exercise 10–21

Entries for trade of fixed asset
Objective 4 - Text page 392

On April 1, Cougar Co., a water distiller, acquired new bottling equipment with a list price of $315,000. Cougar received a trade-in allowance of $50,000 on the old equipment of a similar type, paid cash of $30,000, and gave a series of five notes payable for the remainder. The following information about the old equipment is obtained from the account in the equipment ledger: cost, $212,500; accumulated depreciation on December 31, the end of the preceding fiscal year, $135,000; annual depreciation, $9,000.

Journalize the entries to record:

(a) the current depreciation of the old equipment to the date of trade-in, and

(b) the transaction on April 1 for financial reporting purposes.

Date	Description	Debit	Credit

Entries for trade of fixed asset
Objective 4 - Text page 392

On October 1, Weissman Co. acquired a new truck with a list price of $125,000.
Weissman received a trade-in allowance of $22,000 on an old truck of similar type,
paid cash of $15,000, and gave a series of five notes payable for the remainder. The
following information about the old truck is obtained from the account in the
equipment ledger: cost, $82,500; accumulated depreciation on December 31, the
end of the preceding fiscal year, $57,500; annual depreciation, $7,500.

Journalize the entries to record:

(a) the current depreciation of the old truck to the date of trade-in, and

(b) the transaction on October 1 for financial reporting purposes.

Date	Description	Debit	Credit

Exercise 10–23

Depreciable cost of asset acquired by exchange
Objective 4 - Text page 392 ✔ a. $50,000

On the first day of the fiscal year, a delivery truck with a list price of $50,000
was acquired in exchange for an old delivery truck and $38,000 cash. The old
truck had a book value of $14,000 at the date of the exchange.

a. Determine the depreciable cost
   for financial reporting purposes.

b. Assuming that the book value of
   the old delivery truck was $9,000,
   determine the depreciable cost for
   financial reporting purposes.

Exercise 10–24

Internal control of fixed assets
Objective 6 - Text page 396

AllNet Co. is a computer software company marketing products in the United States and Canada. While AllNet Co. has over 90 sales offices, all accounting is handled at the company's headquarters in Cleveland, Ohio.

AllNet Co. keeps all its fixed asset records on a computerized system. The computer maintains a subsidiary ledger of all fixed assets owned by the company and calculates depreciation automatically. Whenever a manager at one of the ninety sales offices wants to purchase a fixed asset, a purchase request is submitted to headquarters for approval. Upon approval, the fixed asset is purchased and the invoice is sent back to headquarters so that the asset can be entered into the fixed asset system.

A manager who wants to dispose of a fixed asset simply sells or disposes of the asset and notifies headquarters to remove the asset from the system. Company cars and personal computers are frequently purchased by employees when they are disposed of. Most pieces of office equipment are traded in when new assets are acquired.

What internal control weakness exists in the procedures used to acquire and dispose of fixed assets at AllNet Co.?

Exercise 10–25

Depletion entries
Objective 7 - Text page 397 ✔ a. $5,100,000

Boxer Co. acquired mineral rights for $18,000,000. The mineral deposit is estimated at 30,000,000 tons. During the current year, 8,500,000 tons were mined and sold for $6,500,000.

a. Determine the amount
   of depletion expense
   for the current year.

b. Journalize the adjusting entry to recognize the expense.

Date	Description	Debit	Credit

Amortization entries
Objective 8 - Text page 398 ✔ a. $56,750

Nitro Company acquired patent rights on January 3, 1997, for $935,000. The patent has a useful life equal to its legal life of 20 years. On January 5, 2000, Nitro successfully defended the patent in a lawsuit at a cost of $170,000.

a. Determine the patent
   amortization expense
   for the current year
   ended December 31,
   2000.

b. Journalize the adjusting entry to recognize the amortization.

Date	Description	Debit	Credit

Exercise 10–27

Balance sheet presentation
Objective 9 - Text page 399

How many errors can you find in the following partial balance sheet?

Gazette Company
Balance Sheet
December 31, 20—

Assets

Total current assets $297,500

	Replacement Cost	Accumulated Depreciation	Book Value
Property, plant, and equipment:			
Land	$ 65,000	$ 20,000	$ 45,000
Buildings	160,000	76,000	84,000
Factory equipment	450,000	192,000	258,000
Office equipment	120,000	77,000	43,000
Patents	60,000	—	60,000
Goodwill	45,000	—	45,000
Total property, plant, and equipment	$900,000	$365,000	535,000

Ratio of Fixed Assets to Long-Term Liabilities		
Procter & Gamble	**(in millions)**	
	1996	**1995**
Property, plant, equip. (net)	$11,118	$11,026
Long-term liabilities (debt)	$ 4,670	$ 5,161
Ratio of fixed assets	2.4	2.1

Use: To indicate the margin of safety to long-term creditors

Exercise 10–28

Ratio of fixed assets to long-term liabilities
Objective 10 - Text page 400

The financial statements for **Hershey Foods Corporation** are presented in Appendix G at the end of the text.

a. Compute the ratio of fixed assets (property, plant, and equipment) to long-term liabilities (long-term debt) as of December 31, 1996 and 1995.

b. What conclusions can be drawn from these ratios concerning Hershey's ability to borrow additional funds on a long-term basis?

Activity 10–5 Into the Real World

Applying for patents, copyrights, and trademarks

Go to the Internet and review the procedures for applying for a patent, a copyright, and a trademark. One Internet site that is useful for this purpose is:
www.idresearch.com

Prepare a written summary of these procedures.

Compare three depreciation methods
Objective 2 ✔ 1999: straight-line depreciation, $45,000

" Roche Company purchased waterproofing equipment on January 2, 1999, for $195,000. The equipment was expected to have a useful life of 4 years, or 45,000 operating hours, and a residual value of $15,000. The equipment was used for 8,900 hours during 1999, 13,100 hours in 2000, 14,500 hours in 2001, and 8,500 hours in 2002. "

Carl Fisher
CEO Roche Company

Instructions

Determine the amount of depreciation expense for the years ended December 31, 1999, 2000, and 2001, and 2002, by (a) the straight-line method, (b) the units-of-production method, and (c) the declining-balance method, using twice the straight-line rate. Also determine the total depreciation expense for the four years by each method.

Depreciation Expense

Year	Straight-Line Method	Units-of-Production Method	Declining-Balance Method
1999			
2000			
2001			
2002			
Total			

Calculations

Straight-line (SL)   Declining-balance (DB)

Units-of-production (UOP)

Blank Page

Depreciation by two methods;
trade of fixed asset
Objectives 2, 4 ✔ 1. b. Year 1, $100,000 depreciation expense; 2. $245,000

New tire retreading equipment, acquired at a cost of $200,000 at the beginning of a fiscal year, has an estimated useful life of 4 years and an estimated residual value of $15,000. The manager requested information regarding the effect of alternative methods on the amount of depreciation expense each year. On the basis of the data presented to the manager, the declining-balance method was selected.

In the first week of the fourth year, the equipment was traded in for similar equipment priced at $250,000. The trade-in allowance on the old equipment was $30,000, cash of $20,000 was paid, and a note payable was issued for the balance.

Instructions

1. Determine the annual depreciation expense for each of the estimated 4 years of use, the accumulated depreciation at the end of each year, and the book value of the equipment at the end of each year by:
   (a) the straight-line method.

Year	Depreciation Expense	Accumulated Depreciation, End of Year	Book Value, End of Year

   (b) the declining-balance method (at twice the straight-line rate).

Year	Depreciation Expense	Accumulated Depreciation, End of Year	Book Value, End of Year

2. For financial reporting purposes, determine the cost of the new equipment acquired in the exchange.

Continued

3. Journalize the entry to record the exchange.

Date	Description	Debit	Credit

4. Journalize the entry to record the exchange, assuming that
   the trade-in allowance was $18,000 instead of $30,000.

Date	Description	Debit	Credit

Compare three depreciation methods
Objective 2 ✔ 1999: straight-line depreciation, $120,000

" Westby Company purchased packaging equipment on January 3, 1999, for $375,000. The equipment was expected to have a useful life of 3 years, or 24,000 operating hours, and a residual value of $15,000. The equipment was used for 6,500 hours during 1999, 11,600 hours in 2000, and 5,900 hours in 2001. "

Carol King
Owner

Instructions

Determine the amount of depreciation expense for the years ended December 31, 1999, 2000, and 2001, by (a) the straight-line method, (b) the units-of-production method, and (c) the declining-balance method, using twice the straight-line rate. Also determine the total depreciation expense for the three years by each method.

Depreciation Expense

Year	Straight-Line Method	Units-of-Production Method	Declining-Balance Method
1999			
2000			
2001			
Total			

Calculations

Straight-line (SL)   Declining-balance (DB)

Units-of-production (UOP)

Blank Page

Depreciation by two methods;
trade of fixed asset
Objectives 2, 4 ✔ 1. b. Year 1: $100,000 depreciation expense; 2. $292,400

New lithographic equipment, acquired at a cost of $250,000 at the beginning of a fiscal year, has an estimated useful life of 5 years and an estimated residual value of $20,000. The manager requested information regarding the effect of alternative methods on the amount of depreciation expense each year. On the basis of the data presented to the manager, the declining balance method was selected.

In the first week of the fifth year, the equipment was traded in for similar equipment priced at $300,000. The trade-in allowance on the old equipment was $40,000, cash of $30,000 was paid, and a note payable was issued for the balance.

Instructions

1. Determine the annual depreciation expense for each of the estimated 5 years of use, the accumulated depreciation at the end of each year, and the book value of the equipment at the end of each year by:
   (a) the straight-line method.

Year	Depreciation Expense	Accumulated Depreciation, End of Year	Book Value, End of Year

   (b) the declining-balance method (at twice the straight-line rate).

Year	Depreciation Expense	Accumulated Depreciation End of Year	Book Value End of Year

2. For financial reporting purposes, determine the cost of the new equipment acquired in the exchange.

Continued

3. Journalize the entry to record the exchange.

Date	Description	Debit	Credit

5. Journalize the entry to record the exchange, assuming that
   the trade-in allowance was $25,000 instead of $40,000.

Date	Description	Debit	Credit

Chapter 11

Current Liabilities

Payables are the opposite of receivables. They are debts owed by an enterprise to its creditors. Money claims against a firm may be created in many ways. For example, payables are created by purchases of merchandise or services on account, loans from banks, and purchases of equipment and marketable securities on a credit basis. At a point in time, a business may also owe its employees for wages or salaries accrued, banks or other creditors for interest accrued on notes, and governmental agencies for taxes.

Some types of current liabilities, such as accounts payable, have been discussed in earlier chapters. Additional types of current liabilities, including liabilities arising from payrolls, vacation pay, pensions, notes payable, and product warranties, are discussed in this chapter.

Learning objectives are listed for the exercises and problems that follow. Use the information to the right to determine the nature of the objective and the page number to refer to your textbook for a discussion of the topic.

Blank Page

Current liabilities
Objective 1 - Text page 421 ✔ Total current liabilities, $130,150

Tech World Magazine Inc. sold 3,200 annual subscriptions of *Tech World* for $36 during December 2000. These new subscribers will receive monthly issues, beginning in January 2001. In addition, the business had taxable income of $125,000 during the first calendar quarter of 2001. The federal tax rate is 35%. A quarterly tax payment will be made on April 7, 2001.

Prepare the current liabilities section of the balance sheet for Tech World Magazine Inc. on March 31, 2001.

Exercise 11–2

Entries for discounting notes payable
Objective 2 - Text page 421

Star Bright Lighting Co. issues a 60-day note for $300,000 to Builtwell Wholesale Supply Co. for merchandise inventory. Builtwell discounts the note at 9%.

a. Journalize the borrower's entries to record:
   1. the issuance of the note.
   2. the payment of the note at maturity.

Date	Description	Debit	Credit

b. Journalize the creditor's entries to record:
   1. the receipt of the note.
   2. the receipt of payment of the note at maturity.

Date	Description	Debit	Credit

Exercise 11–3

Name:

Evaluate alternative notes
Objective 2 - Text page 421   ✔ a. $2,000

A borrower has two alternatives for a loan:

(1) issue an $80,000, 90-day, 10% note or

(2) issue an $80,000, 90-day note that the creditor discounts at 10%.

a. Calculate the amount of the interest expense for each option.

b. Determine the proceeds received by the borrower in each situation.

c. Which alternative is more favorable to the borrower? Explain.

Exercise 11–4

Entries for notes payable
Objective 2 - Text page 421

A business issued a 60-day, 12% note for $25,000 to a creditor on account.
Journalize the entries to record

a. the issuance of the note and

b. the payment of the note at maturity, including interest.

Date	Description	Debit	Credit

Exercise 11–5

Fixed asset purchases with note
Objective 2 - Text page 421

On June 30, Mario Game Company purchased land for $250,000 and a building for $730,000, paying $280,000 cash and issuing an 8% note for the balance, secured by a mortgage on the property. The terms of the note provide for 20 semiannual payments of $35,000 on the principal plus the interest accrued from the date of the preceding payment.

Journalize the entry to record:

(a) the transaction on June 30,

(b) the payment of the first installment on December 31, and

(c) the payment of the second installment the following June 30.

Date	Description	Debit	Credit

Exercise 11–6

Accrued product warranty
Objective 3 - Text page 423

Precision Audio Company warrants its products for one year. The estimated product warranty is 3% of sales. Assume that sales were $400,000 for January. In February, a customer received warranty repairs requiring $200 of parts and $600 of labor.

a. Journalize the adjusting entry required at January 31, the end of the first month of the current year, to record the accrued product warranty.

b. Journalize the entry to record the warranty work provided in February.

Date	Description	Debit	Credit

Contingent liabilities
Objective 3 - Text page 423

Several months ago, Endurance Battery Company experienced a hazardous materials spill at one of its plants. As a result, the Environmental Protection Agency (EPA) fined the company $150,000. The company is contesting the fine. In addition, an employee is seeking $600,000 damages related to the spill. Lastly, a homeowner has sued the company for $100,000. The homeowner lives 20 miles form the plant, but believes that the incident has reduced the home's resale value by $100,000.

Endurance Battery's legal counsel believes that it is probable that the EPA fine will stand. In addition, counsel indicates that an out-of-court settlement of $300,000 has recently been reached with the employee. The final papers will be signed next week. Counsel believes that the homeowner's case is much weaker and will be decided in favor of Endurance. Other litigation related to the spill is possible, but the damage amounts are uncertain.

a. Journalize the contingent liabilities associated
   with the hazardous materials spill.

Date	Description	Debit	Credit

b. Prepare a footnote
   disclosure relating
   to this incident.

Exercise 11–8

Calculate payroll
Objective 4 - Text page 425 ✔ b. Net pay, $786.50

An employee earns $20 per hour and 1 1/2 times that rate for all hours in excess of 40 hours per week. Assume that the employee worked 50 hours during the week, and that the gross pay prior to the current week totaled $59,760. Assume further that the social security tax rate was 6.0% (on earnings up to $70,000), the Medicare tax rate was 1.5%, and federal income tax to be withheld was $231.

a. Determine the gross pay for the week.

b. Determine the net pay for the week.

Exercise 11–9

Calculate payroll
Objective 4 - Text page 425 ✔ Administrator net pay, $853.20

Prism Business Consultants has three employees—a consultant, a computer programmer, and an administrator. The following payroll information is available for each employee.

For the current pay period, the computer programmer worked 43 hours and the administrator worked 48 hours. For the current pay period, the federal income tax withheld for the consultant was $840. The federal income tax withheld for the computer programmer and the administrator can be determined from the wage bracket withholding table in Exhibit 3 in the chapter. Assume further that the social security tax rate was 6.0% on the first $70,000 of annual earnings, and the Medicare tax rate was 1.5%.

Determine the gross pay and the net pay for each of the three employees for the current pay period.

	Consultant	Computer Programmer	Administrator
Regular earnings rate	$3,000 per week	$28 per hour	$22 per hour
Overtime earnings rate	Not applicable	1 1/2 times hourly rate	1 1/2 times hourly rate
Gross pay prior to current pay period	$108,700	$69,100	$39,100
Number of withholding allowances	1	0	3
Regular earnings	_____	_____	_____
Overtime earnings	_____	_____	_____
Gross pay	_____	_____	_____
Less:			
Social security tax	_____	_____	_____
Medicare tax	_____	_____	_____
Federal income tax withheld	_____	_____	_____
Net pay	_____	_____	_____

Summary payroll data
Objectives 4, 5 ✔ a. (3) Total earnings, $200,000

In the following summary of data for a payroll period,
some amounts have been intentionally omitted:

Earnings:
1. At regular rate .... $_____
2. At overtime rate 28,500
3. Total earnings .... $_____

Accounts debited:
11. Factory Wages 124,300
12. Sales Salaries .... $_____
13. Office Salaries 34,300

Deductions:
4. Social security tax.......... $11,500
5. Medicare tax 3,000
6. Income tax withheld 28,200
7. Medical insurance 1,050
8. Union dues .... $_____
9. Total deductions.............. 45,000
10. Net amount paid 155,000

a. Calculate the amounts omitted in lines (1), (3), (8), and (12),
writing your answer on the appropriate line.

b. Journalize the entry to record the payroll accrual.

Date	Description	Debit	Credit

c. Journalize the entry to record the payment of the payroll.

Date	Description	Debit	Credit

d. From the data given in this exercise
and your answer to (a), would you
conclude that this payroll was paid
sometime during the first few weeks
of the calendar year? Explain.

Payroll internal control procedures
Objective 5 - Text page 430

Memphis Sounds is a retail store specializing in the sale of jazz compact discs and cassettes. The store employs 3 full-time and 10 part-time workers. The store's weekly payroll averages $1,800 for all 13 workers.

Memphis Sounds uses a personal computer to assist with the preparing of paychecks. Each week, the store's accountant collects employee time cards and enters the hours worked into the payroll program. The payroll program calculates each employee's pay and prints a paycheck. The accountant uses a check-signing machine to sign the paychecks. Next, the store's owner authorizes the transfer of funds from the store's regular bank account to the payroll account.

For the week of May 1C, the accountant accidentally recorded 400 hours worked instead of 40 hours for one of the full-time employees.

Does Memphis
Sounds have internal
controls in place to
catch this error?
If so, how will this
error be detected?

Internal control procedures
Objective 5 - Text page 430

Sure-Grip Tools is a small manufacturer of home workshop power tools. The company employs 30 production workers and 10 administrative persons. The following procedures are used to process the company's weekly payroll. State whether each of the procedures is appropriate or inappropriate after considering the principles of internal control. If a procedure is inappropriate, describe the appropriate procedure.

a. Whenever a salaried employee is terminated, Personnel authorizes Payroll to remove the employee from the payroll system. However, this procedure is not required when an hourly worker is terminated. Hourly employees only receive a paycheck if their time card shows hours worked. The computer automatically drops an employee from the payroll system when that employee has six consecutive weeks with no hours worked.

b. Whenever an employee receives a pay raise, the supervisor must fill out a wage adjustment form, which is signed by the company president. This form is used to change the employee's wage rate in the payroll system.

c. All employees are required to record their hours worked by clocking in and out on a time clock. Employees must clock out for lunch break. Due to congestion around the time clock area at lunch time, management has not objected to having one employee clock in and out for an entire department.

d. Paychecks are signed by using a check-signing machine. This machine is located in the main office, so that it can be easily accessed by anyone needing a check signed.

e. Sure-Grip maintains a separate checking account for payroll checks. Each week, the total net pay for all employees is transferred from the company's regular bank account to the payroll account.

Exercise 11–13

Payroll tax entries
Objective 5 - Text page 430 ✔ a. $36,015

According to a summary of the payroll of Tender Heart Publishing Co., $460,000 was subject to the 6.0% social security tax and $510,000 was subject to the 1.5% Medicare tax. Also, $15,000 was subject to state and federal unemployment taxes.

a. Calculate the employer's payroll taxes, using the following rates: state unemployment, 4.3%; federal unemployment, 0.8%.

b. Journalize the entry to record the accrual of payroll taxes.

Date	Description	Debit	Credit

Exercise 11–14

Payroll procedures
Objective 5 - Text page 430

The fiscal year for Homestead Stores Inc. ends on June 30. In addition, the company computes and reports payroll taxes on a fiscal-year basis. Thus, social security and FUTA maximum earnings limitations apply to the fiscal-year payroll.

What is wrong with these procedures for accounting for payroll taxes?

Accrued vacation pay
Objective 6 - Text page 438

A business provides its employees with varying amounts of vacation per year, depending on the length of employment. The estimated amount of the current year's vacation pay is $187,200. Journalize the adjusting entry required on January 31, the end of the first month of the current year, to record the accrued vacation pay.

Date	Description	Debit	Credit

Exercise 11–16

Pension plan entries
Objective 6 - Text page 438

Forever Memories Inc. operates a chain of photography stores. The company maintains a defined contribution pension plan for its employees. The plan requires quarterly installments to be paid to the funding agent, Interstate Insurance Company, by the fifteenth of the month following the end of each quarter. Assuming that the pension cost is $175,000 for the quarter ended December 31, journalize entries to record:

(a) the accrued pension liability on December 31 and

(b) the payment to the funding agent on January 15.

Date	Description	Debit	Credit

Solvency Measures — Quick Ratio

	Noble Co.	Hart Co.
Quick assets:		
Cash	$ 100,000	$ 55,000
Cash equivalents	47,000	65,000
Accounts receivable (net)	84,000	472,000
Total	$231,000	$592,000
Current liabilities	$220,000	$740,000
Quick ratio	1.05	.8

Use: To indicate instant debt-paying ability

Exercise 11–17

Quick ratio
Objective 7 - Text page 440

The financial statements for **Hershey Foods Corporation** are presented in Appendix G at the end of the text.

a. Compute the quick ratio as of December 31, 1995 and 1996.

b. What conclusions can be drawn from these data as to Hershey's ability to meet its current liabilities?

Liability transactions
Objectives 2, 3

The following items were selected from among the transactions
completed by Renaissance Products Co. during the current year:

Feb. 15. Purchased merchandise on account from Ranier Co., $14,000, terms n/30.

Mar. 17. Issued a 30-day, 9% note for $14,000 to Ranier Co., on account.

Apr. 16. Paid Ranier Co. the amount owed on the note of March 17.

July 15. Borrowed $20,000 from Security Bank, issuing a 90-day, 12% note.

   25. Purchased tools by issuing a $60,000, 120-day note to Sun Supply Co., which
        discounted the note at the rate of 13%.

Oct. 13. Paid Security Bank the interest due on the note of July 15 and renewed the loan by
        issuing a new 30-day, 15% note for $20,000. (Journalize both the debit and credit to the
        notes payable account.)

Nov. 12. Paid Security Bank the amount due on the note of October 13.

   22. Paid Sun Supply Co. the amount due on the note of July 25.

Dec. 1. Purchased office equipment from Valley Equipment Co. for $75,000, paying $15,000
        and issuing a series of ten 12% notes for $6,000 each, coming due at 30-day intervals.

   17. Settled a product liability lawsuit with a customer for $35,000, payable in January.
        Renaissance accrued the loss in a litigation claims payable account.

   31. Paid the amount due Valley Equipment Co. on the first note in the series issued on
        December 1.

Instructions

1. Using a blank **Form GJ**, journalize the transactions.

2. Journalize the adjusting entry for each of the following accrued expenses at
    the end of the current year:

    a. Product warranty cost, $15,450.

    b. Interest on the nine remaining notes owed to Valley Equipment Co.

Blank Page

**Wage and tax statement data
on employer FICA tax**
Objectives 4, 5 ✔ 2. (e) $23,160

Sunrise Bread Company began business on January 2 of last year. Salaries were paid to
employees on the last day of each month, and social security tax, Medicare tax, and federal
income tax were withheld in the required amounts. An employee who is hired in the middle of
the month receives half the monthly salary for that month. All required payroll tax reports were
filed, and the correct amount of payroll taxes was remitted by the company for the calendar
year. Before the Wage and Tax Statements (Form W-2) could be prepared for distribution to
employees and for filing with the Social Security Administration, the employees' earnings
records were inadvertently destroyed.

None of the employees resigned
or were discharged during the
year, and there were no changes
in salary rates. The social
security tax was withheld at the
rate of 6.0% on the first $70,000
of salary and Medicare tax at
the rate of 1.5% on salary. Data
on dates of employment, salary
rates, and employees' income
taxes withheld, which are
summarized as follows, were
obtained from personnel
records and payroll records.

Employee	Date First Employed	Monthly Salary	Monthly Income Tax Withheld
Alvarez	Jan. 16	$6,400	$1,376.00
Conrad	Nov. 1	3,000	544.20
Felix	Jan. 2	2,500	447.25
Lydall	July 16	4,200	783.30
Porter	Jan. 2	6,700	1,497.45
Soong	May 1	2,800	463.40
Walker	Feb. 16	5,000	1,027.00

Instructions

1. Calculate the amounts to be reported on each employee's Wage and Tax
   Statement (Form W-2) for the year, arranging the data in the following form:

Employee	Gross Earnings	Federal Income Tax Withheld	Social Security Tax Withheld	Medicare Tax Withheld
Alvarez				
Conrad				
Felix				
Lydall				
Porter				
Soong				
Walker				

Continued

2. Calculate the following employer payroll taxes for the year:

(a) social security .... $_____

(b) Medicare .... $_____

(c) state unemployment compensation at 4.2%
      on the first $7,000 of each employee's earnings .... $_____

(d) federal unemployment compensation at 0.8%
      on the first $7,000 of each employee's earnings .... $_____

(e) total .... $_____

Liability transactions
Objectives 2, 3

The following items were selected from among the transactions
completed by Pride Polymers during the current year:

Apr. 7. Borrowed $12,000 from First Financial Corporation, issuing a 60-day, 12%
          note for that amount.

May 10. Purchased equipment by issuing a $60,000, 120-day note to Milford
         Equipment Co., which discounted the note at the rate of 10%.

June 6. Paid First Financial Corporation the interest due on the note of April 7 and
          renewed the loan by issuing a new 30-day, 16% note for $12,000. (Record
          both the debit and credit to the notes payable account.)

July 6. Paid First Financial Corporation the amount due on the note of June 6.

Aug. 3. Purchased merchandise on account from Hamilton Co., $25,000, terms n/30.

Sep. 2. Issued a 60-day, 15% note for $25,000 to Hamilton Co., on account.

      7. Paid Milford Equipment Co. the amount due on the note of May 10.

Nov. 1. Paid Hamilton Co. the amount owed on the note of September 2.

     15. Purchased store equipment from Shingo Equipment Co. for $80,000, paying
          $17,000 and issuing a series of seven 12% notes for $9,000 each, coming due
          at 30-day intervals.

Dec. 15. Paid the amount due Shingo Equipment Co. on the first note in the series
          issued on November 15.

     21. Settled a product liability lawsuit with a customer for $50,000, to be paid in
          January. Pride Polymers accrued the loss in a litigation claims payable
          account.

Instructions

1. Using a blank **Form GJ**, journalize the transactions.

2. Journalize the adjusting entry for each of the following accrued expenses
   at the end of the current year:

   b. Product warranty cost, $9,500.
   b. Interest on the six remaining notes owed to Shingo Equipment Co.

Blank Page

**Wage and tax statement data
and employer FICA tax**
Objectives 4, 5 ✔ 2. (e) $24,701.70

Sanchez Company began business on January 2 of last year. Salaries were paid to employees on the last day of each month, and social security tax, Medicare tax, and federal income tax were withheld in the required amounts. An employee who is hired in the middle of the month receives half the monthly salary for that month. All required payroll tax reports were filed, and the correct amount of payroll taxes was remitted by the company for the calendar year. Before the Wage and Tax Statements (Form W-2) could be prepared for distribution to employees and for filing with the Social Security Administration, the employees' earnings records were inadvertently destroyed.

None of the employees resigned or were discharged during the year, and there were no changes in salary rates. The social security tax was withheld at the rate of 6.0% on the first $70,000 of salary and Medicare tax at the rate of 1.5% on salary. Data on dates of employment, salary rates, and employees' income taxes withheld, which are summarized as follows, were obtained from personnel records and payroll records.

Employee	Date First Employed	Monthly Salary	Monthly Income Tax Withheld
Albright	June 2	$5,400	$1,137.00
Charles	Jan. 2	6,500	1,426.25
Given	Mar. 1	3,700	686.35
Nelson	Jan. 2	4,200	783.30
Quinn	Nov. 15	3,800	722.00
Ramsey	Apr. 15	3,000	535.50
Wu	Jan. 16	7,000	1,564.40

Instructions

1. Calculate the amounts to be reported on each employee's Wage and Tax Statement (Form W-2) for the year, arranging the data in the following form:

Employee	Gross Earnings	Federal Income Tax Withheld	Social Security Tax Withheld	Medicare Tax Withheld
Albright				
Charles				
Given				
Nelson				
Quinn				
Ramsey				
Wu				

Continued

2. Calculate the following employer payroll taxes for the year:

   (a) social security .... $_____

   (b) Medicare .... $_____

   (c) state unemployment compensation at 3.8%
        on the first $7,000 of each employee's earnings .... $_____

   (d) federal unemployment compensation at 0.8%
        on the first $7,000 of each employee's earnings .... $_____

   (e) total .... $_____

Chapter 12

Corporations: Organization, Capital Stock Transactions, and Dividends

If you own stock in a corporation, you are interested in how the stock is performing in the market. If you are considering buying stocks, you are interested in what your rights are as a stockholder and what kind of returns you might expect from the stock.

Although you may not own any stock, you probably buy services or products from corporations, and you may work for a corporation. Understanding the corporate form of organization will help you in your role as a stockholder, a consumer, or an employee. In this chapter, we discuss the characteristics of corporations, as well as how corporations account for stocks.

Learning objectives are listed for the exercises and problems that follow. Use the information to the right to determine the nature of the objective and the page number to refer to your textbook for a discussion of the topic.

Objective 1 — **Nature of a Corporation 465**
Describe the nature of the corporate form of organization.

Objective 2 — **Stockholders' Equity 467**
List the two main sources of stockholders' equity.

Objective 3 — **Sources of Paid-in Capital 468**
List the major sources of paid-in capital, including the various classes of stock.

Objective 4 — **Issuing Stock 471**
Journalize the entries for issuing stock.

Objective 5 — **Treasury Stock Transactions 474**
Journalize the entries for treasury stock transactions.

Objective 6 — **Stock Splits 475**
State the effect of stock splits on corporate financial statements.

Objective 7 — **Accounting for Dividends 476**
Journalize the entries for cash dividends and stock dividends.

Objective 8 — **Financial Analysis and Interpretation 479**
Compute and interpret the dividend yield on common stock.

Blank Page

Exercise 12–1

Dividends per share
Objective 3 - Text page 468 ✔ Preferred stock, 3rd year: $4.00

Davenport Inc., a developer of radiology equipment, has stock
outstanding as follows: 15,000 shares of $4 (4%) nonparticipating,
noncumulative preferred stock of $100 par, and 250,000 shares of $75 par
common. During its first five years of operations, the following amounts
were distributed as dividends: first year, none; second year, $45,000;
third year, $90,000; fourth year, $200,000; fifth year, $240,000. Calculate
the dividends per share on each class of stock for each of the five years.

Working
Papers
Plus

Chapter 12

Description	1st Year	2nd Year	3rd Year	4th Year	5th Year
Total Preferred Stock					
Total Common Stock					
Dividend Totals	0	45,000	90,000	200,000	240,000
Per Share Preferred					
Per Share Common					

Exercise 12–2

Dividends per share
Objective 3 - Text page 468 ✔ Preferred stock, 4th year: $8.00

Taft Inc., a computer software development firm, has stock outstanding
as follows: 25,000 shares of $3 (3%) cumulative, nonparticipating
preferred stock of $100 par, and 100,000 shares of $50 par common.
During its first five years of operations, the following amounts were
distributed as dividends: first year, none; second year, $20,000; third
year, $80,000; fourth year, $220,000; fifth year, $180,000. Calculate the
dividends per share on each class of stock for each of the five years.

Description	1st Year	2nd Year	3rd Year	4th Year	5th Year
Total Preferred Stock					
Total Common Stock					
Dividend Totals	0	20,000	80,000	220,000	180,000
Per Share Preferred					
Per Share Common					

Exercise 12–3

Entries for issuing par stock
Objective 4 - Text page 47⁻ ✔ b. $420,000

On June 5, Szabo Inc., a marble contractor, issued for cash 15,000 shares of $18 par common stock at $24, and on August 7, it issued for cash 5,000 shares of $10 par preferred stock at $12.

a. Journalize the entries for June 5 and August 7.

Date	Description	Debit	Credit

b. What is the total amount invested (total paid-in capital) by all stockholders as of August 7?

Exercise 12–4

Entries for issuing no-par stock
Objective 4 - Text page 471 ✔ b. $175,500

On January 3, Elco Corp., a carpet wholesaler, issued for cash 2,500 shares of no-par common stock (with a stated value of $50) at $65, and on May 15, it issued for cash 1,000 shares of $10 par preferred stock at $13.

a. Journalize the entries for January 3 and May 15, assuming that the common stock is to be credited with the stated value.

Date	Description	Debit	Credit

b. What is the total amount invested (total paid-in capital) by all stockholders as of May 15?

Exercise 12–5

Issuing stock for assets other than cash
Objective 4 - Text page 471

On April 10, Morriss Corporation, a wholesaler of hydraulic lifts, acquired land in exchange for 1,500 shares of $50 par common stock with a current market price of $82. Journalize the entry to record the transaction.

Date	Description	Debit	Credit

Exercise 12–6

Selected stock transactions
Objective 4 - Text page 47⁻

The Guitar Corp., an electric guitar retailer, was organized by Patty Hilderbrand, Ed Petty, and Kathy Yan. The charter authorized 50,000 shares of common stock with a par of $10. The following transactions affecting stockholders' equity were completed during the first year of operations:

a. Issued 800 shares of stock at par to Petty for cash.

b. Issued 100 shares of stock at par to Hilderbrand for promotional services rendered in connection with the organization of the corporation, and issued 900 shares of stock at par to Hilderbrand for cash.

c. Purchased land and a building from Yan. The building is mortgaged for $25,000 for 22 years at 9%, and there is accrued interest of $500 on the mortgage note at the time of the purchase. It is agreed that the land is to be priced at $30,000 and the building at $40,000, and that Yan's equity will be exchanged for stock at par. The corporation agreed to assume responsibility for paying the mortgage note and the accrued interest.

Journalize the entries to record the transactions.

Date	Description	Debit	Credit

Issuing stock
Objective 4 - Text page 471

Biomed Inc., with an authorization of 20,000 shares of preferred stock and 100,000 shares of common stock, completed several transactions involving its stock on July 1, the first day of operations. The trial balance at the close of the day follows:

Cash	450,000	
Land	90,000	
Buildings	60,000	
Preferred $5 Stock, $100 par		100,000
Paid-In Capital in Excess of Par—Preferred Stock		50,000
Common Stock, $50 par		320,000
Paid-In Capital in Excess of Par—Common Stock		130,000
	600,000	600,000

All shares within each class of stock were sold at the same price. The preferred stock was issued in exchange for the land and buildings.

Journalize the two entries to record the transactions summarized in the trial balance.

Date	Description	Debit	Credit

Issuing stock
Objective 4 - Text page 47⁻

Office Products Inc., a wholesaler of office products, was organized on January 7 of the current year, with an authorization of 50,000 shares of $3 noncumulative preferred stock, $100 par, and 250,000 shares of $20 par common stock.
The following selected transactions were completed during the first year of operations:

Jan.   7. Issued 30,000 shares of common stock at par for cash.
          9. Issued 900 shares of common stock at par to an attorney in payment of legal fees for organizing the corporation.
Feb.   4. Issued 8,500 shares of common stock in exchange for land, buildings, and equipment with fair market prices of $60,000, $120,000, and $12,000, respectively.
Mar. 15. Issued 5,000 shares of preferred stock at $101 for cash.

Journalize the transactions.

Date	Description	Debit	Credit

Treasury stock transactions
Objective 5 - Text page 474 ✔ b. $3,000 credit

Heavenly Inc. bottles and distributes spring water. On July 1 of the current year,
Heavenly Inc. reacquired 3,000 shares of its common stock at $40 per share. On
August 10, Heavenly Inc. sold 1,500 of the reacquired shares at $43 per share. The
remaining 1,500 shares were sold at $39 per share on December 19.

a. Journalize the transactions of July 1, August 10, and December 19.

Date	Description	Debit	Credit

b. What is the balance in
   Paid-In Capital from Sale
   of Treasury Stock on
   December 31 of the current
   year?

c. Where will the balance in
   Paid-In Capital from Sale
   of Treasury Stock be
   reported on the balance
   sheet?

d. For what reasons might
   Heavenly Inc. have
   purchased the treasury
   stock?

Exercise 12–10

Treasury stock transactions
Objective 5 - Text page 474 ✔ b. $44,000 credit

Spray Inc. develops and produces spraying equipment for lawn maintenance and industrial uses. On October 1 of the current year, Spray Inc. reacquired 7,500 shares of its common stock at $89 per share. On November 15, 2,000 of the reacquired shares were sold at $93 per share, and on December 28, 4,000 of the reacquired shares were sold at $98.

a. Journalize the transactions of October 1, November 15, and December 28.

Date	Description	Debit	Credit

b. What is the balance in Paid-In Capital from Sale of Treasury Stock on December 31 of the current year?

c. What is the balance in Treasury Stock on December 31 of the current year?

d. How will the balance in Treasury Stock be reported on the balance sheet?

Effect of stock split
Objective 6 - Text page 475 ✔ a. 75,000 shares

Flanagan Corporation wholesales ovens and ranges to restaurants throughout the Northeast. Flanagan Corporation, which had 15,000 shares of common stock outstanding, declared a 5-for-1 stock split (4 additional shares for each share issued).

a. What will be the
   number of shares
   outstanding after
   the split?

b. If the common stock
   had a market price of
   $175 per share before
   the stock split, what
   would be an
   approximate market
   price per share after
   the split?

Exercise 12–12

Effect of cash dividend and stock split
Objectives 6, 7

Indicate whether the following actions would (+) increase, (–) decrease, or (0) not affect Collier Inc.'s total assets, liabilities, and stockholders' equity:

	Assets	Liabilities	Stockholders' Equity
(1) Declaring a cash dividend	_____	_____	_____
(2) Paying the cash dividend declared in (1)	_____	_____	_____
(3) Declaring a stock dividend	_____	_____	_____
(4) Issuing stock certificates for the stock dividend declared in (3)	_____	_____	_____
(5) Authorizing and issuing stock certificates in a stock split	_____	_____	_____

Exercise 12–13

Entries for cash dividends
Objective 7 - Text page 476

The dates of importance in connection with a cash dividend of $60,000 on a corporation's common stock are January 3, January 27, and February 15. Journalize the entries required on each date.

Date	Description	Debit	Credit

Exercise 12–14   Name: _____

Entries for stock dividends
Objective 7 - Text page 476 ✔ b. (1) $342,500 (3) $642,000

" Quick-Fix Inc. is an HMO for twelve businesses in the Cincinnati area. The following account balances appear on the balance sheet of Quick-Fix Inc.: Common stock (50,000 shares authorized), $10 par, $300,000; Paid-in capital in excess of par—common stock, $42,500; and Retained earnings, $299,500. The board of directors declared a 2% stock dividend when the market price of the stock was $16 a share. Quick-Fix Inc. reported no income or loss for the current year. "

Dave Campbell
Board Member

a. Journalize the entries to record (1) the declaration of the dividend, capitalizing an amount equal to market value, and (2) the issuance of the stock certificates.

Date	Description	Debit	Credit

b. Determine the following amounts before the stock dividend was declared:

(1) total paid-in capital .... _____

(2) total retained earnings .... _____

(3) total stockholders' equity ... _____

c. Determine the following amounts after the stock dividend was declared and closing entries were recorded at the end of the year:

(1) total paid-in capital .... _____

(2) total retained earnings .... _____

(3) total stockholders' equity .. _____

Selected stock and dividend transactions
Objectives 4, 6, 7

Selected transactions completed by SWAT Boating Supply Corporation during the current fiscal year are as follows:

Jan.   9. Split the common stock 3 for 1 and reduced the par from $75 to $25 per share. After the split, there were 150,000 common shares outstanding.

Mar. 1. Declared semiannual dividends of $2 on 5,000 shares of preferred stock and $0.50 on the common stock to stockholders of record on March 25, payable on April 15.

Apr. 15. Paid the cash dividends.

Nov.30. Declared semiannual dividends of $2 on the preferred stock and $0.80 on the common stock (before the stock dividend). In addition, a 2% common stock dividend was declared on the common stock outstanding. The fair market value of the common stock is estimated at $51.

Dec. 30. Paid the cash dividends and issued the certificates for the common stock dividend.

Journalize the transactions.

Date	Description	Debit	Credit

Profitability Measures — The Common Stockholder

Dividend Yield

	2000	1999
Dividends per share of common	$ 0.80	$ 0.60
Market price per share of common	$20.50	$13.50
Dividend yield on common stock	3.9%	4.4%

Use: To indicate the rate of return to common stockholders in terms of dividends

Exercise 12–16

Dividend yield
Objective 8 - Text page 479

The finanical statements for **Hershey Foods Corporation** are presented in Appendix G at the end of the text.

a. Determine Hershey's dividend yield as of December 31, 1996 and 1995 on common stock (exclude Class B Common Stock).

Note: Hershey's common stock price was $43.75 and $32.50 on December 31, 1996 and 1995, respectively.

b. What conclusions can you reach from an analysis of these data?

Profiling a corporation

Select a public corporation you are familiar with or which interests you. Using the Internet, your school library, and other sources, develop a short (2 to 5 pages) profile of the corporation. Include in your profile the following information:

1. Name of the corporation.
2. State of incorporation.
3. Nature of its operations.
4. Total assets for the most recent balance sheet.
5. Total revenues for the most recent income statement.
6. Net income for the most recent income statement.
7. Classes of stock outstanding.
8. Market price of the stock outstanding.
9. High and low price of the stock for the past year.
10. Dividends paid for each share of stock during the past year.

In groups of three or four, discuss each corporate profile. Select one of the corporations, assuming that your group has $100,000 to invest in its stock. Summarize why your group selected the corporation it did and how financial accounting information may have affected your decision. Keep track of the performance of your corporation's stock for the remainder of the term.

Note: Most major corporations maintain "home pages" on the Internet. This home page provides a variety of information on the corporation and often includes the corporation's financial statements. In addition, the New York Stock Exchange Web site (**www.nyse.com**) includes links to the home pages of many listed companies. Financial statements can also be accessed using EDGAR, the electronic archives of financial statements filed with the Securities and Exchange Commission (SEC). The EDGAR Internet address is **www.sec.gov/edgarhp.htm**.

To obtain annual report information, type in a company name on the "Search EDGAR archives" form. EDGAR will list the reports available for the selected company. A company's annual report (along with much more information) is provided in its annual 10-K report to the SEC. Click on the 10-K (or 10-K405) report for the year you wish to download. If you wish, you can save the whole 10-K report to a file, then open it with your word processor.

Dividends on preferred and common stock
Objective 3 ✔ 1. Common dividends in 1996: $5,000

" Gallatin Corp. manufactures mountain bikes and distributes them through retail outlets in Colorado and Montana. Gallatin Corp. has declared the following annual dividends over a six-year period as shown in the table below. During the entire period, the outstanding stock of the company was composed of 10,000 shares of cumulative, nonparticipating, $2 preferred stock, $50 par, and 25,000 shares of common stock, $10 par. We need the information below prepared as soon as possible. Thanks. "

Marcos Garza
President

1. Calculate the total dividends and the per-share dividends declared on each class of stock for each of the six years. There were no dividends in arrears on January 1, 1996.

Year	Total Dividends	Preferred Dividends Total	Preferred Dividends Per Share	Common Dividends Total	Common Dividends Per Share
1996	$25,000				
1997	8,000				
1998	10,000				
1999	4,000				
2000	50,000				
2001	75,500				

2. Calculate the average annual dividend per share for each class of stock for the six-year period.

(a) Preferred stock .... $_____
(b) Common stock .... $_____

3. Assuming that the preferred stock was sold at par and common stock was sold at $10 at the beginning of the six-year period, calculate the percentage return on initial shareholders' investment, based on the average annual dividend per share for:

(a) Preferred stock .... _____%
(b) Common stock .... _____%

Blank Page

Selected stock transactions
Objectives 4, 5, 7

" Robin Corporation sells and services pipe welding equipment in Texas. The following selected accounts appear in the ledger of Robin Corporation on January 1, 2000, the beginning of the current fiscal year. We need your help in completing the items outlined below. "

Joyce Harris
President

Preferred 3% Stock, $100 par	$1,250,000
(20,000 shares authorized, 12,500 shares issued)	
Paid-ln Capital in Excess of Par—Preferred Stock	112,500
Common Stock, $10 par	4,000,000
(600,000 shares authorized, 400,000 shares issued)	
Paid-In Capital in Excess of Par—Common Stock	600,000
Retained Earnings	1,450,000

During the year, the corporation completed a number of transactions affecting the stockholders' equity. They are summarized as follows:

a. Purchased 20,000 shares of treasury common for $380,000.

b. Sold 5,000 shares of treasury common for $135,000.

c. Sold 3,000 shares of preferred 3% stock at $110.

d. Issued 50,000 shares of common stock at $32, receiving cash.

e. Sold 10,000 shares of treasury common for $170,000.

f. Declared cash dividends of $3 per share on preferred stock and $0.25 per share on common stock.

g. Paid the cash dividends.

Instructions

Using a **Form GJ**, journalize the entries to record the transactions. Identify each entry by letter.

Blank Page

Entries for selected corporate transactions
Objectives 4, 5, 7 ✔ 3. $1,850,470

" GPS Enterprises Inc. produces aeronautical navigation equipment. The stockholders' equity accounts of GPS Enterprises Inc., with balances on January 1 of the current fiscal year, are shown below. We need the information outlined below prepared as soon as possible. Thanks. "

Sung Park, President

Common Stock, $10 stated value...	$800,000
(100,000 shares authorized, 80,000 shares issued)	
Paid-In Capital in Excess of Stated Value	180,000
Retained Earnings..	497,750
Treasury Stock (4,000 shares, at cost)......................................	60,000

The following selected transactions occurred during the year:

Jan. 31. Paid cash dividends of $1 per share on the common stock. The dividend had been properly recorded when declared on December 28 of the preceding fiscal year for $76,000.

Mar. 7. Sold all of the treasury stock for $81,000.

May 5. Issued 10,000 shares of common stock for $210,000.

June 11. Received land from the Olinville City Council as a donation. The land had an estimated fair market value of $75,000.

July 30. Declared a 4% stock dividend on common stock, to be capitalized at the market price of the stock, which is $22 a share.

Aug. 27. Issued the certificates for the dividend declared on July 30.

Oct. 8. Purchased 2,000 shares of treasury stock for $42,500.

Dec. 20. Declared an $0.80-per-share dividend on common stock.

     31. Closed the credit balance of the income summary account, $182,500.

     31. Closed the two dividends accounts to Retained Earnings.

Instructions

1. Enter the January 1 balances, shown above, in the T accounts on the next page.

2. Using a **Form GJ**, journalize the entries to record the transactions and post to the nine selected accounts which are listed on the next page.

3. Determine the total stockholders' equity on December 31.

Continued

Common Stock		Treasury Stock

Paid-In Capital in Excess of Stated Value		Paid-In Capital from Sale of Treasury Stock

Retained Earnings		Donated Capital

Stock Dividends		Stock Dividends Distributable

Cash Dividends

Dividends on preferred and common stock
Objective 3 ✔ 1. Common dividends in 1998: $31,000

" TCX Inc. owns and operates movie theaters throughout Georgia and Alabama. TCX Inc. has declared the following annual dividends over a six-year period as shown in the table below. During the entire period, the outstanding stock of the company was composed of 5,000 shares of cumulative, nonparticipating, $10 preferred stock, $100 par, and 20,000 shares of common stock, $10 par. "

John Jordan
President

Instructions

1. Calculate the total dividends and the per-share dividends declared on each class of stock for each of the six years. There were no dividends in arrears on January 1, 1996.

Year	Total Dividends	Preferred Dividends		Common Dividends	
		Total	Per Share	Total	Per Share
1996	$32,000				
1997	65,000				
1998	84,000				
1999	60,000				
2000	72,000				
2001	95,000				

2. Calculate the average annual dividend per share for each class of stock for the six-year period.

   (a) Preferred stock .... $_____
   (b) Common stock .... $_____

3. Assuming that the preferred stock was sold at par and common stock was sold at $15 at the beginning of the six-year period, calculate the percentage return on initial shareholders' investment, based on the average annual dividend per share for:

   (a) Preferred stock .... _____%
   (b) Common stock .... _____%

Selected stock transactions
Objectives 4, 5, 7

Richard Gilberg
President

" The following selected accounts appear in the ledger of KWR Environmental Corporation on July 1, 1999, the beginning of the current fiscal year. We need your help in completing the items outlined below. "

Preferred 4% Stock, $50 par $350,000
    (10,000 shares authorized, 7,000 shares issued)

Paid-In Capital in Excess of Par—Preferred Stock 28,000

Common Stock, $20 par 500,000
    (50,000 shares authorized, 25,000 shares issued)

Paid-In Capital in Excess of Par—Common Stock 90,000

Retained Earnings 537,000

During the year, the corporation completed a number of transactions affecting the stockholders' equity. They are summarized as follows:

a. Issued 5,000 shares of common stock at $30, receiving cash.

b. Sold 1,000 shares of preferred 4% stock at $53.

c. Purchased 2,500 shares of treasury common for $60,000.

d. Sold 1,500 shares of treasury common for $45,000.

e. Sold 500 shares of treasury common for $11,500.

f. Declared cash dividends of $2 per share on preferred stock and $1 per share on common stock.

g. Paid the cash dividends.

Instructions

Using a **Form GJ**, journalize the entries to record the transactions. Identify each entry by letter.

Blank Page

Entries for selected corporate transactions
Objectives 4, 5, 7 ✔ 3. $2,692,090

" Pittard Enterprises Inc. manufactures bathroom fixtures. The stockholders' equity accounts of Pittard Enterprises Inc., with balances on January 1 of the current fiscal year, are as follows: "

Kenneth Martin
Controller

Common Stock, $25 stated value $1,250,000
    (100,000 shares authorized, 50,000 shares issued)
Paid-In Capital in Excess of Stated Value 250,000
Retained Earnings 725,000
Treasury Stock (2,500 shares, at cost) 80,000

The following selected transactions occurred during the year:

Jan. 20. Received land from the city as a donation. The land had an estimated fair market value of $150,000.

29. Paid cash dividends of $1 per share on the common stock. The dividend had been properly recorded when declared on December 30 of the preceding fiscal year for $47,500.

Mar. 3. Issued 6,000 shares of common stock for $240,000.

Apr. 1. Sold all of the treasury stock for $105,000.

July 1. Declared a 2% stock dividend on common stock, to be capitalized at the market price of the stock, which is $42 a share.

Aug. 11. Issued the certificates for the dividend declared on July 1.

Nov. 20. Purchased 2,500 shares of treasury stock for $90,000.

Dec. 21. Declared a $0.50-per-share dividend on common stock.

31. Closed the credit balance of the income summary account, $169,400.

31. Closed the two dividends accounts to Retained Earnings.

Instructions

1. Enter the January 1 balances, shown above, in the T accounts on the next page.

2. Using a **Form GJ**, journalize the entries to record the transactions and post to the nine selected accounts which are listed on the next page.

3. Determine the total stockholders' equity on December 31.

Continued

Common Stock

Treasury Stock

Paid-In Capital in Excess of Stated Value

Paid-In Capital from
Sale of Treasury Stock

Retained Earnings

Donated Capital

Stock Dividends Distributable

Stock Dividends

Cash Dividends

Chapter 13

Corporations: Income and Taxes, Stockholders' Equity, and Investments in Stocks

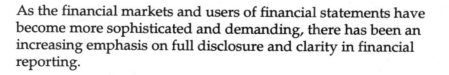

As the financial markets and users of financial statements have become more sophisticated and demanding, there has been an increasing emphasis on full disclosure and clarity in financial reporting.

Objective 1 — **Corporate Income Taxes 498**
Journalize the entries for corporate income taxes, including deferred income taxes.

Objective 2 — **Unusual Items that Affect the Income Statement 501**
Prepare an income statement reporting the following unusual items: discontinued operations, extraordinary items, and changes in accounting priciples.

Objective 3 — **Earnings per Common Share 503**
Prepare an income statement reporting earnings per share data.

Objective 4 — **Reporting Stockholders' Equity 505**
Prepare financial statement presentations of stockholders' equity.

Objective 5 — **Comprehensive Income 507**
Describe the concept and the reporting of comprehensive income.

Objective 6 — **Accounting for Investments in Stocks 508**
Describe the accounting for investments in stocks.

Objective 7 — **Business Combinations 513**
Describe alternative methods of combining businesses and how consolidated financial statements are prepared.

Objective 8 — **Financial Analysis and Interpretation 515**
Compute and interpret the price-earnings ratio.

Learning objectives are listed for the exercises and problems that follow. Use the information to the right to determine the nature of the objective and the page number to refer to your textbook for a discussion of the topic.

Blank Page

Income tax entries
Objective 1 - Text page 498

Journalize the entries to record the following selected transactions of Masters Grave Markers Inc.:

Apr. 15. Paid the first installment of the estimated income tax for the current fiscal year ending December 31, $60,000. No entry had been made to record the liability.

June 15. Paid the second installment of $60,000.

Sep. 15. Paid the third installment of $60,000.

Dec. 31. Recorded the estimated income tax liability for the year just ended and the deferred income tax liability, based on the transactions above and the following data:

    Income tax rate 40%
    Income before income tax $850,000
    Taxable income according to tax return 700,000

Jan. 15. Paid the fourth installment of $100,000.

Date	Description	Debit	Credit

Working Papers Plus

Chapter 13

Exercise 13-2

Extraordinary item
Objective 2 - Text page 50⁻

A company received life insurance proceeds on the death of its president before the end of its fiscal year. It intends to report the amount in its income statement as an extraordinary item.

Would this be in
conformity with
generally accepted
accounting
principles? Discuss.

Exercise 13-3

Extraordinary item
Objective 2 - Text page 501

On May 11, 1996, **ValuJet** tragically lost its Flight 592 en route from Miami to Atlanta. One hundred and ten people lost their lives. The crash cost ValuJet millions of dollars, including $2 million the company paid to the Federal Aviation Administration (FAA) to compensate it for the costs of the special inspections that were conducted. Do you believe that the costs related to this crash should be reported as an extraordinary item on the 1996 income statement of ValuJet?

Identifying extraordinary items
Objective 2 - Text page 501

Assume that the amount of each of the following items is material to the financial statements. Classify each item as either normally recurring (NR) or extraordinary (E).

_____ a. Salaries of corporate officers.

_____ b. Gain on sale of land condemned for public use.

_____ c. Uncollectible accounts expense.

_____ d. Interest revenue on notes receivable.

_____ e. Uninsured flood loss. (Flood insurance is unavailable because of periodic flooding in the area.)

_____ f. Loss on sale of fixed assets.

_____ g. Uninsured loss on building due to hurricane damage. The firm was organized in 1920 and had not previously incurred hurricane damage.

_____ h. Loss on disposal of equipment considered to be obsolete because of development of new technology.

Exercise 13–5

Income statement
Objectives 2, 3 - Text pages 501 and 503 ✔ Net income $87,000

Ocean-Way Inc. produces and distributes equipment for sailboats. On the basis of the following data for the current fiscal year ended April 30, prepare a multiple-step income statement for Ocean-Way Inc., including an analysis of earnings per share in the form illustrated in this chapter. There were 20,000 shares of $100 par common stock outstanding throughout the year. Use a **Form 2C** for your income statement.

Administrative expenses	$ 36,750
Cost of merchandise sold	620,000
Cumulative effect on prior years of changing to a different depreciation method (decrease in income)	50,000
Gain on condemnation of land (extraordinary item)	37,750
Income tax reduction applicable to change in depreciation method	18,200
Income tax applicable to gain on condemnation of land	7,750
Income tax reduction applicable to loss from discontinued operations	45,500
Income tax applicable to ordinary income	105,200
Loss on discontinued operations	114,500
Sales	985,500
Selling expenses	65,750

Exercise 13-6

Income statement

Objectives 2, 3 - Text pages 501 and 503 ✔ Correct EPS for net income, $13.55

Ultra Sound Inc. sells automotive and home stereo equipment. It has 50,000 shares of $100 par common stock and 10,000 shares of $2, $100 par cumulative preferred stock outstanding as of December 31, 2000. It also holds 10,000 shares of common stock as treasury stock as of December 31, 2000. How many errors can you find in the following income statement for the year ended December 31, 2000?

Ultra Sound Inc.
Income Statement
For the Year Ended December 31, 2000

Net sales		$8,450,000
Cost of merchandise sold		6,100,000
Gross profit		$2,350,000
Operating expenses:		
Selling expenses	$1,020,000	
Administrative expenses	280,000	1,300,000
Income from continuing operations before income tax		$1,050,000
Income tax expense		420,000
Income from continuing operations		$ 530,000
Cumulative effect on prior years' income (decrease)		
of changing to a different depreciation method		
(net of applicable income tax of $36,000)		(92,000)
Correction of error (understatement) in December 31, 1999		
physical inventory (net of applicable income tax of $20,000)		30,000
Income before condemnation of land and discontinued operations		$ 468,000
Extraordinary item:		
Gain on condemnation of land, net of applicable		
income tax of $80,000		120,000
Loss on discontinued operations (net of applicable		
income tax of $64,000)		(96,000)
Net income		$ 492,000

Earnings per common share:	
Income from continuing operations	$10.60
Cumulative effect on prior years' income (decrease) of	
changing to a different depreciation method	(1.84)
Correction of error (understatement) in December 31, 1999	
physical inventory	0.60
Income before extraordinary item and discontinued operations	$ 9.36
Extraordinary item	2.40
Loss on discontinued operations	(1.92)
Net income	$ 9.84

Reporting paid-in capital
Objective 4 - Text page 505 ✔ Total paid-in capital, $1,628,000

The following accounts and their balances were selected from the unadjusted trial balance of FastCo Inc., a freight forwarder, at December 31, the end of the curent fiscal year:

Preferred $1 Stock, $50 par	$ 500,000
Paid-In Capital in Excess of Par—Preferred Stock	75,000
Common Stock, no par, $10 stated value	750,000
Paid-In Capital in Excess of Par—Common Stock	140,000
Paid-In Capital from Sale of Treasury Stock	13,000
Donated Capital	150,000
Retained Earnings	1,230,000

Prepare the Paid-In Capital portion of the Stockholders' Equity section of the balance sheet. There are 100,000 shares of common stock authorized and 50,000 shares of preferred stock authorized.

Exercise 13–8

Stockholders' equity section of balance sheet
Objective 4 - Text page 505 ✔ Total stockholders' equity, $582,000

The following accounts and their balances appear in the ledger of McCopy Inc. on September 30 of the current year:

Common Stock, $10 par $250,000
Paid-In Capital in Excess of Par 40,000
Paid-In Capital from Sale of Treasury Stock 7,000
Retained Earnings 310,000
Treasury Stock 25,000

Prepare the Stockholders' Equity section of the balance sheet as of September 30. Thirty thousand shares of common stock are authorized, and 2,500 shares have been reacquired.

Exercise 13–9

Stockholders' equity section of balance sheet
Objective 4 - Text page 505 ✔ Total stockholders' equity, $2,637,500

Le'Car Inc. retails racing products for BMWs, Porsches, and Ferraris. The following accounts and their balances appear in the ledger of Le'Car Inc. on December 31, the end of the current year:

Common Stock, $10 par .... $ 800,000
Paid-In Capital in Excess of Par—Common Stock 127,500
Paid-In Capital in Excess of Par—Preferred Stock 37,500
Paid-In Capital from Sale of Treasury Stock—Common 15,000
Preferred $2 Stock, $100 par 500,000
Retained Earnings 1,252,500
Treasury Stock—Common 95,000

Ten thousand shares of preferred and 150,000 shares of common stock are authorized. There are 5,000 shares of common stock held as treasury stock.

Using a blank sheet of paper, prepare the Stockholders' Equity section of the balance sheet as of December 31, the end of the current year.

Exercise 13–10 _____   Name: _____

Retained earnings statement
Objective 4 - Text page 505

McArthur Corporation, a manufacturer of industrial pumps, reports the following results for the year ending August 31, 2000:

Retained earnings, September 1, 1999 .... $1,356,800
Net income 472,000
Cash dividends declared 100,000
Stock dividends declared 85,000

Prepare a retained earnings statement for the fiscal year ended August 31, 2000.

Exercise 13–11 _____

Stockholders' equity section of balance sheet
Objective 4 - Text page 505 ✔ Corrected total stockholders' equity, $1,435,000

How many errors can you find in the following Stockholder's Equity section of the balance sheet prepared as of the end of the current year?

Stockholders' Equity

Paid-in capital:
  Preferred $2 stock, cumulative, $100 par
    (2,500 shares authorized and issued) $250,000
  Excess of issue price over par .... 60,000 $ 310,000
  Retained earnings 340,000
  Treasury stock (4,000 shares at cost) 75,000
  Dividends payable 60,000
    Total paid-in capital .... $ 785,000
Common stock, $15 par (50,000 shares
  authorized, 40,000 shares issued) $810,000
Donated capital 50,000
Organization costs 120,000   980,000
Total stockholders' equity $1,765,000

Exercise 13–12

Statement of stockholders' equity
Objective 4 - Text page 505 ✔ Total stockholders' equity, Dec. 31, $1,787,000

Use textbook and blank paper to solve this exercise.

Exercise 13–13

**Temporary investments in
marketable securities**
Objective 6 - Text page 508

During its first year of operations, Loran Corporation
purchased the following securities as a temporary investment:

Security	Shares Purchased	Cost	Cash Dividends Received
Geer Inc.	5,000	$18,000	$1,500
Jones Corp.	3,000	24,000	600

a. Journalize the purchase of the temporary investments for cash.

b. Journalize the receipt of the dividends.

Date	Description	Debit	Credit

**Financial statement reporting
of temporary investments**
Objectives 5, 6 - Text pages 507 and 508 ✔ b. Comprehensive income, $127,800

Using the data for Loran Corporation in Exercise 13-13, assume that as of December 31, 2000, the Geer Inc. stock had a market value of $5 per share and the Jones Corp. stock had a market value of $10 per share. For the year ending December 31, 2000, Loran Corporation had net income of $120,000. Its tax ratio is 40%.

a. Prepare the balance sheet
    presentation for the
    temporary investments.

b. Prepare a statement of
    income and comprehensive
    income presentation for the
    temporary investments.

Exercise 13–15

**Entries for investment in stock, receipt of
dividends, and sale of shares**
Objective 6 - Text page 508

On February 3, Adair Corporation acquired 1,500 shares of the 40,000
outstanding shares of TZ Co. common stock at 60 1/2 plus commission charges
of $510. On August 13, a cash dividend of $1 per share and a 4% stock dividend
were received. On November 15, 500 shares were sold at 62, less commission
charges of $275.

Journalize the entries to record (a) the purchase of the stock, (b) the receipt of
dividends, and (c) the sale of the 500 shares.

Date	Description	Debit	Credit

Exercise 13–16

Equity method
Objective 6 - Text page 508

The following note to the consolidated financial statements for
The Goodyear Tire and Rubber Co. relates to the principles
of consolidation used in preparing the financial statements:

*The Company's investments in 20% to 50% owned companies in which it has
the ability to exercise significant influence over operating and financial policies
are accounted for by the equity method. Accordingly, the Company's share of
the earnings of these companies is included in consolidated net income.*

Is it a requirement
that Goodyear use
the equity method
in this situation?
Explain.

**Entries using equity method for
stock investment**
Objective 6 - Text page 508

" At a total cost of $9,000,000, Eastern Corporation acquired
75,000 shares of Southern Corp. common stock as a long-term
investment. My corporation uses the equity method of
accounting for this investment. Southern Corp. has 250,000
shares of common stock outstanding, including the shares
acquired by Eastern Corporation. Journalize the entries by
Eastern Corporation to record the following information: "

Jason Chartier
Eastern Corporation, CEO

a. Southern Corp. reports net income of $500,000 for the current period.

b. A cash dividend of $1.20 per common share is paid by Southern Corp.
    during the current period.

Date	Description	Debit	Credit

**Eliminations for consolidated
income statement**
Objective 7 - Text page 513 ✔ a. (1) $100,000; b. $1,285,000

For the current year ended June 30, the results of operations of Montana Corporation and its wholly owned subsidiary, Blue Sky Enterprises, are as follows:

	Montana Corporation		Blue Sky Enterprises	
Sales		$2,150,000		$650,000
Cost of merchandise sold	$725,000		$340,000	
Selling expenses	255,000		75,000	
Administrative expenses	85,000		35,000	
Interest expense (revenue)	(12,000)	1,053,000	12,000	462,000
Net income		$1,097,000		$188,000

During the year, Montana sold merchandise to Blue Sky for $100,000. The merchandise was sold by Blue Sky to nonaffiliated companies for $150,000. Montana's interest revenue was realized from a long-term loan to Blue Sky.

a. Determine the amounts to be eliminated from the following items in preparing a consolidated income statement for the current year:

   (1) sales .... _____

   (2) cost of merchandise sold .... _____

b. Determine the consolidated net income.

Analyzing Stock Investments

Accounting: Earnings Per Share

$$\frac{\text{Net Income}}{\text{Common Shares}} = \text{Earnings Per Share}$$

Investing: Price - Earnings Ratio

$$\frac{\text{Market Price Per Share}}{\text{Earnings Per Share}} = \text{Price-Earnings Ratio}$$

Price – Earnings Ratio

The price-earnings ratio represents how much the market is willing to pay per dollar of a company's earnings. This indicates the market's assessment of a firm's <u>growth potential</u> and <u>future earnings prospects</u>.

An example:	2000	1999
Market price per share	$20.50	$13.50
Earnings per share	$1.64	$1.35
Price-earnings ratio	12.5	10.0

The price-earnings ratio indicates that a share of common stock was selling for 10 times earnings for 1999 and 12.5 times for 2000.

Exercise 13–19

Price-earnings ratio
Objective 8 - Text page 515

The finanical statements for **Hershey Foods Corporation** are presented in Appendix G at the end of the text.

a. Determine the price-earnings ratio for Hershey Foods Corporation for 1996 and 1995. The market price of Hershey Foods common stock was 43 3/4 and 32 1/2 on December 31, 1996 and 1995, respectively. (Use only the Class A common stock.)

b. What conclusions can you reach by considering the price-earnings ratio?

Extraordinary items and discontinued operations

In groups of three or four students, search company anual reports, news releases, or the Internet for extraordinary items and announcements of discontinued operations. Identify the most ususual extraordinary item in your group. Also, select a discontinued operation of a well-known company that might be familiar to other students or might interest them.

Prepare a brief analysis of the earnings per share impact of both the extraordinary item and the discontinued operation. Estimate the *potential* impact on the company's market price by multiplying the current price-earnings ratio by the earnings per share amount of each item.

One Internet site that has annual reports is EDGAR (Electronic Data Gathering, Analysis, and Retrieval), the electronic archives of financial statements filed with the Securities and Exchange Commission. The EDGAR address is: **www.sec.gov/edgarhp.htm**

To obtain annual report information, type in a company name on the "Search EDGAR archives" form. EDGAR will list the reports available for the selected company. A company's annual report (along with other information) is provided in its annual 10-K report to the SEC. Click on the 10-K (or 10-K405) report for the year you wish to download. If you wish, you can save the whole 10-K report to a file, then open it with your word processor.

Income tax allocation
Objective 1 ✔ 1. Year-end balance, 3rd year, $51,500

" Differences between the accounting methods applied to accounts and
financial reports and those used in determining taxable income yielded
the following amounts for the first four years of our corporation's
operations: "

	First Year	Second Year	Third Year	Fourth Year
Income before income taxes	$250,000	$340,000	$420,000	$495,000
Taxable income	170,000	282,500	428,750	510,000

" The income tax rate for each of the four years was 40% of
taxable income, and each year's taxes were promptly paid.
Using the following instructions, your assignment is to complete
the table below. "

Christin Roberts
Controller

Instructions

1. Determine for each year the amounts described in the following table.

2. Total the first three amount columns.

Year	Income Tax Deducted on Income Statement	Income Tax Payments for the Year	Deferred Income Tax Payable	
			Year's Addition (Deduction)	Year-End Balance
First				
Second				
Third				
Fourth				
Total				

Blank Page

Income tax allocation

Objective 1 ✔ 1. Year-end balance, 3rd year, $70,500

" Differences between the accounting methods applied to accounts and financial reports and those used in determining taxable income yielded the following amounts for the first four years of our corporation's operations: "

	First Year	Second Year	Third Year	Fourth Year
Income before income tax	$320,000	$450,000	$400,000	$649,000
Taxable income	250,000	360,000	383,750	678,750

" The income tax rate for each of the four years was 40% of taxable income, and each year's taxes were promptly paid. Using the following instructions, your assignment is to complete the table below. "

Rick Lindgren
V. P. Finance

Instructions

1. Determine for each year the amounts described in the following table.

2. Total the first three amount columns.

Year	Income Tax Deducted on Income Statement	Income Tax Payments for the Year	Deferred Income Tax Payable	
			Year's Addition (Deduction)	Year-End Balance
First				
Second				
Third				
Fourth				
Total				

Chapter 14

Bonds Payable and Investments in Bonds

Cash and other assets may be obtained by a corporation through issuing its stock. A corporation may also finance operations through retained earnings, which in some cases is accompanied by the issuance of stock dividends. A corporation may finance its operations by borrowing money on a long-term basis. This chapter discusses accounting principles and concepts related to the issuance of long-term debt.

Learning objectives are listed for the exercises and problems that follow. Use the information to the right to determine the nature of the objective and the page number to refer to your textbook for a discussion of the topic.

Objective 1 — Financing Corporations 537
Compute the potential impact of long-term borrowing on the earnings per share of a corporation.

Objective 2 — Characteristics of Bonds Payable 539
Describe the characteristics of bonds.

Objective 3 — The Present-Value Concept and Bonds Payable 539
Compute the present value of bonds payable.

Objective 4 — Accounting for Bonds Payable 543
Journalize entries for bonds payable.

Objective 5 — Bond Sinking Funds 547
Describe bond sinking funds.

Objective 6 — Bond Redemption 548
Journalize entries for bond redemptions.

Objective 7 — Investments in Bonds 549
Journalize entries for the purchase, interest, discount and premium amortization, and sale of bond investments.

Objective 8 — Corporation Balance Sheet 552
Prepare a corporation balance sheet.

Objective 9 — Financial Analysis and Interpretation 554
Compute and interpret the number of times interest charges earned.

Blank Page

Exercise 14–1   Name: _____

Effect of financing on earnings per share
Objective 1 - Text page 537   ✔ a. $0.30

Nevin Co., which produces and sells skiing equipment, is financed as follows:

Bonds payable, 10% (issued at face amount) $2,000,000
Preferred $9 stock (nonparticipating), $100 par 2,000,000
Common stock, $10 par 2,000,000

Working
Papers
Plus

Chapter 14

Income tax is estimated at 40% of income.

Determine the earnings per share of common stock, assuming that the income before bond interest and income tax is (a) $600,000, (b) $1,000,000, and (c) $2,500,000.

	$600,000	$1,000,000	$2,500,000
Earnings before bond interest & income tax	$600,000	$1,000,000	$2,500,000
Bond interest			
Balance			
Income tax			
Net income			
Dividends on preferred stock			
Earnings available for common stock			
Earnings per share on common stock			

Exercise 14–2

Evaluating alternative financing plans
Objective 1 - Text page 537

Based upon the data in Exercise 14–1, discuss factors other than earnings per share that should be considered in evaluating such financing plans.

Exercise 14-3
_____

Present value of amounts due
Objective 3 - Text page 539 ✔ a. $8,164

Determine the present value of $10,000 to be received in three years, using an interest rate of 7%, compounded annually, as follows:

a. By successive
   divisions.
   (Round to the
   nearest dollar.)

b. By using the
   present value
   table in textbook
   Exhibit 3.

Exercise 14-4
_____

Present value of annuity
Objective 3 - Text page 539 ✔ a. $17,129

Determine the present value of $5,000 to be received at the end of each of four years, using an interest rate of 6 1/2%, compounded annually, as follows:

a. By successive
   computations, using
   the present value
   table in textbook
   Exhibit 3.

b. By using the present
   value table in
   textbook Exhibit 4.

Exercise 14-5
_____

Present value of an annuity
Objective 3 - Text page 539 ✔ $511,334.40

On January 1, 2000, you win
$1,000,000 in the state lottery. The
$1,000,000 prize will be paid in
equal installments of $40,000 over
25 years. The payments will be
made on December 31 of each
year, beginning on December 31,
2000. If the current interest rate is
6%, determine the present value
of your winnings. Use the present
value tables in Appendix A of
your textbook.

_____

Exercise 14–6

Present value of an annuity
Objective 3 - Text page 539

Assume the same data as in Exercise 14–5, except that the current interest rate is 12%. Will the present value of your winnings using an interest rate of 12% be one-half the present value of your winnings using an interest rate of 6%? Why or why not?

Exercise 14–7

Present value of bonds payable; discount
Objectives 3, 4 ✔ $9,227,796

Beall Co. produces and sells bottle capping equipment for soft drink and spring water bottlers. To finance its operations, Beall Co. issued $10,000,000 of five-year, 8% bonds with interest payable semiannually at an effective interest rate of 10%. Determine the present value of the bonds payable, using the present value tables in textbook Exhibits 3 and 4.

Exercise 14–8

Present value of bonds payable; premium
Objectives 3, 4 ✔ $5,188,439

Whitsell Automotive Alarms Co. issued $5,000,000 of five-year, 12% bonds with interest payable semiannually, at an effective interest rate of 11%. Determine the present value of the bonds payable, using the present value tables in textbook Exhibits 3 and 4.

Exercise 14–9

Bond price
Objectives 3, 4 - Text pages 539 and 543

IBM Corporation 8 3/8% bonds due in 2019 were reported in
The Wall Street Journal as selling for 115 on October 7, 1997.

Were the bonds
selling at a premium
or at a discount on
October 7, 1997?
Explain.

Exercise 14–10

Entries for issuing bonds
Objective 4 - Text page 543

"Wilmer Co. produces and distributes fiber optic cable for use
by telecommunications companies. We issued $7,500,000 of 20-
year, 8% bonds on April 1 of the current year, with interest
payable on April 1 and October 1. Our fiscal year is the calendar
year. Journalize the entries to record the following selected
transactions for the current year."

J. J. Wilmer, Owner

Apr. 1. Issued the bonds for cash at their face amount.
Oct. 1. Paid the interest on the bonds.
Dec. 31. Recorded accrued interest for three months.

Date	Description	Debit	Credit

**Entries for issuing bonds and amortizing
discount by straight-line method**
Objective 4 - Text page 543 ✔ b. $917,753

On the first day of its fiscal year, Ryland Company issued $8,000,000 of five-year, 10% bonds to finance its operations of producing and selling home electronics equipment. Interest is payable semiannually. The bonds were issued at an effective interest rate of 12%, resulting in Ryland Company receiving cash of $7,411,236.

a. Journalize the entries to record the following:

1. Sale of the bonds.

2. First semiannual interest payment. (Amortization of discount is to be recorded annually.)

3. Second semiannual interest payment.

4. Amortization of discount at the end of the first year, using the straight-line method. (Round to the nearest dollar.)

Date	Description	Debit	Credit

b. Determine the amount of the bond interest expense for the first year.

**Computing bond proceeds, entries
for bond issuing, and amortizing
premium by straight-line method**
Objectives 3, 4 - Text pages 539 and 543

" Markle Corporation wholesales oil and grease products
to equipment manufacturers. On March 1, 2000, we
issued $5,000,000 of five-year, 12% bonds at an effective
interest rate of 10%. Interest is payable semiannually on
March 1 and September 1. Please journalize the entries to
record the following transactions. "

Charles Connell
General Manager

a. Sale of bonds on March 1, 2000. (Use the tables of present values in
textbook Exhibits 3 and 4 to determine the bond proceeds.)

b. First interest payment on September 1, 2000, and amortization of bond
premium for six months, using the straight-line method. (Round to the
nearest dollar.)

Date	Description	Debit	Credit

Calculations

**Entries for issuing and
calling bonds; loss**
Objectives 4, 6 - Text pages 543 and 548

" Gier Corp., a wholesaler of office furniture, issued $9,000,000 of 20-year, 8% callable bonds on March 1, 2000, with interest payable on March 1 and September 1. Our fiscal year is the calendar year. We need your help in understanding the transactions listed below. Thanks. "

Susan Lofelmaker
General Manager

Journalize the entries to record the following selected transactions:

2000
Mar. 1. Issued the bonds for cash at their face amount.
Sep. 1. Paid the interest on the bonds.

2004
Sep. 1. Called the bond issue at 101 1/2, the rate provided in the bond indenture. (Omit entry for payment of interest.)

Date	Description	Debit	Credit

Exercise 14–14

**Entries for issuing and
calling bonds; gain**
Objectives 4, 6 - Text pages 543 and 548

" Mosser Corp. produces and sells automotive and aircraft safety belts. To finance our operations, we issued $12,000,000 of 30-year, 7% callable bonds on June 1, 1999, with interest payable on June 1 and December 1. Our fiscal year is the calendar year. We need your help in understanding the transactions listed below. Thanks. "

Harry Mosser, Owner

Journalize the entries to record the following selected transactions:

1999
June 1. Issued the bonds for cash at their face amount.
Dec. 1. Paid the interest on the bonds.

2005
Dec. 1. Called the bond issue at 99, the rate provided in the bond indenture.
(Omit entry for payment of interest.)

Date	Description	Debit	Credit

Reporting bonds
Objectives 5, 6, 8 - Text pages 547, 548, and 552

At the beginning of the current year, two bond issues (MM and QQ) were outstanding. During the year, bond issue MM was redeemed and a significant loss on the redemption of bonds was reported as Other Expense on the income statement. At the end of the year, bond issue QQ was reported as a current liability because its maturity date was early in the following year. A sinking fund of cash and securities sufficient to pay the series QQ bonds was reported in the balance sheet as *Investments*.

Can you find any
flaws in the
reporting practices
related to the two
bond issues?

Exercise 14–16

Amortizing discount on bond investment
Objective 7 - Text page 549

A company purchased a $1,000, 20-year zero-coupon bond for $189 to yield 8.5% to maturity. How is the interest revenue computed?

Exercise 14–17

**Entries for purchase and sale
of investment in bonds; loss**
Objective 7 - Text page 549

Crone Co. sells optical supplies to opticians and ophthalmologists. Journalize the entries to record the following selected transactions of Crone Company:

a. Purchased for cash $200,000 of Lambert Co. 6% bonds at 103 plus accrued interest of $2,000.

b. Received first semiannual interest.

c. At the end of the first year, amortized $250 of the bond premium.

d. Sold the bonds at 99 plus accrued interest of $4,000. The bonds were carried at $203,500 at the time of the sale.

Date	Description	Debit	Credit

**Entries for purchase and sale
of investment in bonds; gain**
Objective 7 - Text page 549

Rockne Company develops and sells graphics software for use by architects. Journalize the entries to record the following selected transactions of Rockne Company:

a. Purchased for cash $150,000 of Culp Co. 6% bonds at 97 plus accrued interest of $1,500.

b. Received first semiannual interest.

c. Amortized $200 on the bond investment at the end of the first year.

d. Sold the bonds at 99 plus accrued interest of $3,000. The bonds were carried at $148,000 at the time of the sale.

Date	Description	Debit	Credit

Solvency Measures — The Long-Term Creditor

Number of Times Interest Charges Earned

	1997	1996
Income before income tax	$ 900,000	$ 800,000
Add interest expense	$ 300,000	$ 250,000
Amount available for interest	$1,200,000	$1,050,000
Number of times earned	4.0 times	4.2 times

Use: To assess the risk to debtholders in terms of number of times interest charges were earned

---

Exercise 14–19

Number of times interest charges earned
Objective 9 - Text page 554

The financial statements for **Hershey Foods Corporation** are presented in Appendix G at the end of the text.

a. Determine the number of times interest charges were earned for the years ended December 31, 1996 and 1995. (The makeup of "interest expense, net" as reported on the income statement is described in Note 6 to the statements. Use only the interest on long-term and lease obligations and short-term debt in your computation.)

b. What conclusions can be drawn from the data concerning the risk of the debtholders for the interest payments and the general financial strength of Hershey?

Amortize discount by interest method
Text page 556 ✔ b. $892,029

On the first day of its fiscal year, Ryland Company issued $8,000,000 of five-year, 10% bonds to finance its operations of producing and selling home electronics equipment. Interest is payable semiannually. The bonds were issued at an effective interest rate of 12%, resulting in Ryland Company receiving cash of $7,411,236.

a. Journalize the entries to record the following:

  1. Sale of the bonds.

  2. First semiannual interest payment. (Amortization of discount is to be recorded annually.)

  3. Second semiannual interest payment.

  4. Amortization of discount at the end of the first year, using the interest method. (Round to the nearest dollar.)

Date	Description	Debit	Credit

b. Compute the amount of the bond interest expense for the first year.

Appendix Exercise 14-21

Amortize premium by interest method

Text page 557 ✔ b. $537,073

Markle Corporation wholesales oil and grease products to equipment manufacturers. On March 1, 2000, Markle Corporation issued $5,000,000 of five-year, 12% bonds at an effective interest rate of 10%, receiving cash of $5,386,072. Interest is payable semiannually on March 1 and September 1. Markle Corporation's fiscal year begins on March 1.

a. Journalize the entries to record the following:

    1. First interest payment on September 1, 2000. (Amortization of premium is to be recorded annually.)

    2. Second interest payment on March 1, 2001.

    3. Amortization of premium at the end of the first year, using the interest method. (Round to the nearest dollar.)

Date	Description	Debit	Credit

b. Determine the bond interest expense for the first year.

**Computing bond proceeds;
amortizing premium by interest
method, and interest expense**
Text page 557 ✔ a. $10,386,057 ✔ b. $30,697

" Fabian Co. produces and sells spray painting equipment for
construction contractors. On the first day of our fiscal year, we
issued $10,000,000 of five-year, 11% bonds at an effective interest
rate of 10%, with interest payable semiannually. We need your
help. Please compute the following, presenting figures used in
your computations, rounding to the nearest dollar. "

Ben Rodriquez
President

a. The amount of cash
proceeds from the sale of
the bonds. (Use the tables
of present values in
textbook Exhibits 3 and 4.)

b. The amount of premium
to be amortized for the
first semiannual interest
payment period, using the
interest method.

c. The amount of premium
to be amortized for the
second semiannual
interest payment period,
using the interest method.

d. The amount of the bond
interest expense for the
first year.

Activity 14–5 Into the Real World

Investing in bonds

Select a bond from listings that appear daily in *The Wall Street Journal*, and summarize the information related to the bond you select. Include the following information in your summary:

1. Contract rate of interest
2. Year when the bond matures
3. Current yield (effective rate of interest)
4. Closing price of bond (indicate date)
5. Other information noted about the bond, such as whether it is a zero-coupon bond (see the Explanatory Notes to the listings)

In groups of three or four, share the information you developed about the bond you selected. As a group, select one bond to invest $100,000 in and prepare a justification for your choice for presentation to the class. For example, your justification should include a consideration of risk and return.

Activity 14–6 Into the Real World

Bond ratings

Moody's Investors Service maintains a Web site at **www.Moodys.com**. One of the services offered at this site is a listing of announcements of recent bond rating changes. Visit this site and read over some of these announcements. Write down several of the reasons provided for rating downgrades and upgrades. If you were a bond investor or bond issuer, would you care if Moody's changed the rating on your bonds? Why or why not?

Problem 14–1A   Name: _____

Effect of financing on earnings per share
Objective 1 ✔ 1. Plan 3: $7.36

Three different plans for financing a $10,000,000 corporation are under consideration
by its organizers. Under each of the following plans, the securities will be issued at
their par or face amount and the income tax rate is estimated at 40% of income.

	Plan 1	Plan 2	Plan 3
12% bonds			$ 5,000,000
Preferred 8% stock, $100 par		$ 5,000,000	2,500,000
Common stock, $10 par	$10,000,000	5,000,000	2,500,000
Total	$10,000,000	$10,000,000	$10,000,000

Instructions

1. Determine for each plan the earnings per share of common stock, assuming
   that the income before bond interest and income tax is $4,000,000.

	Plan 1	Plan 2	Plan 3
Earnings before interest and income tax			
Deduct interest on bonds			
Income before income tax			
Deduct income tax			
Net income			
Dividends on preferred stock			
Available for dividends on common			
Shares of common stock outstanding			
Earnings per share on common stock			

2. Determine for each plan the earnings per share of common stock, assuming
   that the income before bond interest and income tax is $1,000,000.

	Plan 1	Plan 2	Plan 3
Earnings before interest and income tax			
Deduct interest on bonds			
Income before income tax			
Deduct income tax			
Net income			
Dividends on preferred stock			
Available for dividends on common			
Shares of common stock outstanding			
Earnings per share on common stock			

Continued

3. Discuss the
   advantages and
   disadvantages of
   each plan.

**Present value; bond premium; entries
for bonds payable transactions**
Objectives 3, 4 ✔ 3. $268,844

" Willard Corporation produces and sells burial vaults. On July 1,
2000, we issued $5,000,000 of ten-year, 12% bonds at an effective
interest rate of 10%. Interest on the bonds is payable semiannually on
December 31 and June 30. The fiscal year of the company is the
calendar year. Please complete the items below. "

Samuel Whitefish,
President

Instructions

1. Journalize the entry to record the amount of the cash proceeds from the sale of
   the bonds. Use the tables of present values in Appendix A to compute the cash
   proceeds, rounding to the nearest dollar.

Date	Description	Debit	Credit

2. Journalize the entries to record the following:

   a. The first semiannual interest payment on December 31, 2000, and the
      amortization of the bond premium, using the straight-line method.
      (Round to the nearest dollar.)

   b. The interest payment on June 30, 2001, and the amortization of the bond
      premium, using the straight-line method.

Date	Description	Debit	Credit

Continued

3. Determine the total
   interest expense for 2000.

4. Will the bond proceeds
   always be greater than
   the face amount of the
   bonds when the contract
   rate is greater than the
   market rate of interest?
   Explain.

**Present value; bond discount; entries
for bonds payable transactions**
Objectives 3, 4 ✔ 3. $694,407

" On July 1, 1999, Geyser Corporation, a wholesaler of used robotic
equipment, issued $12,000,000 of ten-year, 11% bonds at an effective
interest rate of 12%. Interest on the bonds is payable semiannually on
December 31 and June 30. The fiscal year of the company is the
calendar year. Please complete the items below. "

Terrie Cam, President

Instructions

1. Journalize the entry to record the amount of the cash proceeds from the sale of
the bonds. Use the tables of present values in Appendix A to compute the
cash proceeds, rounding to the nearest dollar.

Date	Description	Debit	Credit

2. Journalize the entries to record the following:

   a. The first semiannual interest payment on December 31, 1999, and the
   amortization of the bond discount, using the straight-line method.
   (Round to the nearest dollar.)

   b. The interest payment on June 30, 2000, and the amortization of the bond
   discount, using the straight-line method.

Date	Description	Debit	Credit

Continued

3. Determine the total interest expense for 1999.

4. Will the bond proceeds always be less than the face amount of the bonds when the contract rate is less than the market rate of interest? Explain.

Effect of financing on earnings per share
Objective 1 ✔ 1. Plan 3: $7.60

Three different plans for financing a $15,000,000 corporation are under consideration by its organizers. Under each of the following plans, the securities will be issued at their par or face amount, and the income tax rate is estimated at 40% of income.

	Plan 1	Plan 2	Plan 3
12% bonds			$ 6,250,000
Preferred 4% stock, $50 par		$ 7,500,000	5,000,000
Common stock, $30 par	$15,000,000	7,500,000	3,750,000
Total	$15,000,000	$15,000,000	$15,000,000

Instructions

1. Determine for each plan the earnings per share of common stock, assuming that the income before bond interest and income tax is $3,000,000.

	Plan 1	Plan 2	Plan 3
Earnings before interest and income tax			
Deduct interest on bonds			
Income before income tax			
Deduct income tax			
Net income			
Dividends on preferred stock			
Available for dividends on common			
Shares of common stock outstanding			
Earnings per share on common stock			

2. Determine for each plan the earnings per share of common stock, assuming that the income before bond interest and income tax is $1,450,000.

	Plan 1	Plan 2	Plan 3
Earnings before interest and income tax			
Deduct interest on bonds			
Income before income tax			
Deduct income tax			
Net income			
Dividends on preferred stock			
Available for dividends on common			
Shares of common stock outstanding			
Earnings per share on common stock			

Continued

3. Discuss the
   advantages and
   disadvantages
   of each plan.

**Present value; bond premium; entries
for bonds payable transactions**
Objectives 3, 4 ✔ 3. $509,422

" Leibee Inc. produces and sells voltage regulators. On July 1,
1999, we issued $10,000,000 of ten-year, 10 1/2% bonds at an
effective interest rate of 10%. Interest on the bonds is payable
semiannually on December 31 and June 30. The fiscal year of
my company is the calendar year. Please complete the items
below. "

Sherry Moore
President

Instructions

1. Journalize the entry to record the amount of the cash proceeds from the sale of
   the bonds. Use the tables of present values in Appendix A to compute the cash
   proceeds, rounding to the nearest dollar.

Date	Description	Debit	Credit

2. Journalize the entries to record the following:

   a. The first semiannual interest payment on December 31, 1999, including
      the amortization of the bond premium, using the straight-line method.

   b. The interest payment on June 30, 2000, and the amortization of the bond
      premium, using the straight-line method.

Date	Description	Debit	Credit

Continued

3. Determine the total interest expense for 1999.

4. Will the bond proceeds always be greater than the face amount of the bonds when the contract rate is greater than the market rate of interest? Explain.

**Present value; bond discount; entries
for bonds payable transactions**
Objectives 3, 4 ✔ 3. $346,733

> " On July 1, 1999, Cyrano Communications Equipment Inc. issued
> $7,500,000 of ten-year, 8% bonds at an effective interest rate of 10%.
> Interest on the bonds is payable semiannually on December 31 and
> June 30. The fiscal year of our company is the calendar year. Please
> complete the items below. "

Steven Walker,President

Instructions

1. Journalize the entry to record the amount of the cash proceeds from the sale of
   the bonds. Use the tables of present values in Appendix A to compute the
   cash proceeds, rounding to the nearest dollar.

Date	Description	Debit	Credit

2. Journalize the entries to record the following:

   a. The first semiannual interest payment on December 31, 1999, and the
      amortization of the bond discount, using the straight-line method.
      (Round to the nearest dollar.)

   b. The interest payment on June 30, 2000, and the amortization of the bond
      discount, using the straight-line method.

Date	Description	Debit	Credit

Continued

3. Determine the total
   interest expense for 1999.

4. Will the bond proceeds
   always be less than the
   face amount of the
   bonds when the contract
   rate is less than the
   market rate of interest?
   Explain.

Chapter 15

Statement of Cash Flows

The basic financial statements are the (1) income statement, (2) retained earnings statement (or statement of owner's equity), (3) balance sheet, and (4) statement of cash flows. The preparation and use of the first three statements were thoroughly described and illustrated in previous chapters. This chapter presents the basic preparation and use of the statement of cash flows.

Learning objectives are listed for the exercises and problems that follow. Use the information to the right to determine the nature of the objective and the page number to refer to your textbook for a discussion of the topic.

Objective 1 — **Purpose of the Statement of Cash Flows 577**
Explain why the statement of cash flows is one of the basic financial statements.

Objective 2 — **Reporting Cash Flows 577**
Summarize the types of cash flow activities reported in the statement of cash flows.

Objective 3 — **Statement of Cash Flows—The Indirect Method 581**
Prepare a statement of cash flows, using the indirect method.

Objective 4 — **Statement of Cash Flows—The Direct Method 589**
Prepare a statement of cash flows, using the direct method.

Objective 5 — **Financial Analysis and Interpretation 593**
Calculate and interpret the free cash flow.

Blank Page

**Cash flows from operating
activities—net loss**
Objective 2 - Text page 577

On its income statement for the current year, Marconi Company reported
a net loss of $65,000 from operations. On its statement of cash flows, it
reported $20,000 of cash flows from operating activities.

Working
Papers
Plus

Chapter 15

Explain this
apparent
contradiction
between the loss
and the positive
cash flows.

Exercise 15–2

Effect of transactions on cash flows
Objective 2 - Text page 577 ✔ c. Cash payment, $501,000

State the effect (cash receipt or payment and amount) of each of the following
transactions, considered individually, on cash flows:

a. Paid dividends of $1.50 per share. There were 30,000 shares
 issued and 5,000 shares of treasury stock. .... _____

b. Purchased a building by paying $30,000 cash and issuing a
 $90,000 mortgage note payable. .... _____

c. Retired $500,000 of bonds, on which there was $2,500 of
 unamortized discount, for $501,000. .... _____

d. Purchased land for $120,000 cash. .... _____

e. Sold a new issue of $100,000 of bonds at 101. .... _____

f. Purchased 5,000 shares of $30 par common stock as treasury
 stock at $50 per share. .... _____

g. Sold 5,000 shares of $30 par common stock for $45 per share. . _____

h. Sold equipment with a book value of $42,500 for $41,000. .... _____

Exercise 15–3

Classifying cash flows
Objective 2 - Text page 577

Identify the type of cash flow activity for each of the following events (operating, investing, or financing):

a. Paid cash dividends. .... _____
b. Sold long-term investments. .... _____
c. Issued bonds. .... _____
d. Issued common stock. .... _____
e. Sold equipment. .... _____
f. Net income. .... _____
g. Issued preferred stock. .... _____
h. Redeemed bonds. .... _____
i. Purchased patents. .... _____
j. Purchased treasury stock. .... _____
k. Purchased buildings .... _____

Exercise 15–4

**Cash flows from operating activities—
indirect method**
Objective 3 - Text page 531

Indicate whether each of the following would be added to or deducted from net income in determining net cash flow from operating activities by the indirect method:

a. Decrease in accounts receivable .... _____
b. Amortization of patent.. _____
c. Depreciation of fixed assets... _____
d. Decrease in salaries payable.. _____
e. Decrease in accounts payable .... _____
f. Loss on disposal of fixed assets .... _____
g. Increase in notes payable due in 90 days .... _____
h. Amortization of goodwill .... _____
i. Increase in notes receivable due in 90 days .... _____
j. Decrease in prepaid expenses .... _____
k. Increase in merchandise inventory .... _____
l. Gain on retirement of long-term debt............................... _____

**Cash flows from operating activities—
indirect method**
Objectives 2, 3 - Text pages 577 and 581   ✔ a. Cash flows from operating activities, $153,850

" The net income reported on the income statement for the current year was $134,800. Depreciation recorded on equipment and a building amounted to $27,400 for the year. Balances of the current asset and current liability accounts at the beginning and end of the year are shown below. Your assignment is to prepare the cash flows from operating activities. "

Monique Tam
Controller

	End of Year	Beginning of Year	Changes Debit	Credit
Cash	$ 23,500	$37,400		
Accounts receivable (net)	84,500	80,350		
Inventories	100,200	94,300		
Prepaid expenses	4,970	5,300		
Accounts payable (mdse. creditors)	71,400	68,900		
Salaries payable	5,320	6,450		

a. Prepare the cash flows from operating activities section of the statement of cash flows, using the indirect method.

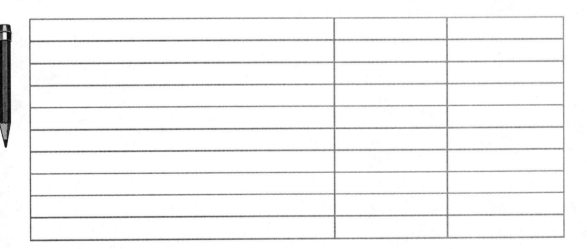

b. If the direct method had been used, would the net cash flow from operating activities have been the same? Explain.

**Cash flows from operating activities—
indirect method**

Objective 3 - Text page 581   ✔ a. Cash flows from operating activities, $537,800

" The net income reported on my income statement for the current year was $465,000. Depreciation recorded on store equipment for the year amounted to $96,800. Balances of the current asset and current liability accounts at the beginning and end of the year are shown below. I'm looking for a new accountant and would like to evaluate your work. Please prepare the cash flows from operating activities. "

Alvin McNeil
Owner

	End of Year	Beginning of Year	Changes Debit	Credit
Cash	$345,000	$386,000		
Accounts receivable (net)	554,300	567,800		
Merchandise inventories	693,000	672,400		
Prepaid expenses	27,000	24,000		
Accounts payable (mdse. creditors)	510,000	527,400		
Wages payable	39,500	36,000		

Prepare the cash flows from operating activities section of a statement of cash flows, using the indirect method.

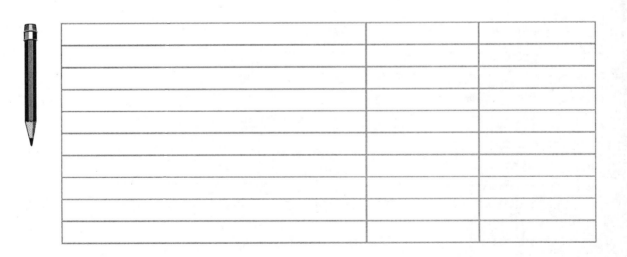

Exercise 15–7

Determining cash payments to stockholders
Objective 3 - Text page 581

The board of directors declared cash dividends totaling $240,000 during the current year. The comparative balance sheet indicates dividends payable of $50,000 at the beginning of the year and $60,000 at the end of the year. What was the amount of cash payments to stockholders during the year?

Exercise 15–8

Reporting changes in equipment on statement of cash flows
Objective 3 - Text page 581

An analysis of the general ledger accounts indicates that office equipment, which had cost $245,000 and on which accumulated depreciation totaled $95,000 on the date of sale, was sold for $130,000 during the year. Using this information, indicate the items to be reported on the statement of cash flows.

Exercise 15–9

Reporting changes in equipment on statement of cash flows
Objective 3 - Text page 581

An analysis of the general ledger accounts indicates that delivery equipment, which had cost $39,000 and on which accumulated depreciation totaled $23,000 on the date of sale, was sold for $20,000 during the year. Using this information, indicate the items to be reported on the statement of cash flows.

Exercise 15–10

**Reporting land transactions
on statement of cash flows**
Objective 3 - Text page 581

On the basis of the details of the following fixed asset account,
indicate the items to be reported on the statement of cash flows:

ACCOUNT	LAND			ACCOUNT NO.	
				Balance	
Date	Item	Debit	Credit	Debit	Credit
2000					
Jan. 1	Balance			400,000	
Feb. 5	Purchased for cash	250,000		650,000	
Oct. 30	Sold for $95,000		80,000	570,000	

Exercise 15–11

**Reporting stockholders' equity items
on statement of cash flows**
Objective 3 - Text page 581

Use the textbook exercise and blank paper to solve this exercise.

Exercise 15–12

**Reporting land acquisition for
cash and mortgage note on
statement of cash flows**
Objective 3 - Text page 581

On the basis of the details of the following asset account,
indicate the items to be reported on the statement of cash flows:

ACCOUNT	LAND			ACCOUNT NO.	
				Balance	
Date	Item	Debit	Credit	Debit	Credit
2000					
Jan. 1	Balance			450,000	
Feb. 10	Purchased for cash	125,000		575,000	
Nov.20	Purchased with long-term mortgage note	200,000		775,000	

**Determining net income from net cash
flow from operating activities**
Objective 3 - Text page 581   ✔ Net income $89,150

Rose Mustain
Controller

" Tiger Golf Inc. reported a net cash flow from operating activities of $102,500 on its statement of cash flows for the year ended December 31, 2000. The following information was reported in the cash flows from operating activities section of the statement of cash flows, using the indirect method. We have misplaced our cash flow statement and would like to engage your services to reconstruct the cash flow from operations as indicated below. Thanks! "

Decrease in income taxes payable ..... $ 1,400
Decrease in inventories 6,200
Depreciation 15,400
Gain on sale of investments 9,450
Increase in accounts payable 9,100
Increase in prepaid expenses 1,000
Increase in accounts receivable 5,500

Determine the net income reported by Tiger Golf Inc. for the year ended December 31, 2000.

Calculations

Exercise 15–14

Cash flows from operating activities
Objective 3 - Text page 581   ✔ Cash flows from operating activities, $743,400

" Selected data from the income statement and statement of cash flows of **Toys "R" Us, Inc.,** for the year ending February 1, 1997, are shown below. Please prepare the cash flows from operations using the indirect method. "

Judy Johnston, Investor

Income Statement Data (dollars in thousands)

Net earnings	$427,400
Depreciation and amortization	206,400
Deferred portion of current period tax expense (noncash expense)	23,400

Statement of Cash Flows Data (dollars in thousands)

Increase in accounts receivable	$ 14,300
Increase in merchandise inventories	194,600
Increase in prepaid expenses and other operating assets	10,100
Increase in accounts payable, accrued expenses, and taxes	261,400
Increase in income tax payable	43,800

Prepare the cash flows from operating activities section of the statement of cash flows (using the indirect method) for Toys "R" Us, Inc., for the year ending February 1, 1997.

Exercise 15–15   Name: _____

**Cash flows from operating activities—
direct method**
Objective 4 - Text page 589   ✔ a. $865,000

The cash flows from operating activities are reported by the direct method on the
statement of cash flows. Determine the following:

a. If sales for the current year were
   $820,000 and accounts receivable
   decreased by $45,000 during the year,
   what was the amount of cash received
   from customers?

b. If income tax expense for the current
   year was $64,000 and income tax
   payable decreased by $6,000 during
   the year, what was the amount of cash
   payments for income tax?

Exercise 15–16

**Determining selected amounts for cash flows
from operating activities—direct method**
Objective 4 - Text page 589   ✔ b. $311,700

Selected data taken from the accounting records of Hi Gain Electronics
Company for the current year ended December 31 are as follows:

	Balance January 1	Balance December 31
Accrued expenses (operating expenses)	$ 14,300	$11,100
Accounts payable (merchandise creditors)	112,000	90,000
Inventories	83,400	76,500
Prepaid expenses	21,000	19,500

During the current year, the cost of merchandise sold was $870,000
and the operating expenses other than depreciation were $310,000.
The direct method is used for presenting the cash flows from
operating activities on the statement of cash flows.

Determine the amount reported on the statement of cash flows for:

(a) cash payments
    for merchandise

(b) cash payments
    for operating
    expenses.

Exercise 15–17

**Cash flows from operating activities—
direct method**

Objective 4 - Text page 589   ✔ Cash flows from operating activities, $101,800

The income statement of Tru-Blu Greeting Card Company for
the current year ended June 30 is as follows:

Sales		$865,000
Cost of merchandise sold		525,000
Gross profit		$340,000
Operating expenses:		
Depreciation expense	$ 45,000	
Other operating expenses	210,400	
Total operating expenses		255,400
Income before income tax		$ 84,600
Income tax expense		35,000
Net income		$ 49,600

Changes in the balances of selected accounts from the
beginning to the end of the current year are as follows:

	Increase (Decrease)
Accounts receivable (net)	$(27,000)
Inventories	11,200
Prepaid expenses	(2,400)
Accounts payable (merchandise creditors)	(18,300)
Accrued expenses (operating expenses)	10,700
Income tax payable	(3,400)

Prepare the cash flows from operating activities section
of the statement of cash flows, using the direct method.

Cash flows from operating activities— direct method
Objective 4 - Text page 589   ✔ Cash flows from operating activities, $75,450

The income statement for Wholly Donut Company for the current year ended June 30 and balances of selected accounts at the beginning and the end of the year are as follows:

Sales		$683,000
Cost of merchandise sold		395,700
Gross profit		$287,300
Operating expenses:		
Depreciation expense	$ 49,500	
Other operating expenses	172,600	
Total operating expenses		222,100
Income before income tax		$ 65,200
Income tax expense		28,600
Net income		$ 36,600

	End of Year	Beginning of Year
Accounts receivable (net)	$85,000	$82,000
Inventories	98,600	85,000
Prepaid expenses	6,100	8,150
Accounts payable (merchandise creditors)	76,600	71,100
Accrued expenses (operating expenses)	4,250	5,850
Income tax payable	1,600	1,600

Prepare the cash flows from operating activities section of the statement of cash flows, using the direct method.

Statement of cash flows
Objective 3 - Text page 581

List the errors you find in the following statement of cash flows. The cash balance at the beginning of the year was $70,700. All other figures are correct.

Monarch Games Inc.
Statement of Cash Flows
For the Year Ended December 31, 2000

Cash flows from operating activities:			
Net income, per income statement		$100,500	
Add: Depreciation	$ 49,000		
Increase in accounts receivable	9,500		
Gain on sale of investments	5,000	63,500	
		$164,000	
Deduct: Increase in accounts payable	$ 4,400		
Increase in inventories	18,300		
Decrease in accrued expenses	1,600	24,300	
Net cash flow from operating activities			$139,700
Cash flows from investing activities:			
Cash received from sale of investments		$ 85,000	
Less: Cash paid for purchase of land	$ 90,000		
Cash paid for purchase of equipment	150,100	240,100	
Net cash flow used for investing activities			(155,100)
Cash flows from financing activities:			
Cash received from sale of common stock		$107,000	
Cash paid for dividends		36,800	
Net cash flow provided by financing activities			143,800
Increase in cash			$128,400
Cash at the end of the year			105,300
Cash at the beginning of the year			$233,700

Financial Analysis and Interpretation

Free Cash Flow

Cash flow from operations	$100,500
Less: Cash used to purchase fixed assets to maintain capacity	(75,000)
Less: Cash used for dividends	(24,000)
Free cash flow	$ 1,500

Use: To measure operating cash flow available for corporate purposes after providing sufficient fixed asset additions to maintain current productive capacity and dividends.

Exercise 15–20

Free cash flow
Objective 5 - Text page 593

The financial statements for **Hershey Foods Corporation** are presented in Appendix G at the end of the text.

a. Determine the free cash flow for 1995 and 1996 from the statements of cash flows. Assume that 80% of the capital additions for each year are used to maintain productive capacity and that the remaining 20% adds to productive capacity.

b. What conclusions can you draw from your analysis?

This activity will require two teams to retrieve statement of cash flow information from the Internet. One team is to obtain the most recent year's statement of cash flows for **Intel Corporation**, and the other team the most recent year's statement of cash flows for **America Online (AOL)**.

The statement of cash flows is part of the annual report information that is a required disclosure to the Securities Exchange Commission (SEC). The SEC, in turn, provides this information on the Internet through its EDGAR (Electronic Data Gathering, Analysis, and Retrieval) service. The Edgar address is **www.sec.gov/edgarhp.htm**.

To obtain annual report information, type in a company name on the "Search EDGAR archives" form. EDGAR will list the reports available for the selected company. A company's annual report (along with much more information) is provided in its annual 10-K report to the SEC. Click on the 10-K (or 10-K405) report for the year you wish to download. If you wish, you can save the whole 10-K report to a file, then open it with your word processor.

As a group, compare the two statements of cash flows. How are Intel and America Online similar or different regarding cash flows?

Statement of cash flows—indirect method
Objective 3   ✔ Net cash flow from operating activities, $72,800

" The comparative balance sheet of Idaho Al's Golf Shops Co. for December 31, 2000 and 1999, is shown below. Using the information below, please prepare a statement of cash flows using the indirect method. We haven't prepared this statement in the past but our investors are now requiring it. "

John Swensson, Founder

	Dec. 31, 2000	Dec. 31, 1999	Changes Debit	Changes Credit
Assets				
Cash	$ 86,400	$ 51,600		
Accounts receivable (net)	132,400	112,600		
Inventories	153,400	141,300		
Investments	0	115,000		
Land	85,000	0		
Equipment	785,000	635,000		
Accumulated depreciation	(265,000)	(211,500)		
	$977,200	$844,000		
Liabilities and Stockholders' Equity				
Accounts payable (mdse. creditors)	$ 85,000	$ 70,600		
Accrued expenses (operating exps.)	4,700	6,700		
Dividends payable	20,000	15,000		
Common stock, $10 par	60,000	40,000		
Paid-in capital in excess of par	220,000	100,000		
Retained earnings	587,500	611,700		
	$977,200	$844,000		

The following additional information was taken from the records:

   a. The investments were sold for $132,000 cash.
   b. Equipment and land were acquired for cash.
   c. There were no disposals of equipment during the year.
   d. The common stock was issued for cash.
   e. There was a $55,800 credit to Retained Earnings for net income.
   f. There was a $80,000 debit to Retained Earnings for cash dividends declared.

Instructions

Prepare a statement of cash flows, using the indirect method of presenting cash flows from operating activities. Use a blank **Form 3C** for the statement. You may also use a blank **Form 4C** to prepare a work sheet if desired.

Blank Page

Statement of cash flows—direct method
applied to Problem 15–1A
Objective 4   ✔ Net cash flow from operating activities, $72,800

The comparative balance sheet of Idaho Al's Golf Shops Co. for December 31, 2000 and 1999, is shown in Problem 15–1A, which is included in this manual. The income statement for the year ended December 31, 2000, is as follows:

Idaho Al's Golf Shops Co.
Income Statement
For the Year Ended December 31, 2000

Sales		$693,200
Cost of merchandise sold		394,500
Gross profit		$298,700
Operating expenses:		
Depreciation expense	$ 53,500	
Other operating expenses	172,900	
Total operating expenses		226,400
Operating income		$ 72,300
Other income:		
Gain on sale of investments		17,000
Income before income tax		$ 89,300
Income tax expense		33,500
Net income		$ 55,800

The following additional information was taken from the records:

a. The investments were sold for $132,000 cash.
b. Equipment and land were acquired for cash.
c. There were no disposals of equipment during the year.
d. The common stock was issued for cash.
e. There was an $88,000 debit to Retained Earnings for cash dividends declared.

Instructions

Prepare a statement of cash flows, using the direct method of presenting cash flows from operating activities. Use a **Form 3C** for the statement. You may also use a **Form 4C** to prepare a work sheet if desired.

Blank Page

Problem 15–1B Mother Nature Health Foods Inc.   Name: _____

Statement of cash flows—indirect method
Objective 3   ✔ Net cash flow from operating activities, $95,500

" The comparative balance sheet of Mother Nature Health Foods Inc. for June 30, 2000 and 1999, is shown below. Using the information below, please prepare a statement of cash flows using the indirect method. We haven't prepared this statement in the past but our investors are now requiring it. "

Chantel Medeiros, Founder

	June 30, 2000	June 30, 1999	Changes Debit	Credit
Assets				
Cash	$ 93,400	$ 57,800		
Accounts receivable (net)	125,000	123,500		
Inventories	146,500	108,900		
Investments	0	65,000		
Land	145,000	0		
Equipment	367,600	278,600		
Accumulated depreciation	(110,900)	(87,400)		
	$766,600	$546,400		
Liabilities and Stockholders' Equity				
Accounts payable (mdse. creditors)	$ 82,400	$ 74,000		
Accrued expenses (operating exps.)	6,700	6,000		
Dividends payable	18,400	15,700		
Common stock, $10 par	100,000	70,000		
Paid-in capital in excess of par	320,000	200,000		
Retained earnings	239,100	180,700		
	$766,600	$546,400		

The following additional information was taken from the records of Mother Nature Health Foods Inc.:

a. Equipment and land were acquired for cash.
b. There were no disposals of equipment during the year.
c. The investments were sold for $95,000 cash.
d. The common stock was issued for cash.
e. There was a $132,000 credit to Retained Earnings for net income.
f. There was a $73,600 debit to Retained Earnings for cash dividends declared.

Instructions

Prepare a statement of cash flows, using the indirect method of presenting cash flows from operating activities. Use a blank **Form 3C** for the statement. You may also use a blank **Form 4C** to prepare a work sheet if desired.

Blank Page

Statement of cash flows—direct method
applied to Problem 15–1B
Objective 4   ✔ Net cash flow from operating activities, $95,500

The comparative balance sheet of Mother Nature Health Foods Inc. for June 30, 2000 and 1999, is shown in Problem 15–1B, which is included in this manual. The income statement for the year ended June 30, 2000, is as follows:

Sales	$724,700
Cost of merchandise sold	423,100
Gross profit	$301,600
Operating expenses:	
Depreciation expense ....$ 23,500	
Other operating expenses 102,900	
Total operating expenses	126,400
Operating income	$175,200
Other income:	
Gain on sale of investments	30,000
Income before income tax	$205,200
Income tax expense	73,200
Net income	$132,000

The following additional information was taken from the records of Mother Nature Health Foods Inc.:

  a. Equipment and land were acquired for cash.
  b. There were no disposals of equipment during the year.
  c. The investments were sold for $95,000 cash.
  d. The common stock was issued for cash.
  e. There was a $73,600 debit to Retained Earnings for cash dividends declared.

Instructions

Prepare a statement of cash flows, using the direct method of presenting cash flows from operating activities. Use a **Form 3C** for the statement. You may also use a **Form 4C** to prepare a work sheet if desired.

Blank Page

Chapter 16

Financial Statement Analysis

The financial condition and the results of operations of business enterprises are of interest to many users. These user groups include owners, managers, creditors, governmental agencies, employees, and prospective owners and creditors. The basic financial statements provide much of the information users need to make economic decisions about business enterprises.

Learning objectives are listed for the exercises and problems that follow. Use the information to the right to determine the nature of the objective and the page number to refer to your textbook for a discussion of the topic.

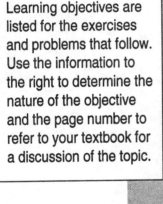

Blank Page

Vertical analysis of income statement
Objective 1 - Text page 626   ✔ 2000 net income: $52,800; 8% of sales

Revenue and expense data for Cabot Cabinet Co. are as follows:

Working
Papers
Plus

Chapter 16

	2000	1999
Sales	$660,000	$600,000
Cost of goods sold	389,400	384,000
Selling expenses	105,600	84,000
Administrative expenses	66,000	54,000
Income tax expense	46,200	42,000

a. Prepare an income statement in comparative form, stating
   each item for both 2000 and 1999 as a percent of sales.

Cabot Cabinet Co.
Comparative Income Statement
For Years Ended December 31, 2000 and 1999

	2000		1999	
	Amount	Percent	Amount	Percent

b. Comment on the
   significant changes
   disclosed by the
   comparative
   income statement.

Exercise 16-2

Vertical analysis of income statement

Objective 1 - Text page 626   ✔ a. 1997 operating income, 9.2% of revenues

The following comparative income statement (in thousands of dollars) for the years ending February 2, 1997, and January 31, 1996, was adapted from the 1997 annual report of **Dell Computer Corporation**:

| | 1997 | | 1996 | |
	Amount	Percent	Amount	Percent
Revenues	$7,759,000	_____	$5,296,000	_____
Costs and expenses:				
Cost of sales	6,093,000	_____	$4,229,000	_____
Gross profit	$1,666,000	_____	$1,067,000	_____
Selling, distribution,				
and administrative expenses	952,000	_____	690,000	_____
Operating income	$ 714,000	_____	$ 377,000	_____

a. Prepare a comparative income statement for 1997 and 1996 in vertical form, stating each item as a percent of revenues. Round to one digit after the decimal place.

b. Based upon the 1996 income statement, comment on the significant changes.

Common-size income statement

Objective 1 - Text page 626   ✔ a. Keystone net income: $642,000; 9.2% of sales

Revenue and expense data for the current calendar year for Keystone Publishing Company and for the publishing industry are as follows. The Keystone Publishing Company data are expressed in dollars. The publishing industry averages are expressed in percentages.

	Keystone Publishing Company	Keystone Common-Size Percentages	Publishing Industry Average
Sales	$7,070,000	_____	100.5%
Sales returns and allowances	70,000	_____	0.5
Cost of goods sold	4,900,000	_____	69.0
Selling expenses	560,000	_____	9.0
Administrative expenses	490,000	_____	8.2
Other income	42,000	_____	0.6
Other expense	100,000	_____	1.4
Income tax expense	350,000	_____	5.0

a. Prepare a common-size income statement comparing the results of operations for Keystone Publishing Company with the industry average. Round to one digit after the decimal place.

b. As far as the data permit, comment on significant relationships revealed by the comparisons.

Exercise 16-4

Vertical analysis of balance sheet

Objective 1 - Text page 626   ✔ Retained earnings, Dec. 31, 2000, 33.75%

Balance sheet data for Fisher Fabrics Company on December 31, the end of the fiscal year, are as follows:

	2000	1999
Current assets	$280,000	$260,000
Property, plant, and equipment	480,000	400,000
Intangible assets	40,000	41,000
Current liabilities	100,000	71,000
Long-term liabilities	180,000	220,000
Common stock	250,000	200,000
Retained earnings	270,000	210,000

Prepare a comparative balance sheet for 2000 and 1999, stating each asset as a percent of total assets and each liability and stockholders' equity item as a percent of the total liabilities and stockholders' equity. Round to two digits after the decimal place.

Fisher Fabrics Company
Comparative Balance Sheet
December 31, 2000 and 1999

	2000		1999	
	Amount	Percent	Amount	Percent

Horizontal analysis of the income statement

Objective 1 - Text page 626   ✔ a. Net income increase, 73.9%

Income statement data for Neon Flashlight Company for the year
ended December 31, 2000 and 1999, are as follows:

	2000	1999
Sales	$940,000	$850,000
Cost of goods sold	610,000	580,000
Gross profit	$330,000	$270,000
Selling expenses	$126,000	$137,000
Administrative expenses	44,000	53,500
Total operating expenses	$170,000	$190,500
Income before income tax	$160,000	$ 79,500
Income tax expense	60,000	22,000
Net income	$100,000	$ 57,500

a. Prepare a comparative income statement with horizontal analysis,
   indicating the increase (decrease) for 2000 when compared with
   1999. Round to one digit after the decimal place.

Neon Flashlight Company
Comparative Income Statement
For the Years Ended December 31, 2000 and 1999

	2000	1999	Increase (Decrease)	
	Amount	Amount	Amount	Percent

b. What conclusions can
   be drawn from the
   horizontal analysis?

Exercise 16-6

Current position analysis
Objective 2 - Text page 631　✔ Current year working capital, $360,000

The following data were abstracted from the
balance sheet of Precision Engine Company:

	Current Year	Preceding Year
Cash	$ 89,500	$139,000
Marketable securities	110,000	98,000
Accounts and notes receivable (net)	190,500	153,000
Inventories	250,500	222,000
Prepaid expenses	19,500	38,000
Accounts and notes payable (short-term)	245,000	203,500
Accrued liabilities	55,000	56,500

a. Determine for each year:

  (1) the working capital

  (2) the current ratio

  (3) the acid-test ratio

b. What conclusions can be
   drawn from these data as
   to the company's ability
   to meet its currently
   maturing debts?

Current position analysis
Objective 2 - Text page 631

The bond indenture for the 10-year, 9 1/2% debenture bonds dated January 2, 1999, required working capital of $350,000, a current ratio of 1.5, and an acid-test ratio of 1 at the end of each calendar year until the bonds mature. At December 31, 2000, the three measures were computed as follows:

1. Current assets:

Cash	$295,000	
Marketable securities......................................	148,000	
Accounts and notes receivable (net)	172,000	
Inventories	300,000	
Prepaid expenses	135,000	
Goodwill..	150,000	
Total current assets		$1,200,000
Current liabilities:		
Accounts and short-term notes payable	$500,000	
Accrued liabilities	250,000	
Total current liabilities		750,000
Working capital...		$ 450,000

2. Current ratio = 1.6 ($1,200,000 / $750,000)
3. Acid-test ratio = 1.2 ($615,000 / $500,000)

a. Can you find any errors
in the determination of
the three measures of
current position analysis?

b. Is the company satisfying
the terms of the bond
indenture?

Exercise 16-8

Accounts receivable analysis
Objective 2 - Text page 631   ✔ a. Accounts receivable turnover, current year, 6.0

The following data are taken from the financial statements of North Company. Terms of all sales are 1/10, n/60.

	Current Year	Preceding Year
Accounts receivable, end of year	$ 572,000	$ 408,333
Monthly average accounts receivable (net)	476,667	350,000
Net sales on account	2,860,000	2,450,000

a. Determine for each year: (1) the accounts receivable turnover and (2) the number of days' sales in receivables. Round to one digit after the decimal place.

b. What conclusions can be drawn from these data concerning accounts receivable and credit policies?

Exercise 16-9

Inventory analysis
Objective 2 - Text page 631
✔ Inventory turnover, current year, 8.0

The following data were abstracted from the income statement of Cascade Instruments Inc.:

	Current Year	Preceding Year
Sales	$7,400,000	$5,200,000
Beginning inventories	642,500	607,500
Cost of goods sold	5,280,000	3,750,000
Ending inventories	677,500	642,500

a. Determine for each year: (1) the inventory turnover and (2) the number of days' sales in inventory. Round to one digit after the decimal place.

b. What conclusions can be drawn from these data concerning the inventories?

**Ratio of liabilities to stockholders' equity and
number of times interest charges earned**
Objective 2 - Text page 631   ✔ a. Ratio of liabilities to stockholders' equity, Dec. 31, 2000, 0.56

The following data were taken from the
financial statements of Mountain Spring
Water Co. for December 31, 2000 and 1999:

	December 31, 2000	December 31, 1999
Accounts payable	$ 200,000	$ 400,000
Current maturities of serial bonds payable	400,000	400,000
Serial bonds payable, 12%, issued 1995, due 2004	1,600,000	2,000,000
Common stock, $1 par value	100,000	100,000
Paid-in capital in excess of par	1,000,000	1,000,000
Retained earnings	2,860,000	2,400,000

The income before income tax was $780,000 and $216,000
for the years 2000 and 1999, respectively.

a. Determine the ratio of
   liabilities to stockholders'
   equity at the end of each
   year. Round to two digits
   after the decimal place.

b. Determine the number of
   times the bond interest
   charges are earned during
   the year for both years.

c. What conclusions can be
   drawn from these data as
   to the company's ability to
   meet its currently maturing
   debts?

Exercise 16-11

Profitability ratios
Objective 3 - Text page 637   ✔ a. Ratio earned on total assets, 2001, 14%

The following selected data were taken from the
financial statements of Ohio Cement Co. for
December 31, 2001, 2000, and 1999:

	December 31, 2001	December 31, 2000	December 31, 1999
Total assets	$3,200,000	$2,800,000	$2,000,000
Notes payable (8% interest)	500,000	500,000	500,000
Common stock	900,000	900,000	900,000
Preferred $10 stock. $100 par, cumulative, nonparticipating (no change during year)	300,000	300,000	300,000
Retained earnings	1,430,000	1,050,000	250,000

The 2001 net income was $380,000, and the 2000 net income was $800,000.
No dividends on common stock were declared between 1999 and 2001.

a. Determine the rate
   earned on total assets,
   the rate earned on
   stockholders' equity,
   and the rate earned on
   common stockholders'
   equity for the years
   2000 and 2001. Round
   to one digit after the
   decimal place.

b. What conclusions
   can be drawn from
   these data as to the
   company's
   profitability?

Six measures of solvency or profitability
Objectives 2, 3   ✔ c. Ratio of net sales to assets, 1.44

The following data were taken from the financial statements
of Premium Printers Inc. for the current fiscal year:

Property, plant, and equipment (net)			$1,000,000
Liabilities:			
Current liabilities		$400,000	
Mortgage note payable, 10%, issued 1990, due 2005		800,000	
Total liabilities			$1,200,000
Stockholders' equity			
Preferred $4 stock, $80 par, cumulative,			
nonparticipating (no change during year)			$ 400,000
Common stock, $10 par (no change during year)			1,200,000
Retained earnings:			
Balance, beginning of year	$600,000		
Net income	300,000	$900,000	
Preferred dividends..	$ 20,000		
Common dividends	80,000	100,000	
Balance, end of year...			800,000
Total stockholders' equity			$2,400,000
Net sales			$4,500,000
Interest expense...			$ 80,000

Assuming that long-term investments totaled $175,000 throughout the year and that
total assets were $3,000,000 at the beginning of the year, determine the following,
rounding to two digits after the decimal place:

(a) ratio of fixed
    assets to long-
    term liabilities.

(b) ratio of liabilities
    to stockholders'
    equity.

(c) ratio of net sales
    to assets.

(d) rate earned on
    total assets.

(e) rate earned on
    stockholders'
    equity.

(f) rate earned on
    common
    stockholders'
    equity.

Five measures of solvency or profitability
Objectives 2, 3 ✔ d. Price-earnings ratio, 24

The balance sheet for Aspen Avionics Corporation at the
end of the current fiscal year indicated the following:

Bonds payable, 10% (issued in 1990, due in 2010) $4,000,000
Preferred $10 stock, $100 par 1,000,000
Common stock, $20 par 8,000,000

Income before income tax was $1,000,000, and income taxes were $300,000 for the current year.
Cash dividends paid on common stock during the current year totaled $288,000. The common
stock was selling for $36 per share at the end of the year. Determine each of the following:

(a) number of times
   bond interest
   charges were
   earned.

(b) number of times
   preferred dividends
   were earned.

(c) earnings per share
   on common stock.

(d) price-earnings ratio.

(e) dividends per share
   of common stock.

(f) dividend yield.

Exercise 16-14

Earnings per share, price-earnings ratio, dividend yield
Objective 3 - Text page 637   ✔ b. Price-earnings ratio, 15

The following information was taken from the financial statements of Cool Breeze Air Conditioners Inc. for December 31 of the current fiscal year:

Common stock, $15 par value (no change during the year) $4,500,000
Preferred $8 stock, $100 par, cumulative, nonparticipating
    (no change during the year) 800,000

The net income was $574,000 and the declared dividends on the common stock were $225,000 for the current year. The market price of the common stock is $25.50 per share.

For the common stock, determine the:

(a) earnings per share.

(b) price-earnings
    ratio.

(c) dividends per
    share.

(d) dividend yield.

Exercise 16-15

Earnings per share
Objective 3 - Text page 637   ✔ b. Earnings per share on common stock, $6.50

The net income reported on the income statement of United Fruit Co. was $4,200,000. There were 400,000 shares of $20 par common stock and 200,000 shares of $8 cumulative preferred stock outstanding throughout the current year. The income statement included two extraordinary items: a $1,250,000 gain from condemnation of land and a $250,000 loss arising from flood damage, both after applicable income tax. Determine the per share figures for common stock for:

(a) income before
    extraordinary
    items.

(b) net income.

Horizontal analysis and profitability analysis

Go to the **Microsoft** Web site at **www.microsoft.com** and download Microsoft's comparative income statements for the last three fiscal years as an Excel® file. Next, go to the *Wall Street Journal* and look up Microsoft in the NASDAQ National Market pages. Under this listing, report the price-earnings ratio and dividend yield for Microsoft.

Use the comparative income statement Excel® file to prepare a horizontal analysis for the last two fiscal years (delete the oldest year from the analysis). Use Microsoft's balance sheet and income statement information to determine the rate earned on stockholders' equity for the latest fiscal year. How do these analyses reconcile with Microsoft's price-earnings ratio and dividend yield?

Solvency and profitability analysis

One team should obtain the latest annual report for **Wal-Mart Stores Inc.**, and the other team should obtain the latest **Kmart Corp.** annual report. These annual reports can be obtained from a library or the company's 10K filing with the Securities and Exchange Commission at **www.sec.gov/edgarhp.htm.**

To obtain annual report information, type in the company name on the "Search EDGAR Archives" form. EDGAR will list the reports available for the company. Click on the 10K (or 10-K405) report for the year you wish to download. If you wish, you can save the whole 10K report to a file and then open it with your word processor.

Each team should compute the following for their company:

a. current ratio

b. inventory turnover

c. rate earned on stockholders' equity

d. rate earned on total assets

e. net income as a percentage of sales

f. ratio of liabilities to stockholders' equity

Horizontal analysis for income statement
Objective 1 ✔ 1. Sales, 10% increase

" For 2000, Wang Company reported its most significant decline in net income in years. At the end of the year, I was presented with the condensed comparative income statement shown below. I would appreciate your help in preparing the items shown below. Your analysis and comments are important to me. Thank you."

Hai Wang
President

Wang Company
Comparative Income Statement
For the Years Ended December 31, 2000 and 1999

	2000	1999	Increase (Decrease) Amount	Increase (Decrease) Percent
Sales	$495,000	$450,000		
Sales returns and allowances	5,000	2,000		
Net sales	$490,000	$448,000		
Cost of goods sold	312,000	260,000		
Gross profit	$178,000	$188,000		
Selling expenses	$84,000	$ 70,000		
Administrative expenses	38,500	35,000		
Total operating expenses	$122,500	$105,000		
Income from operations	$ 55,500	$ 83,000		
Other income	2,500	2,000		
Income before income tax	$ 58,000	$ 85,000		
Income tax expense	20,000	28,000		
Net income	$ 38,000	$ 57,000		

Instructions

1. Prepare a comparative income statement with horizontal analysis for the two-year period, using 1999 as the base year. Round to one digit after the decimal place.

2. To the extent the data permit, comment on the significant relationships revealed by the horizontal analysis prepared in (1).

Blank Page

Vertical analysis for income statement
Objective 1   ✔ 1. Net income, 2000, 8.6%

For 2000, Kasouski Company initiated a sales promotion campaign that included the expenditure of an additional $10,000 for advertising. At the end of the year, Leszek Kasouski, the president, is presented with the following condensed comparative income statement:

Kasouski Company
Comparative Income Statement
For the Years Ended December 31, 2000 and 1999

	2000		1999	
	Amount	Percent	Amount	Percent
Sales	$720,000	_____	$650,000	_____
Sales returns and allowances	20,000	_____	15,000	_____
Net sales	$700,000	_____	$635,000	_____
Cost of goods sold	290,000	_____	270,000	_____
Gross profit	$410,000	_____	$365,000	_____
Selling expenses	$200,000	_____	$ 190,000	_____
Administrative expenses	125,000	_____	115,000	_____
Total operating expenses	$325,000	_____	$305,000	_____
Income from operations	$ 85,000	_____	$ 60,000	_____
Other income	10,000	_____	9,000	_____
Income before income tax	$ 95,000	_____	$ 69,000	_____
Income tax expense	35,000	_____	26,000	_____
Net income	$ 60,000	_____	$ 43,000	_____

Instructions

1. Prepare a comparative income statement for the two-year period, presenting an analysis of each item in relationship to net sales for each of the years. Round to one digit after the decimal place.

2. To the extent the data permit, comment on the significant relationships revealed by the vertical analysis prepared in (1).

Blank Page

**Effect of transactions on current
position analysis**
Objective 2   ✔ 1. Current ratio, 2.5

Data pertaining to the
current position of Clarity
Glass Company are
shown to the right:

Cash $256,000
Marketable securities 84,000
Accounts and notes receivable (net) 360,000
Inventories 532,000
Prepaid expenses 18,000
Accounts payable 380,000
Notes payable (short-term) 80,000
Accrued expenses 40,000

Instructions

1. Compute

   (a) the working capital

   (b) the current ratio

   (c) the acid-test ratio.

2. Using the form below, compute the working capital, the current ratio, and
   the acid-test ratio after each of the following transactions, and record the
   results in the appropriate columns. Consider each transaction separately
   and assume that only that transaction affects the data given above. Round
   to two digits after the decimal place.

Transaction	Working Capital	Current Ratio	Acid-Test Ratio
a. Sold marketable securities at no gain or loss, $56,000.	_____	_____	_____
b. Paid accounts payable, $40,000.	_____	_____	_____
c. Purchased goods on account, $80,000.	_____	_____	_____
d. Paid notes payable, $30,000.	_____	_____	_____
e. Declared a cash dividend, $25,000.	_____	_____	_____
f. Declared a common stock dividend on common stock, $28,500.	_____	_____	_____
g. Borrowed cash from bank on a long-term note, $140,000.	_____	_____	_____
h. Received cash on account, $164,000.	_____	_____	_____
i. Issued additional shares of stock for cash, $200,000.	_____	_____	_____
j. Paid cash for prepaid expenses, $10,000.	_____	_____	_____

Blank Page

Horizontal analysis for income statement
Objective 1   ✔ 1. Sales, 20% increase

" For 1999, Better Biscuit Company reported its most significant increase in net income in years. At the end of the year, I was presented with the condensed comparative income statement shown below. I would appreciate your help in preparing the items shown below. Your analysis and comments are important to me — thanks. "

John Newton
President

Better Biscuit Company
Comparative Income Statement
For the Years Ended December 31, 2000 and 1999

	2000	1999	Increase (Decrease) Amount	Percent
Sales	$840,000	$700,000	_____	_____
Sales returns and allowances	5,000	5,000	_____	_____
Net sales	$835,000	$695,000	_____	_____
Cost of goods sold	450,000	400,000	_____	_____
Gross profit	$385,000	$295,000	_____	_____
Selling expenses	$115,000	$100,000	_____	_____
Administrative expenses	49,500	45,000	_____	_____
Total operating expenses	$164,500	$145,000	_____	_____
Income from operations	$220,500	$150,000	_____	_____
Other income	4,500	6,000	_____	_____
Income before income tax	$225,000	$156,000	_____	_____
Income tax expense	70,000	50,000	_____	_____
Net income	$155,000	$106,000	_____	_____

Instructions

1. Prepare a comparative income statement with horizontal analysis for the two-year period, using 1999 as the base year. Round to one digit after the decimal place.

2. To the extent the data permit, comment on the significant relationships revealed by the horizontal analysis prepared in (1).

Blank Page

Vertical analysis for income statement
Objective 1   ✔ 1. Net income, 2000, 5.4%

For 2000, Stainless Exhaust Systems Inc. initiated a sales promotion campaign that included the expenditure of an additional $50,000 for advertising. At the end of the year, Edmundo Gonzalez, the president, is presented with the following condensed comparative income statement:

Stainless Exhaust Systems Inc.
Comparative Income Statement
For the Years Ended December 31, 2000 and 1999

	2000		1999	
	Amount	Percent	Amount	Percent
Sales	$490,000		$460,000	
Sales returns and allowances	10,000		10,000	
Net sales	$480,000		$450,000	
Cost of goods sold	215,000		200,000	
Gross profit	$265,000		$250,000	
Selling expenses	$150,000		$100,000	
Administrative expenses	85,000		80,000	
Total operating expenses	$235,000		$180,000	
Income from operations	$ 30,000		$ 70,000	
Other income	10,000		9,000	
Income before income tax	$ 40,000		$ 79,000	
Income tax expense	14,000		30,000	
Net income	$ 26,000		$ 49,000	

Instructions

1. Prepare a comparative income statement for the two-year period, presenting an analysis of each item in relationship to net sales for each of the years. Round to one digit after the decimal place.

2. To the extent the data permit, comment on the significant relationships revealed by the vertical analysis prepared in (1).

Blank Page

Problem 16-3B Granular Aggregates Inc.

Name: _____

**Effect of transactions on
current position analysis**
Objective 2   ✔ 1. Acid-test ratio, 1.8

Data pertaining to the
current position of
Granular Aggregates Inc.
are shown to the right:

Cash	$143,000
Marketable securities	57,000
Accounts and notes receivable (net)	250,000
Inventories	266,000
Prepaid expenses	9,000
Accounts payable	190,000
Notes payable (short-term)	40,000
Accrued expenses	20,000

Instructions

1. Compute

   (a) the working capital

   (b) the current ratio

   (c) the acid-test ratio.

2. Using the form below, compute the working capital, the current ratio, and
   the acid-test ratio after each of the following transactions, and record the
   results in the appropriate columns. Consider each transaction separately
   and assume that only that transaction affects the data given above. Round
   to two digits after the decimal place.

Transaction	Working Capital	Current Ratio	Acid-Test Ratio
a. Sold marketable securities at no gain or loss, $34,000.	_____	_____	_____
b. Paid accounts payable, $60,000.	_____	_____	_____
c. Purchased goods on account, $50,000.	_____	_____	_____
d. Paid notes payable, $20,000.	_____	_____	_____
e. Declared a cash dividend, $15,000.	_____	_____	_____
f. Declared a stock dividend on common stock, $16,500.	_____	_____	_____
g. Borrowed cash from bank on a long-term note, $120,000.	_____	_____	_____
h. Received cash on account, $86,000.	_____	_____	_____
i. Issued additional shares of stock for cash, $160,000.	_____	_____	_____
j. Paid cash for prepaid expenses, $12,000.	_____	_____	_____

Blank Page

GENERAL JOURNAL

Page

Date	Description	Post. Ref.	Debit	Credit

Form GJ

GENERAL JOURNAL

Page

Date	Description	Post. Ref.	Debit	Credit

Problem: _____   **Name:** _____

GENERAL JOURNAL

Page _____

Date	Description	Post. Ref.	Debit	Credit

Form GJ

Problem: _____   **Name:** _____

GENERAL JOURNAL

Page _____

Date		Description	Post. Ref.	Debit		Credit	

Form GJ

Problem: _____   **Name:** _____

GENERAL LEDGER

ACCOUNT   NO.

Date	Description	Post. Ref.	Debit	Credit	Balance Debit	Balance Credit

ACCOUNT   NO.

Date	Description	Post. Ref.	Debit	Credit	Balance Debit	Balance Credit

ACCOUNT   NO.

Date	Description	Post. Ref.	Debit	Credit	Balance Debit	Balance Credit

ACCOUNT   NO.

Date	Description	Post. Ref.	Debit	Credit	Balance Debit	Balance Credit

Form GL

Problem: _____   **Name:** _____

GENERAL LEDGER

ACCOUNT   **NO.**

Date		Description	Post. Ref.	Debit	Credit	Balance Debit	Credit

ACCOUNT   **NO.**

Date		Description	Post. Ref.	Debit	Credit	Balance Debit	Credit

ACCOUNT   **NO.**

Date		Description	Post. Ref.	Debit	Credit	Balance Debit	Credit

ACCOUNT   **NO.**

Date		Description	Post. Ref.	Debit	Credit	Balance Debit	Credit

Form GL

Problem: _____   **Name:** _____

GENERAL LEDGER

ACCOUNT _____   NO. _____

Date	Description	Post. Ref.	Debit	Credit	Balance Debit	Balance Credit

ACCOUNT _____   NO. _____

Date	Description	Post. Ref.	Debit	Credit	Balance Debit	Balance Credit

ACCOUNT _____   NO. _____

Date	Description	Post. Ref.	Debit	Credit	Balance Debit	Balance Credit

ACCOUNT _____   NO. _____

Date	Description	Post. Ref.	Debit	Credit	Balance Debit	Balance Credit

Form GL

Problem: _____   **Name:** _____

GENERAL LEDGER

ACCOUNT   NO.

Date		Description	Post. Ref.	Debit	Credit	Balance Debit	Credit

ACCOUNT   NO.

Date		Description	Post. Ref.	Debit	Credit	Balance Debit	Credit

ACCOUNT   NO.

Date		Description	Post. Ref.	Debit	Credit	Balance Debit	Credit

ACCOUNT   NO.

Date		Description	Post. Ref.	Debit	Credit	Balance Debit	Credit

Form GL

Problem: _____   **Name:** _____

Form 2C

Problem: _____   **Name:** _____

Form 2C

Problem: _____   **Name:** _____

Form 2C

Problem: _____   **Name:** _____

Form 2C

Problem: _____   **Name:** _____

Form 3C

Problem:

Name:

Form 3C

Problem: _____   **Name:** _____

Form 3C

Problem: _____   **Name:** _____

Form 3C

Problem: _____   **Name:** _____

Form 4C

Problem: _____   **Name:** _____

Form 4C

Problem: _____   **Name:** _____

Form 4C

Problem: _____ **Name:** _____

Form 4C

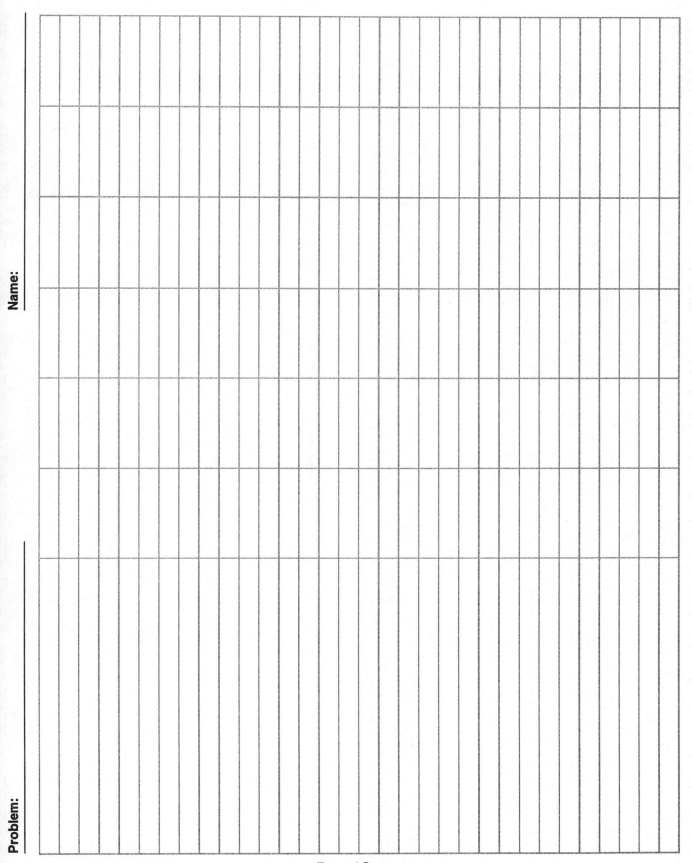

Form 6C

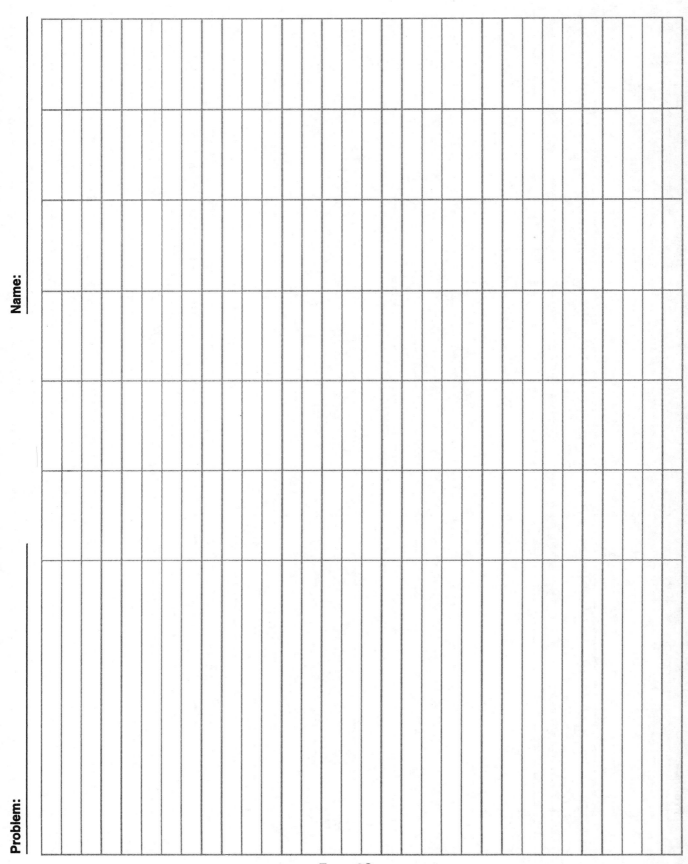

Form 6C

Problem:

Form 6C

Name:

Problem:

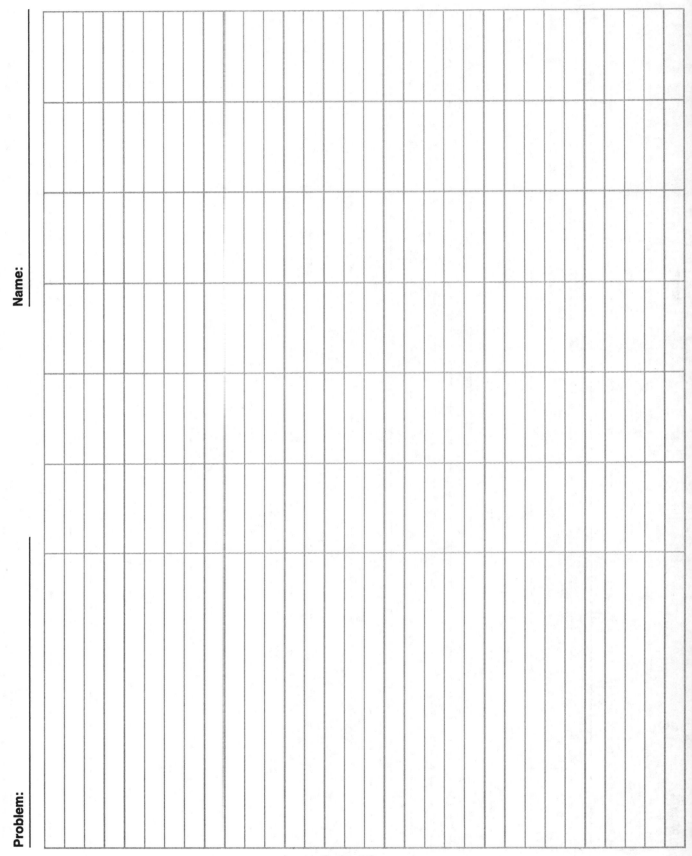

Form 6C

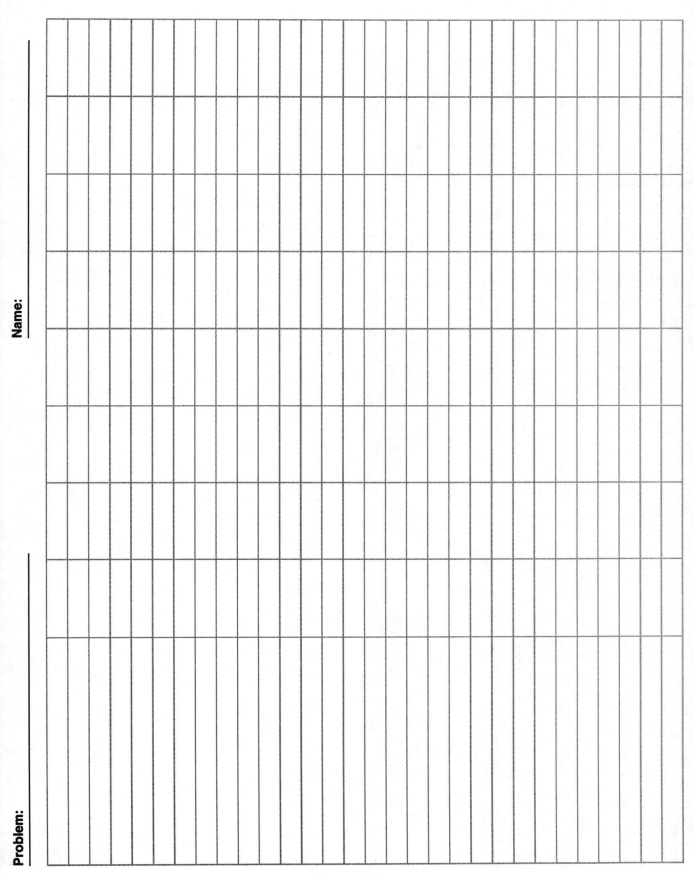

Form 8C

Name:

Problem:

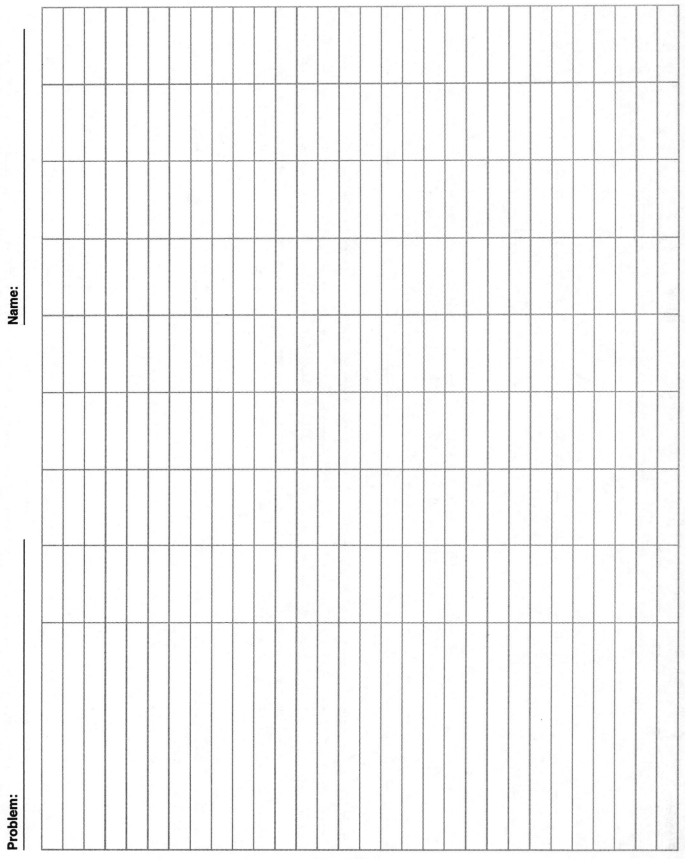

Form 8C

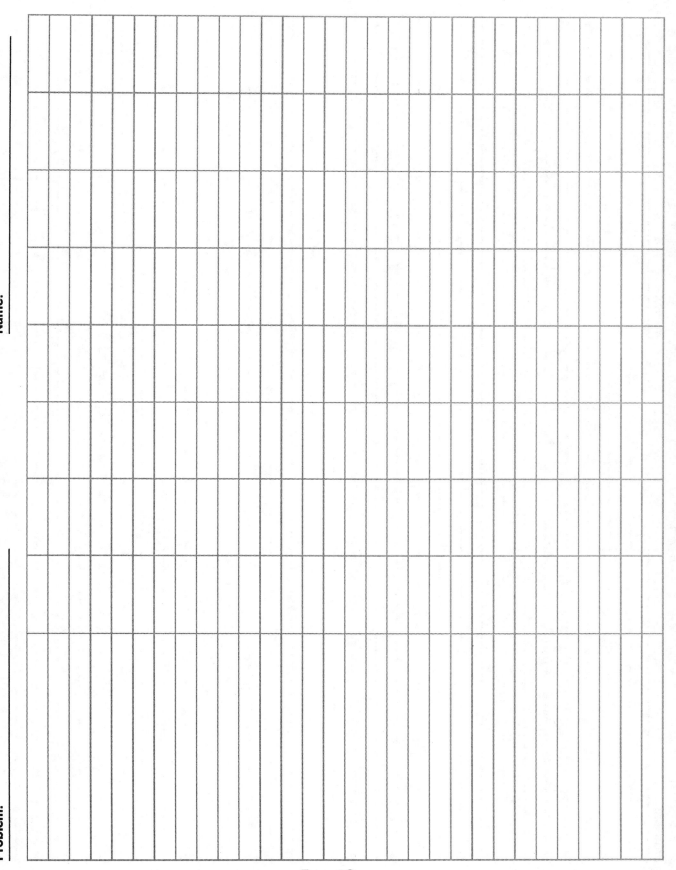

Form 8C

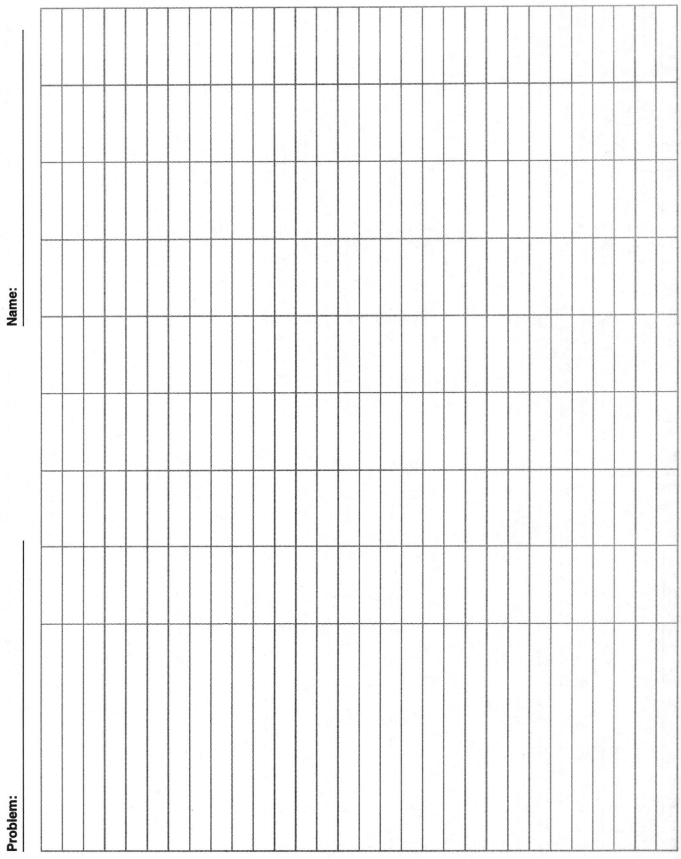

Form 8C

Name:

Problem:

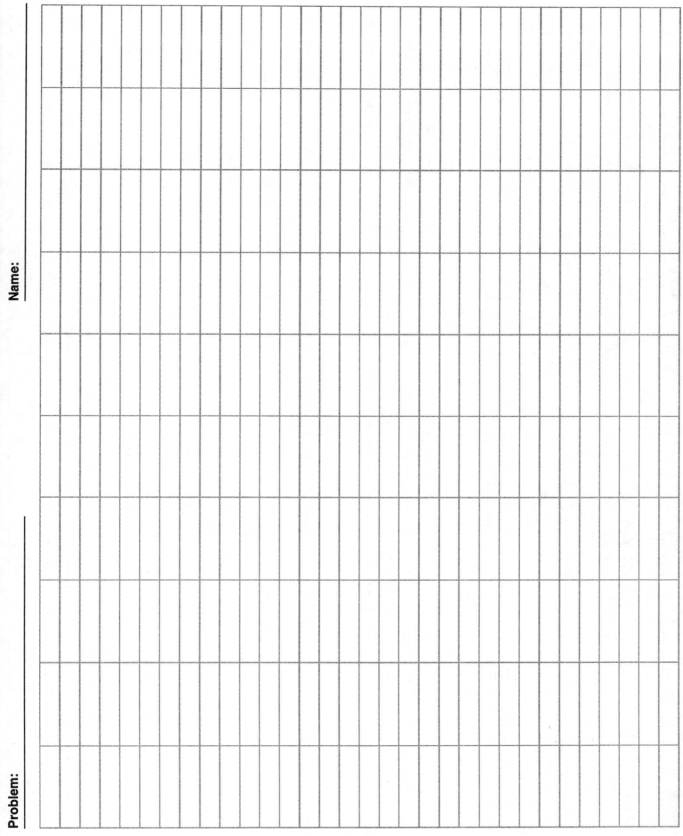

Form 10C

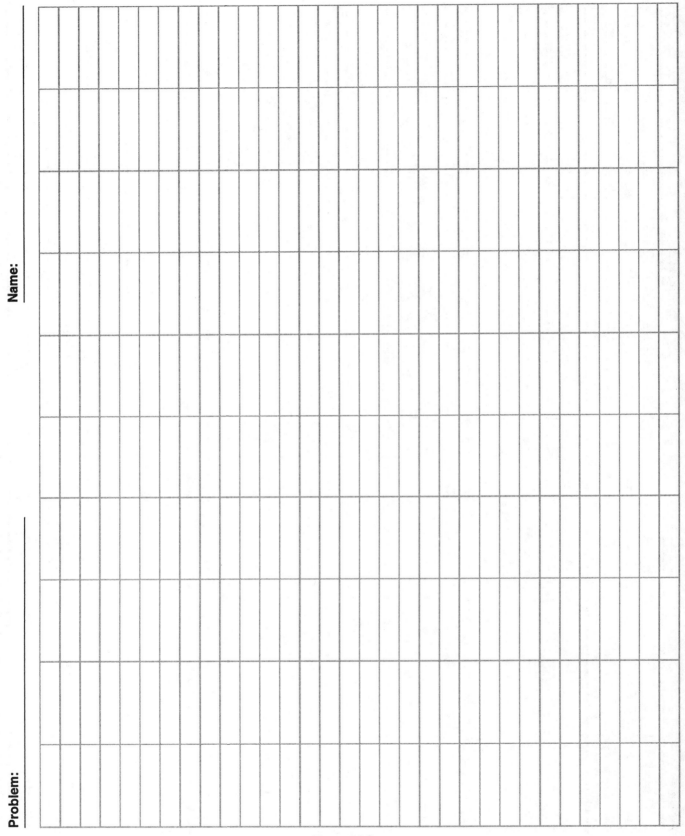

Form 10C

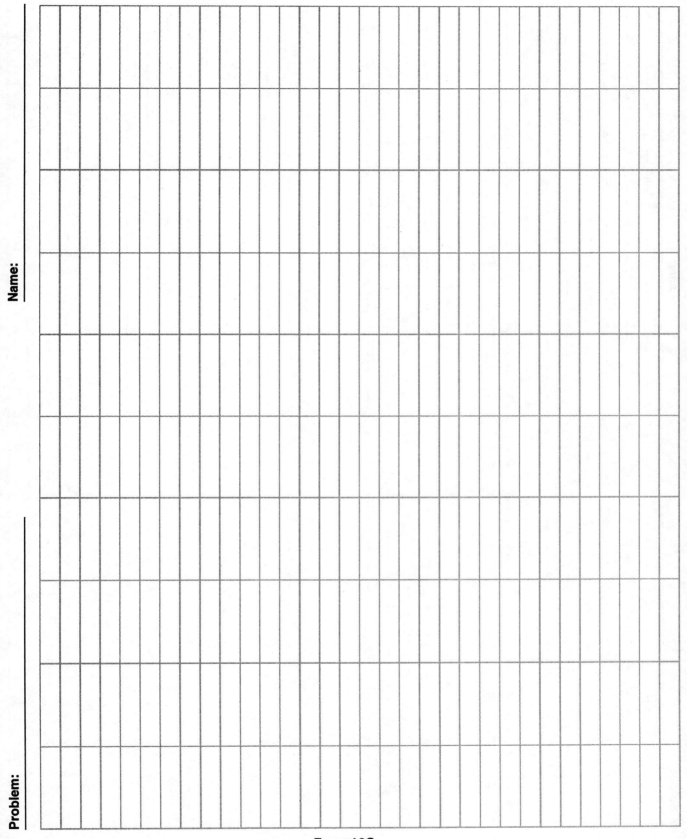

Form 10C

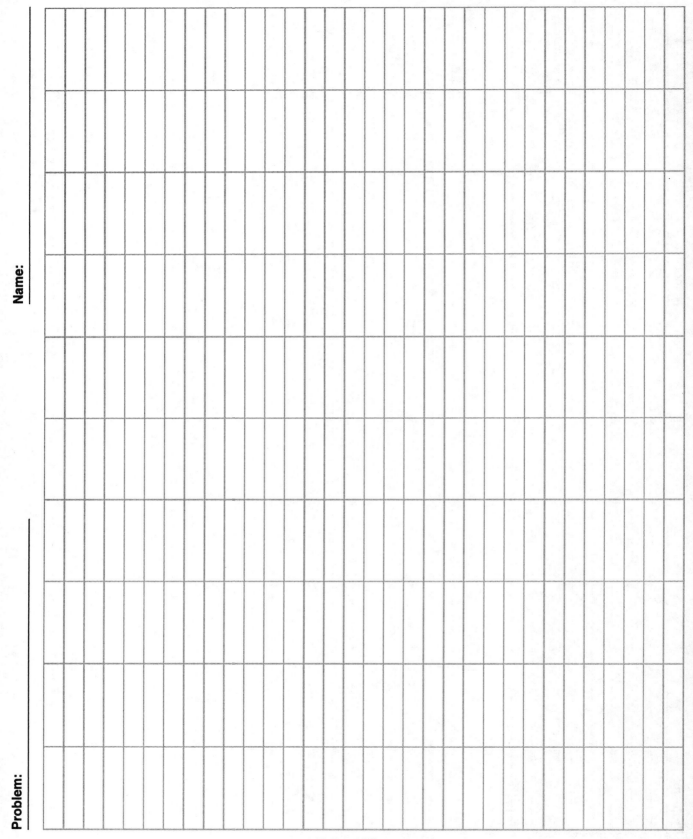

Form 10C

Name: _____

Problem: _____

Account Title	Trial Balance		Adjustments		Income Statement		Balance Sheet	
	Debit	Credit	Debit	Credit	Debit	Credit	Debit	Credit

Form 8W

Problem:

Account Title	Trial Balance		Adjustments		Income Statement		Balance Sheet	
	Debit	Credit	Debit	Credit	Debit	Credit	Debit	Credit

Problem:

Account Title	Trial Balance		Adjustments		Income Statement		Balance Sheet	
	Debit	Credit	Debit	Credit	Debit	Credit	Debit	Credit

Name: _____

Problem: _____

Account Title	Trial Balance		Adjustments		Income Statement		Balance Sheet	
	Debit	Credit	Debit	Credit	Debit	Credit	Debit	Credit

Form 8W

Problem:

Account Title	Trial Balance		Adjustments		Adjusted Balances		Income Statement		Balance Sheet	
	Debit	Credit	Debit	Credit	Debit	Credit	Debit	Credit	Debit	Credit

Form 10W

Account Title	Trial Balance		Adjustments		Adjusted Balances		Income Statement		Balance Sheet	
	Debit	Credit	Debit	Credit	Debit	Credit	Debit	Credit	Debit	Credit

Name:

Problem:

Account Title	Trial Balance		Adjustments		Adjusted Balances		Income Statement		Balance Sheet	
	Debit	Credit	Debit	Credit	Debit	Credit	Debit	Credit	Debit	Credit

Form 10W

Problem:

Account Title	Trial Balance		Adjustments		Adjusted Balances		Income Statement		Balance Sheet	
	Debit	Credit	Debit	Credit	Debit	Credit	Debit	Credit	Debit	Credit

Name:

Problem:

	A	B	C	D	E	F	G
1							
2							
3							
4							
5							
6							
7							
8							
9							
10							
11							
12							
13							
14							
15							
16							
17							
18							
19							
20							
21							
22							
23							
24							
25							
26							
27							
28							

Form ES

Name:

Problem:

	A	B	C	D	E	F	G
1							
2							
3							
4							
5							
6							
7							
8							
9							
10							
11							
12							
13							
14							
15							
16							
17							
18							
19							
20							
21							
22							
23							
24							
25							
26							
27							
28							

Form ES

Name:

Problem:

	A	B	C	D	E	F	G
1							
2							
3							
4							
5							
6							
7							
8							
9							
10							
11							
12							
13							
14							
15							
16							
17							
18							
19							
20							
21							
22							
23							
24							
25							
26							
27							
28							

Form ES

Name:

Problem:

	A	B	C	D	E	F	G
1							
2							
3							
4							
5							
6							
7							
8							
9							
10							
11							
12							
13							
14							
15							
16							
17							
18							
19							
20							
21							
22							
23							
24							
25							
26							
27							
28							

Form ES

Problem: _____   **Name:** _____

GENERAL JOURNAL

Page _____

Date	Description	Post. Ref.	Debit	Credit

Form GJ

GENERAL JOURNAL

Page _____

Date	Description	Post. Ref.	Debit	Credit

Form GJ

Problem: _____   **Name:** _____

GENERAL JOURNAL

Page

Date		Description	Post. Ref.	Debit		Credit	

Form GJ

GENERAL JOURNAL

Page

Date	Description	Post. Ref.	Debit	Credit

Problem: _____   **Name:** _____

GENERAL JOURNAL

Page

Date	Description	Post. Ref.	Debit	Credit

Form GJ

Problem: _____   **Name:** _____

GENERAL JOURNAL

Page ___

Date	Description	Post. Ref.	Debit	Credit

Form GJ

Problem: _____   Name: _____

GENERAL JOURNAL

Page _____

Date		Description	Post. Ref.	Debit		Credit	

Form GJ

Problem: _____   **Name:** _____

GENERAL JOURNAL

Page

Date	Description	Post. Ref.	Debit	Credit

Form GJ

Problem: _____   Name: _____

GENERAL JOURNAL

Page _____

Date	Description	Post. Ref.	Debit		Credit	

Form GJ

Problem: _____   **Name:** _____

GENERAL JOURNAL

Page _____

Date	Description	Post. Ref.	Debit	Credit

Form GJ

Problem: _____ **Name:** _____

GENERAL JOURNAL

Page _____

Date	Description	Post. Ref.	Debit	Credit

Form GJ

Problem: _____ **Name:** _____

GENERAL JOURNAL

Page _____

Date	Description	Post. Ref.	Debit		Credit	

Form GJ